KV-625-250

STUDIES IN ENVIRONMENTAL POLLUTION

The geography of pollution   C. M. Wood *et al.*

The estimation of pollution damage   P. J. W. Saunders

CHRISTOPHER WOOD

Town planning and pollution control

Manchester University Press

© 1976 C. M. Wood

Published by
MANCHESTER UNIVERSITY PRESS
Oxford Road, Manchester M13 9PL

ISBN 0 7190 0635 X

L. I. H. E.
THE MARKLAND LIBRARY

Accession No. 76219

Class No. 914.202
WOO

Catal.
14.10.82 GE

Printed in Great Britain
by Eyre and Spottiswoode Ltd at Grosvenor Press,
Northarbour Road, Portsmouth.

CONTENTS

LIST OF FIGURES

STUDIES IN ENVIRONMENTAL POLLUTION

GENERAL INTRODUCTION

It is apparent that the recent growth in public concern over environmental pollution has not been matched by a corresponding increase in understanding about the form it takes, the sources from which it originates, its effects or the manner in which it is (or can be) controlled. In part this is a problem of communication and in part a problem of research technique and objective. Confronted by a large, uncharted territory, it is tempting to retreat into some small corner, applying the tools of one's discipline to an aspect of one environmental medium's problem.

However, waste creation and disposal, whether in gaseous, liquid, solid or noise form, are interrelated problems. Similarly, the significance of scientific research into the effects of pollution or the technical methods of controlling it can be established only with reference to the type of society in which the pollution phenomenon occurs. Equally, the examination of appropriate pollution control levels and the administrative instruments by which these are achieved is a hollow exercise unless the necessary scientific backing is to hand. In short, a genuinely interdisciplinary approach to the whole problem of waste is ideally required.

It is considerations of this kind which have led to the introduction of this series and which have conditioned its form. It is intended for three types of reader. First, the academic reader who is anxious to gain a wider understanding of environmental pollution, particularly from the standpoint of disciplines other than his own. Second, those who are engaged in a professional capacity, technical or administrative, in some aspect of pollution control. Finally, the more general reader, who, we hope, will be attracted by the thoroughness of treatment, achieved with the minimum of technical terminology.

There is, in the series, a deliberate intention to treat the subject matter in an objective manner but, in so doing, not to avoid contentious issues. Apart from the existence of conflicting evidence and interpretation on some important issues, there are also differences of view on the research methods by which knowledge will be advanced. These are important matters which require careful examination.

Finally it should be clear that though the monographs in this series share the same broad purpose, the particular treatment in each is the responsibility of the author and is not necessarily accepted by other contributors to the series.

Norman Lee

PREFACE

Many would regard pollution control and planning as an unlikely pair of topics to be joined together. And yet are they so unlikely a match? Pollution and amenity are bound up together, as, of course, are amenity and planning. Over the last year or two there have been increasing signs of recognition that planning can help to control pollution, and pollution is now coupled with dereliction as being a possible deterrent to footloose industry. It has been stated that, armed with a knowledge of pollution control powers, the planner should be better able to see how planning control may be able to plug a gap in the laws of pollution or otherwise assist in preventing pollution.[1] This book attempts to demonstrate that planning can and should help to control pollution.

The study has developed with the help and encouragement of Dr Norman Lee of the Department of Economics, University of Manchester, and Professor David Robinson of the Department of Town and Country Planning of the same university. Pairing the subjects of planning and pollution was a logical step for a planner who had once been a chemist—particularly as I was employed as a member of an interdisciplinary research project on pollution. David Robinson arranged for Norman Lee and I to give three seminars at the Town and Country Planning Summer School[2] which led to an article in the *Journal of the Royal Town Planning Institute*.[3] This was considerably expanded to form a chapter of the Pollution Research Unit's final report to the Science and Social Service Research Councils[4] and the section on powers was further refined to be published as a separate article.[5] (Chapter 3 draws very heavily on this.) Further development of the book took place while undertaking a second research project, arising from the first, at the Pollution Research Unit[6,7] and, subsequently, while working on a number of pollution-related commissions with Land Use Consultants, London.

I wish to record my great thanks, therefore, to David Robinson and to Norman Lee. A large number of other people have been very generous with help and advice. Among these I am particularly grateful to Jim McLoughlin, Senior Lecturer, Department of Law, University of Manchester; Stuart Gulliver of Warrington New Town Development Corporation; Les Coffey and Peter Walton, formerly of the Strategic Plan for the North West; Mr F. G. Sugden, Middlesbrough Borough Council Chief Environmental Health Officer; Mr W. Bean, Cleveland County Planning Officer; Mr Pat Hurley, Metropolitan Borough of Sandwell Planning Department; Mr M. Paddock, City of Birmingham Environmental Department; Mr P. E. Goode, City of Birmingham Planning Department; Mr R. E. Weston, Shell Refining and Marketing UK Ltd; Miss R. Paine, Cheshire County Planning Department; Mr A. J. Eberlein, Shell Chemicals UK Ltd; Mr H. Barrett, Hampshire County Planning Department; Jack Richards, Manchester City Environmental Health Department; Peter Saunders, formerly of the Pollution Research Unit; Mr J. Beighton, Deputy Chief Alkali Inspector; Messrs S. J. Hart, G. G. Jones and R. H. Smith, District Alkali Inspectors; Mr P. B. Richards, Assistant Director, Planning Inspectorate, Department of the Environment; and Mr H. G. Poore, Senior Principal, Department of the Environment. In acknowledging their help I assume full responsibility for any errors and for the interpretation of the information they have provided.

I am also grateful to Max Nicholson, John Herbert and Cliff Tandy, the Principals of Land Use Consultants, who have given me their encouragement and the time to write this book. I have received such helpful assistance from various libraries that I feel bound to acknowledge the aid of the staff at the University of Manchester Arts Library, the University of Manchester Architecture and Planning Library, the Manchester Central Reference Library, the Department of the Environment Library, and particularly the advice and enthusiasm of the Kingston Polytechnic librarians. I gratefully acknowledge the generosity of *The Guardian,* who gave me permission to use their photographs (frontispiece, 2–7, 10, A1), of Cliff Tandy (1, 11, A2) and of Land Use Consultants (8). Finally, I should like to thank my wife, Jo, without whom this book would not have been written, together with Sue Eyre and Shirley Hare, without whom it would not have been typed.

Christopher Wood

REFERENCES
1 Boynton, J. K. (1973) The law relating to pollution *JRTPI, 59* 41.
2 Lee, N., and Wood, C. M. (1971) Economics of pollution in relation to planning *Proc. Town and Country Planning Summer School, Southampton,* 43–4.
3 Lee, N., and Wood, C. M. (1972) Planning and pollution *JRTPI, 58* 153–8.
4 Pollution Research Unit (1972) *Environmental pollution: a research report* 625–57, University of Manchester, Manchester.
5 Wood, C. M. (1973) Powers and responsibilities of local planning authorities in controlling pollution *JPL (1973)* 635–41.
6 Wood, C. M., Lee, N., Luker, J. A., and Saunders, P. J. W. (1974) *The geography of pollution: a study of Greater Manchester* Manchester University Press, Manchester.
7 Saunders, P. J. W., and Wood, C. M. (1974) Plants and air pollution *Landscape Design, No. 105* 28–30.

CHAPTER 1

L. I. H. E.
THE MARKLAND LIBRARY
STAND PARK RD., LIVERPOOL, L16 9JD

Introduction

A coal spoil tip close to housing which, having burnt out, is now being quarried for red shale. Planning control of pollution has perhaps been most readily associated with solid waste dereliction and other forms of land pollution in the past, not always effectively.

Four fundamental questions can be posed about the relationship between town planning and pollution control:

1 Does land use planning have a distinctive role in the control of pollution, given the existence of various other pollution control authorities, each with their own powers and jurisdictions?

2 Do planning powers and responsibilities which relate to the control of pollution exist?

3 Are such powers and responsibilities, and the manner in which they are discharged, consistent with the optimum level of pollution control?

4 Does town planning embody a range of techniques appropriate to the implementation of its role in pollution control?

These questions can be satisfactorily examined only in the light of a number of theoretical and practical issues:

1 The potential of planning to bridge gaps in present methods of controlling pollution.
2 The potential instruments which could strengthen the power of town planning to control pollution.
3 The overall potential effectiveness of planning as a method of pollution control.
4 The selection of appropriate objectives and criteria for pollution control by land use planning.
5 The reconciliation of conflicting considerations. These relate both to conflicts between different pollution control objectives and to conflicts between pollution control and other planning objectives.
6 The range of potential techniques for pollution control available to planners.
7 Do planning authorities accept that they have a distinctive role in the control of pollution?
8 Do local planning authorities adequately discharge their powers and responsibilities relating to the control of pollution?
9 How effectively do planning authorities control pollution?
10 What are the principles guiding local planning authorities in the utilisation of pollution control techniques and powers?
11 How are pollution control considerations modified by the planning authority's other objectives?
12 Do planners use the pollution control techniques which are available to them?

These theoretical and operational issues are developed in the chapters which follow (2–10). Chapter 11 draws a number of conclusions from these chapters before moving on to provide answers to the four fundamental questions posed at the outset.

Chapter 2 consists of a brief review of the pollution process. Pollution is defined, set in the context of a wider range of problems, and classified into air, water, land, noise and other categories. Methods of controlling pollution and the powers and jurisdiction of the various control authorities are then briefly described in order to establish whether planning could play a distinctive role and to ascertain the potential position of the planning authority amongst these bodies.

(Appendix 1 provides a short guide to pollution for planners: sources, types, effects and control of air, noise, water and land pollution; trends in pollution; sources of pollution data; sources of advice on pollution problems.)

Chapter 3 describes the existing English planning powers and responsibilities in the control of pollution. It reviews the powers contained in Acts of Parliament and in statutory instruments and discusses the duties to control pollution which are incumbent upon local planning authorities. This chapter also deals with the responsibilities urged upon planning authorities by a number of circulars which, while not statutory duties, should be discharged wherever possible.

Chapter 4 is concerned with the nature of planning as a method of pollution control and presents the main theoretical discussion. Commencing with a discussion of criteria, the difficulties of the optimal control theory approach to pollution control are contrasted with those embodied in the setting and observance of standards by local planning authorities. The chapter then examines the distinctive role of planning in relation to the stages of the pollution process and to the other control authorities. The various problems involved in the use of planning as a method of pollution control are mentioned, particular reference being made to the reconciliation of conflicting planning objectives, the effectiveness of planning control and its operation in the absence of specific directives.

Chapter 5, the last of the mainly theoretical chapters, describes the planning techniques available for controlling air, noise, water and land pollution at both the plan-making and the development control stages of the planning process. Most of the theoretical issues raised earlier will have been examined at this point, but one or two can only be dissected once the practical issues have been analysed (for example, the potential effectiveness of planning as a method of pollution control) and must await Chapter 11.

Chapter 6 commences the treatment of pollution control in planning practice. It deals with the discussion of pollution in large-scale plans: regional and sub-regional studies. As a case study it describes the work of the team which prepared the Strategic Plan for the North West. The team's final report demonstrates the development of planning thought on pollution control and illustrates a number of issues.

Chapter 7 summarises the approach of new town plans to pollution control. The case study chosen is Warrington New Town, whose

designated area is based upon an existing town which has experienced
a number of pollution problems.

Chapter 8 deals with structure plan formulation. It mentions the
recognition of pollution as a problem in old-style development plans
and then very briefly reviews the treatment of pollution in published
structure plans. It analyses the provisions for pollution control contained in three structure plans, Warley, Teesside and South
Hampshire.

Chapter 9 is concerned with a single case study in structure plan
implementation: the improvement of the South Hampshire sub-
region's sewerage and sewage disposal system. The alternative
approaches to long overdue provision for improved disposal typify
the problem of reconciling pollution control with other objectives.

Chapter 10 presents a number of development control decisions in
which pollution control was an issue. Case studies dealing with pollution from a works extension, pollution in a new housing development
and pollution arising during redevelopment in a city centre are
described. There are a number of distinctions to be drawn between
the treatment of pollution at this stage in the planning process and its
treatment at the plan-making stage.

Chapters 6–10 provide sufficient material for the practical issues
raised earlier to be analysed. The final chapter draws conclusions
from the comparison of practice with theory, thus rounding off the
examination of the various issues and fundamental questions. Having
identified a number of deficiencies in the planning control of pollution, it recommends organisational and administrative changes (and
suggests topics requiring further research) in order to increase the
effectiveness of town planning control.

However, it is first necessary to define the term 'town planning'.
'Land use planning', 'town and country planning', 'town planning' or
simply 'planning' are all used in Britain as different names for the
same complex process. This process is concerned with control over
the use of land and hence over the whole physical environment.
Statutory land use planning is based upon the dual plan preparation
and development control provisions of the Town and Country Planning Act, 1971. Numerous non-statutory plans, covering regions and
many sub-regions as well as smaller areas such as new towns, exist.
Town planning is administered by local planning authorities with
guidance from central government.

CHAPTER 2

Pollution and its control

Smoke from burning spoil tips. Pollution problems frequently affect more than one medium, and the dumping of solid waste has given rise to both land pollution and air pollution here.

DEFINITION AND NATURE OF POLLUTION

There is no generally accepted definition of pollution, but most contain the concepts embodied in the following: pollution is the introduction by man of waste matter or surplus energy into the environment, directly or indirectly causing damage to persons other than himself, his household or those with whom he has a direct contractual relationship.

Pollution thus originates from the generation of waste matter or surplus energy by human activity. These wastes may be gaseous or particulate emissions, aqueous effluents, solid wastes or surplus energy in the form of radiation, heat, vibration or noise. During their transmission through air or water or on land they are usually diluted but may sometimes be biologically concentrated. They may also be transformed chemically by interaction with the natural environment or with other wastes. Only if the resulting substances cause damage to animate or inanimate objects ('receptors') are they classed as environmental pollutants. 'Pollution damage' embraces direct or indirect effects on man and his environment, whether to human health, materials, agriculture, wild life or to amenity. The distinctions between 'waste' and 'pollution' and between damage resulting from human and from natural sources (for example, air-borne wastes such as sulphur dioxide from volcanoes) are thus crucial. Finally, the term pollution is restricted to situations where damage is inflicted upon people with whom the waste generator has no contractual relationship, thus excluding self-inflicted damage from, say, smoking or damage incurred during employment from, for example, coal dust.

The pollution process
Pollution is seen to be the end result of a process originating in the generation of waste. The various parts of this process, from the different types of waste to the resulting pollution, are represented in Figure 1. It is clear that several methods of pollution control can be employed at different points in the pollution process. Such methods will directly influence the part of the process controlled but may also indirectly affect other parts because of repercussions elsewhere in the process. Pollution damage might be reduced, for example, by limiting waste generation, by requiring more effective waste treatment, by controlling the manner and location of waste disposal, or by suitable protection and siting of sensitive receptors.

Pollution and other environmental problems
It is apparent from Figure 1 that a complex relationship exists between pollution and natural resources, among which must be numbered the human population and the quality of its environment. There is considerable debate about the nature of this relationship, much of which has centred on the effect of economic growth on pollution. Certain contributions to the debate have been weakened by a confusion between wastes and pollution, but a brief outline of the more important points provides a relevant background to an examination of the relationship between planning and pollution.

There are several components of economic growth. It has been asserted that population is the root cause of the pollution problem.[1] It

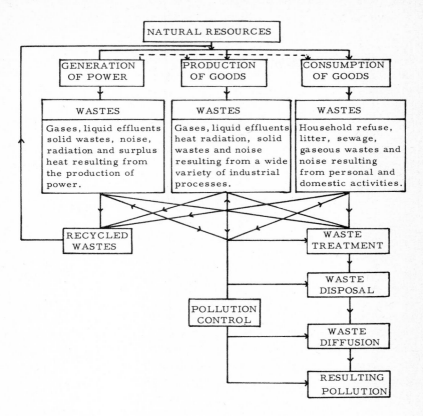

FIGURE 1   The pollution process

is true that quantities of waste generated undoubtedly increase with population but it does not necessarily follow that the pollution resulting from them becomes more severe. If additional controls were applied to abate pollution, it is possible that the problem might become less rather than more serious as population rises.

Similarly, technology has been blamed for causing increasingly severe pollution, it being argued, for example, that the rate of increase in pollutants generated in the United States since the war far exceeds the growth in population and affluence which has occurred.[2] While a relationship undoubtedly exists between advances in technology and the quantities of wastes generated, this argument is not

rigorously applied to pollution (as opposed to wastes). Indeed, there
is considerable evidence to show that the age and structure of industry affect pollution generation, more modern plants causing less pollution per ton of product than older plants manufacturing the same
product.[3]

Elsewhere it has been argued that, while population and technology are important, affluence is the main determinant of potentially
polluting wastes.[4] The controversy is unlikely ever to be completely
resolved, but it does appear that the production of wastes, irrespec-
tive of the pollution to which they give rise, cannot be conclusively
related to a single determinant.

The utilisation of mineral resources is increasing at a very fast rate.
It is apparent that resources would be conserved were the wastes
resulting from consumption and production processes to be re-used
rather than discarded to create pollution.[5] Such an approach has been
strongly advocated,[6] and indeed is practised in a number of industries
(for example, lead). There are technical and financial limitations to
recycling many materials, but the potential for conservation is shown
by the extremely effective measures taken to conserve precious
metals during refining.

Interest in the global effects of pollution upon natural resources
has centred on the climate, although there is also considerable concern about the diffusion of marine pollutants. A number of critics
have pointed to the connection between global pollution and
economic growth[5] but, because of the enormous complexity of the
problem, no conclusive relationships have been established. It
appears that man-made pollution is unlikely to cause significant
changes in the natural environment in the next decade or so, but too
little is known for mankind to be complacent about longer-term
effects.[7]

It is obvious that pollution is closely related to the utilisation of
natural resources. Many of the solutions to both pollution problems
and the wider resource problems of which they form part are known
in that they are technically feasible. The substitution of materials and
processes could be accomplished to conserve the original materials
and limit the quantities of waste discharged to the environment, provided that the necessary financial resources were made available.[8 9]
However, it is generally cheaper, in conventional economic terms, to
continue to ignore these solutions.

Dereliction is another resource problem related to pollution and one which is familiar to planners. The definition of pollution adopted here excludes several types of dereliction (land so damaged by industrial or other development that it is incapable of beneficial use without treatment[10]) but it does include derelict spoil heaps and tips, since these originate from wastes and cause damage to amenity. Both the materials causing the dereliction and the land on which they are deposited could be re-used and the pollution thus 'controlled', the principal barrier being the cost of reclamation.

Classification of pollutants

It is often convenient to classify pollutants according to the environmental medium through which they are principally diffused: air, water (fresh and marine) and land. In many cases the environmental medium affected depends upon the manner of waste disposal. Thus a liquid chemical waste might be incinerated (leading to air pollution), diluted and run to a watercourse (fresh water pollution), or piped or dumped into the sea (marine pollution). The classification is thus somewhat arbitrary, since the environmental media are closely interrelated parts of the natural system. Noise is usually regarded as a separate category of pollution, but radioactivity, pesticides and heavy metals (depending upon their form) may be treated as types of air, water or land pollution, or as a separate group of persistent or multi-media pollutants.

Appendix 1 presents a brief guide to the effects of the main types of pollution and to their control. It also summarises trends in those pollutants for which data are available, describes sources of pollution data and suggests where planners might turn for assistance. However, it is intended to sketch in one or two details here about the main pollutants as background to the succeeding discussion.

Wastes are emitted into the atmosphere as either gases or particles, and are eventually removed by natural self-cleansing processes. The wastes mostly originate from the burning of fuels and the processing of materials. The pollutant concentrations to which they give rise (usually measured by the amount of pollutant per unit volume of air at ground level) are determined by the way in which the pollutant is dispersed, one of the main factors being the height at which emission takes place. Gaseous pollutants are generally quickly and uniformly mixed with a large volume of air. The important common gaseous pollutants include oxides of sulphur, nitrogen and carbon, hydrogen sulphide, hydrogen fluoride, hydrogen chloride, hydrocarbons and ozone. By no means all these pollutants are monitored. Particulate pollutants consist of finely divided liquid or solid matter which may be small enough to remain suspended in the atmosphere for some time. The mainly solid particulates are roughly classified by size as smoke, fume, dust and grit. Their composition varies from unburnt carbon to complex substances including lead and radioactive compounds. Mists consist mostly of liquid particles.[11]

The main sources of noise are transport (road traffic and aircraft), industrial premises and domestic residences, transport noise generally being regarded as being the most significant. Noise monitoring is not yet widely practised (partly because of technical measurement difficulties) but noise levels in the environment can be estimated with reasonable accuracy if the noise properties of the sources are known.[12] Land pollution arises from the disposal of a large range of solid and liquid wastes and from the aerial deposition of trace substances, including pesticides. The former include mineral, industrial and agricultural wastes, domestic refuse and sewage, pesticides and trace metals.

A wide variety of organic and inorganic substances originating as human sewage, industrial and agricultural wastes and run-off from the land, together with limited amounts emitted to the air (through aerial deposition), find their way into the river systems. The volume of water in a river, its velocity, depth and aeration affect the dilution and degradation of these effluents, and thus the water quality at any given point. The numerous water pollutants have not generally been analysed individually, water quality being determined by such measures as biochemical oxygen demand, suspended and dissolved solid content, etc. Separate analyses for metals, phenols, pesticides, nitrates, phosphates and other substances are, however, being conducted with increasing frequency.[13]

The main wastes discharged into the marine environment originate from rivers, atmospheric fall-out, industrial and sewage discharges from pipelines and vessels and from accidental spillages (for example, of oil). With the tightening of controls over inland waste disposal during the 1960's it is suspected that a significant diversion of wastes to the marine environment has occurred.[14] The diffusion and fate of wastes in the sea is more complex than in fresh water because of tidal movements, variations in salinity and the much larger volumes of water involved. The individual pollutants are, however, similar to those found in fresh water, although they may include a wider range of toxic substances.

Despite its convenience, and although most of our knowledge about pollution has tended to relate to particular environmental media, the classification of pollutants by such media has a number of limitations when the pollution process as a whole is examined. It is quite possible that wastes discharged to one medium could be substituted, at a number of different stages in the pollution process, by another set of wastes discharged to a different medium. Similarly, changes in waste treatment may have repercussions on other media, and, once discharged, there is no guarantee that diffusion of waste will be limited to a particular environmental medium (especially in the case of persistent or cumulative substances). These limitations should be recognised, but they do not warrant the abandoning of classification by medium.

POLLUTION CONTROL

It is apparent from Figure 1 that it is possible to impose control at several stages in the pollution process:

1   The location of development which may give rise to pollution can be controlled by determining whether or not the development will take place on a particular site.
2   The process by which a particular product is manufactured can be controlled, to determine whether and how it is made.
3   The nature of the product can be controlled by regulating its composition or construction.
4   The use of the product can be controlled by the imposition of various restrictions on the place, manner and time of that use.
5   The method of treatment of waste can be controlled to ensure that treatment plant of an appropriate specification is installed.
6   The disposal of wastes can be controlled by fixing the place, rate and method of discharge ('end-of-pipe' control).

Pollution control authorities

There are a number of British pollution control authorities exerting control on different pollutants at different stages in the pollution process.[15] Table 1 presents a selective summary of the situation. Control over the manufacturing process is not common, although, for example, Her Majesty's Alkali and Clean Air Inspectorate (now part of the Health and Safety Commission and Executive) does sometimes recommend the cessation of polluting chemical or metallurgical processes, although it has no legal powers to do so. An example of control over the nature of the product is provided by the noise rating of new aircraft engines. Restrictions upon use are again fairly unusual, Department of Trade and Industry regulations on flying times and procedures administered to control noise from aircraft and motor vehicle construction and use regulations enforced by the police to control traffic fumes and noise being the two obvious examples of this type of control. The Alkali Inspectorate imposes control over the method of treatment of waste by insisting that the 'best practicable means' are utilised to reduce air pollution from registered industrial processes.[16] Similar control over certain other processes is administered by environmental health departments.

Control over the disposal of wastes is the most widely practised method of pollution control in Britain. This is the technique employed by local authority environmental health departments, which are responsible for the control of domestic—and of much industrial—air pollution and of certain noise problems. The regional water authorities control the disposal of wastes to inland watercourses and estuaries by imposing 'consent' conditions on discharges. They are involved in a similar way where discharges take place on gathering grounds or close to pumping stations. The sea fisheries committees are concerned with discharges to marine waters other than estuaries, but their limited powers are soon to be transferred to the regional water authorities. This list of pollution control authorities is not by any means exhaustive. For example, the British Waterways Board administer some discharges to canals, and central government exerts considerable control over the large-scale use of radioactive materials.

Although the number of pollution control authorities is extensive, and despite the wide-ranging nature of their powers, the control of pollution still leaves much to be desired. Part of the problem may lie in the lack of comprehensive control over every type of pollutant or even in the lack of uniformity of the geographical areas administered by the pollution control authorities, and part may lie in the absence of a clear consensus among the controlling authorities on pollution control objectives,[17] methods or implementation.[15]

Local planning authority control of pollution
The diffuse and incomplete nature of the administration of pollution control by the various authorities offers considerable opportunities for planning control. The planning authority exerts control at most stages in the pollution process, but its most powerful contribution is potentially at the first of the stages in determining the nature and location of new development and of redevelopment (Table 1). Because pollution originates as waste from production and consumption activities, one of the key variables in pollution control (the geographical point at which additional waste is created) is determined once the location of these activities has been established. Therefore, because of its control over land use, the local planning authority exercises an important influence on the spatial origin of wastes and consequently upon pollution levels and their distribution. Although other bodies, for example the Alkali Inspectorate and the Atomic Energy Authority, may have a considerable voice in the location of certain specialised land uses, the planning authority is undoubtedly the pre-eminent (and ultimate) controlling authority at this stage in the pollution process, whether it recognises the position or not.

Planning control exercised at the later stages of the pollution process is less fundamental. Some indirect control over the manufacturing process and over the method of treatment of waste can be exercised in the case of noise from new developments by, for example, attaching conditions relating to noise emissions. The imposition of conditions relating to the level of noise emitted from a site and the hours of operation of a noisy activity, or insistence upon a particular type of building, could cause the developer to alter the process or install sound-proofing to 'treat the waste', and this use of such conditions represents an important weapon in the pollution control armoury. Local planning authorities are also often responsible for reclaiming derelict land and hence for 'treating' land pollution.

The use of products and the disposal of wastes can both be controlled to a limited extent by the local planning authority. Authorities have a voice in the determination of new road alignments and also possess some control over the use of existing roads, thus influencing traffic pollution. (Authorities also exercise indirect control over air and noise pollution from motor vehicles by deciding the location of

Table 1.   Examples of the types of control administered by pollution

Pollution control authority:	Environmental health inspectors	Regional water authorities	Alkali Inspectorate	Department of Trade and Industry/ Owning local authority	Police/ (Department of the Environment)
Pollutants controlled:	Air and noise pollution	Water pollution	Air pollution from registered works	Aircraft noise pollution	Motor vehicle air and noise pollution
Type of control					
Location		Discharge points	Some voice in location of registered works—no legal powers		Heavy commercial vehicles
Process	Most industrial furnaces		Limited number of industrial processes		
Product				Aircraft engines	(Motor vehicle construction)
Use	Fuels in control areas			Aircraft flights	Motor vehicle operation
Treatment	Furnaces and new domestic fires (approved appliances)		Scheduled processes		
Disposal	Industrial and domestic air and noise pollution	Nearly all discharges to watercourses	Emission standards for four pollutants. In practice, prescriptive limits for others	Aircraft engine noise emissions	Motor vehicle emissions

control authorities

Sea Fisheries Committees/ (Ministry of Ag., Fish and Food)	British Waterways Board	Dept. of the Environment/ Dept. of Energy	Local authority	Local planning authority
Marine pollution	Canal pollution	Radioactive pollutants	Land pollution	All, especially land and noise pollution
(Dumping at sea)		Some voice in location of uses generating radioactive wastes. (Site licences)	Licensing of waste disposal sites	Ultimate authority responsible for location of all new development likely to cause pollution
		Certain atomic processes		Some control over process noise by planning conditions
		Certain radioactive substances	Specification of wastes to be accepted	Some indirect control over road traffic pollutants
			Code of practice governing method of disposal	Land pollution. Some control over noise by sound proofing conditions
Certain marine discharges	Certain discharges to canals (as owner)	Many radioactive material disposals		Control over location of waste disposal activities

traffic generating activities.)

The location of waste disposal is generally determined once a development is approved although the precise location of, for example, a chimney stack is subject to planning approval. However, the local planning authority also allocate land specifically for waste treatment and disposal. These activities (for example, the operation of sewage works and of tips for domestic refuse and industrial solid waste) tend, of themselves, to generate considerable quantities of waste. Apart from determining the location of such activities the planning authority are able to lay down conditions to partially control the resulting pollution. (Certain authorities will also be responsible for licensing solid waste disposal sites under the Control of Pollution Act, 1974.)

It is apparent that the organisation of pollution control in this country leaves a number of opportunities for the local planning authority, should they wish to exercise a pollution control function, despite the fact that, in practice, local planning authorities generally take the view that the control of discharges should be left to those pollution control authorities who are expressly given powers of control. Indeed, land use planning has a considerable effect upon pollution levels, whether this is intentional or not.

REFERENCES
1   Erlich, P. R. and A. H. (1972) *Population, resources, environment* W. H. Freeman, London.
2   Commoner, B. (1972) The environmental cost of economic growth. In Schurr, S. H. (ed.) *Energy, economic growth and the environment* Johns Hopkins University Press, London.
3   Economic Commission for Europe and United Nations (1970) *Problems of air and water pollution arising in the iron and steel industry* UN, New York.
4   Lee, N., and Saunders, P. J. W. (1972) Pollution as a function of affluence and population increase. In Cox, P. R., and Peel, J. (eds.) *Population and pollution* Academic Press, London.
5   Meadows, D. M., Meadows, D. L., Randers, J., and Behrens, W. W. (1972) *The limits to growth* Earth Island, London.
6   Goldsmith, E. (ed.) (1972) *A blueprint for survival* Stacey, London.
7   Massachusetts Institute of Technology (1970) *Man's impact on the global environment* MIT Press, London.
8   Kneese, A. V., and Bohm, P. (1971) *The economics of environment* Macmillan, London.
9   Committee on Resources and Man (1969) *Resources and man* W. H. Freeman, London.

10 Oxenham, J. R. (1966) *Reclaiming derelict land* Faber, London.
11 Stern, A. C. (ed.) (1968) *Air pollution* (three vols) Academic Press, London.
12 Committee on the Problem of Noise (Wilson Committee) (1963) *Final report* Cmnd 2056, HMSO, London.
13 Klein, L. (1967) *River pollution* (three vols) Butterworth, London.
14 Royal Commission on Environmental Pollution (1971) *First report* Cmnd 4585, HMSO, London.
15 McLoughlin, J. (1972) *The law relating to pollution* Manchester University Press, Manchester.
16 Department of the Environment (1969–74) *Annual report on alkali, etc, works* HMSO, London.
17 Lee, N., and Luker, J. A. (1971) An introduction to the economics of pollution *Economics, 9* 19–31.

CHAPTER 3

Powers and responsibilities of local planning authorities in controlling pollution

Aircraft noise seriously affects 2½ million people in the United Kingdom. Local authorities are now told to impose severe restrictions on the types of new development to be permitted in the vicinity of airports.

The powers which planning authorities possess to control pollution are vested in them by the Town and Country Planning Acts (which enable them to control development and to impose conditions upon it), by other acts of parliament and by statutory instruments made under the provisions of these acts. The interpretation of these powers and the definition of authorities' responsibilities are contained in government circulars. The following review does not attempt to summarise the British two-stage system of plan-making and development control, excellent accounts of which exist elsewhere,[1] [2] only to highlight the provisions relevant to pollution control.

STATUTORY POWERS
Acts of Parliament

The Town and Country Planning Act, 1971, requires a local planning authority to institute a survey of their area prior to the preparation of a structure plan. The Act specifies that the structure plan shall be a written statement 'formulating the local planning authority's policy and general proposals in respect of the development and other use of land in that area (including measures for the improvement of the physical environment and the management of traffic)'.[3] Similar provisions apply to the preparation of local plans.[4]

It is clear that waste disposal and pollution control are relevant topics in the survey and are to be considered in proposing measures for the improvement of the physical environment in the structure plan. Indeed a memorandum on the interpretation of the Act stresses that local planning authorities should 'interpret the term "the improvement of the physical environment" in a wide sense. They should, in formulating proposals in a structure or local plan, have regard to the need to combat and prevent pollution, even though responsibility and specific action in this field will often be for other bodies than the local planning authority.'[5] The Act grants local planning authorities the power to serve a discontinuance order if 'it is expedient in the interests of the proper planning of their area (including the interests of amenity), regard being had to the development plan and to any other material consideration.'[6] Amenity, the enhancement of which is one of the central purposes of planning legislation, would appear to encompass pollution, since an order made under the provisions of the Act refers to 'detriment to the amenity of that area by reason of noise, vibration, smell, fumes, smoke, soot, ash, dust or grit.'[7]

Certain types of pollution may be controlled under provisions of the Act. The avoidance of water pollution is clearly one reason why development may be refused as premature with reference to 'any existing deficiency in the provision of water supplies or sewerage services, and the period within which any such deficiency may reasonably be expected to be made good.'[8]

Provision for the abatement of certain types of land pollution is also contained in the Act. Thus, 'if it appears to a local planning authority that the amenity of any part of their area, or of any adjoining area, is seriously injured by the condition of any garden, vacant site or other open land in their area. . . . the authority may serve . . . a notice . . . requiring . . . steps for abating the injury. . . .'[9] This provision obviously embraces the deposit of solid wastes such as rubble, rubbish and litter. However, refuse may be tipped on land already used for that purpose without planning permission provided that the height of the deposit does not exceed the level of the land adjoining the site and that the superficial area of the deposit is not extended.[10]

Any local planning authority may carry out work to enable derelict, neglected or unsightly land to be brought into use or to be improved in appearance.[11] Works may be carried out on land acquired by the authority or on privately owned land with the consent of the persons interested in the land, which may, under certain circumstances, be compulsorily purchased for this purpose. Such areas clearly include land polluted by both toxic and non-toxic solid wastes and by certain liquid wastes.

The Countryside Act, 1968, imposes positive duties on local planning authorities in relation to the countryside. Damage to amenity from land, air, noise and water pollution is encompassed by the provision that 'every public body shall have regard to the desirability of conserving the natural beauty and amenity of the countryside.'[12] There is a specific provision regarding water pollution since local authorities shall 'have due regard to the protection against pollution of any water, whether on the surface or underground, which belongs to statutory water undertakers or which statutory water undertakers are for the time being authorised to take.'[13]

The Land Compensation Act, 1973, also requires local planning authorities to consider pollution in deliberating about certain types of development. Local authorities and other bodies have a duty to compensate owners of land for depreciation in the value of their property caused by 'physical factors' arising from the use of highways, aerodromes and other public works. The physical factors are 'noise, vibration, smell, fumes, smoke and artificial lighting and the discharge on to the land in respect of which the claim is made of any solid or liquid substance.'[14]

Statutory instruments
The two main orders made under the 1971 Town and Country Planning Act are both relevant to the control of pollution. The noise and, especially, air pollution arising from different industrial uses of land is

taken into account in the distinction made between light, general and special industrial buildings in the Use Classes Order.[7] Thus, a light industrial building is 'an industrial building . . . in which the processes carried on or the machinery installed are such as could be carried on or installed in any residential area without detriment to the amenity of that area by reason of noise, vibration, smell, fumes, smoke, soot, ash, dust or grit'. Special industrial buildings, which include all works registrable under the Alkali etc, Works Orders, are grouped according to the character of the offence likely to arise from the process, in order to ensure that the local planning authority is able to control changes of use which might give rise to pollution.

The General Development Order[15] contains provisions relating to water pollution. Where 'development consists of or includes':

1   the carrying out of works or operations in the bed or on the banks of a river or stream;
2   the carrying out of building or other operations or use of land for the purpose of refining or storing mineral oils and their derivatives;
3   the use of land for the deposit of any kind of refuse or waste;
4   the carrying out of building or other operations . . . or use of land for the retention, treatment or disposal of sewage, trade waste or sludge;

the local planning authority are required to consult the water authority exercising functions in the area in which the development is to take place and, in determining the application, to take into account any representations received from the authority.[15] No distinction is drawn in the Order between highway traffic and water authority consultations thus suggesting that the latter are regarded as being as important as the former.

With respect to the deposit of solid wastes, an application for permission for the 'construction of buildings or other operations, or use of land, for the disposal of refuse or waste materials or as a scrap yard or coal yard or for the winning or working of minerals; and the construction of buildings or other operations . . . or use of land, for the purpose of the retention, treatment or disposal of sewage, trade waste or sludge' must be advertised in a local newspaper.[15] These types of development are considerably broader in scope than those listed in the previous (1963) order, and the provision gives local residents the opportunity to make known their opinions about proposals having amenity and pollution implications.

However, despite these safeguards on new development for solid waste disposal, the continuance of tipping activity on land already used for this purpose is not closely controlled. The effect of the provision in the Act relating to waste tipping [10] together with that of the permission in the General Development Order [15] relating to mineral excavations is that an application for planning permission is not required to continue tipping in an excavation already used for that purpose until it is filled to the level of the adjoining land. The continuance of colliery spoil tipping begun before July 1, 1948 is classed as permitted development,[16] provided the site was held for this purpose at the time, even if the area and height of deposits are extended. Since large acreages of land containing excavations are used for tipping, and since the National Coal Board have held large quantities of land for tipping purposes since 1948, there is no planning control over a significant part of the solid waste generated in Britain.

CIRCULARS

These statutory powers and requirements are supplemented by a number of central government circulars which, in effect, give instructions about the planning policies to be adopted in the light of current legislation. The circulars advise or request local planning authorities to consider water, noise, air and land pollution in making certain decisions at both the plan-making and the development control stages of the planning process and to consult the various authorities responsible for pollution control where necessary. (In addition, circulars relating to new road construction and traffic management—for example, that suggesting that road designers should seek to alleviate the problem of noise by means of various techniques[17]—are obviously relevant.)

Plan making

The main circular concerning the preparation of plans[5] states that, in the preparation of structure plans, 'local planning authorities, especially when concerned with the location of major new development, should bear in mind the need to consult river authorities and, as appropriate, joint sewerage boards, main drainage authorities and internal drainage boards as regards available water resources, effluent disposal and land drainage. Consultation should take place with statutory undertakers ... where their interests are likely to be affected by the location of population and of new development'.

Water pollution is clearly an important consideration here, and the same general principles apply also in the case of local plans.

Fresh emphasis to this advice is given in a circular[18] drawing attention to the third report of the Royal Commission on Environmental Pollution which deals with pollution in some estuaries and coastal waters.[19] The circular repeats the Commission's recommendation that planning authorities consult river authorities before passing any plan which would increase the effluent load on an estuary and then states that 'such consultation should be an integral part of the close liaison with public bodies which is essential for realising the benefits of the new planning system'.[18]

A circular asking local planning authorities to bear noise in mind when drawing up their land use and transport policies has been issued.[20] It stresses the use of development plans to prevent the establishment of new industry in places where it could cause nuisance by noise and generally commends the findings of the Wilson Committee[21] to authorities. A more extensive circular dealing with planning and noise from a variety of sources—which reflects a marked change in policy—has also been distributed.[22] Although the circular deals mainly with the control of development it suggests that the principles it contains will have an important bearing on the plan-making activities of planning authorities.

The circular does not merely request local planning authorities to 'consider noise' or 'bear noise in mind' but suggests that a great deal can be done by positive planning to reduce the risk of intrusion of noisy development and to meet existing problems. Further, the possibility of relocating existing sources of noise which are unsuitably sited must not be overlooked where redevelopment is to take place or resources allow. Again, it suggests that noise will often be a factor in the evaluation of alternatives, both in considering the major issues in structure plans and in making more detailed proposals in local plans.[22]

A draft circular relating to planning and clean air, which also demonstrates the positive approach of the noise circular, has been circulated for consultation.[23] It emphasises that greater weight should be given to atmospheric pollution matters than has sometimes been the case in the past, while recognising that factors relating to pollution will have to be weighed with others. The circular states that in preparing plans, local planning authorities will have regard to the

effects of one form of development on another in allocating land for
use for particular purposes. Where areas are allocated for industrial
purposes and are likely to be used for industries of kinds giving rise to
problems as a result of grit, dust or fumes they should consider the
situation of the land in relation to existing or proposed development
which would be affected by the emissions, having regard to topography, prevailing winds and other climatic conditions.

Development control
The use of development control procedures to control pollution is
advised in several circulars. A circular[24] accompanying the General
Development Order stresses that, in carrying out their statutory consultations, authorities are encouraged to continue any consultations
under existing local arrangements with the British Waterways Board
or the appropriate water undertaker where their interests might be
affected. It also states that, in addition, it is desirable that regional
water authorities should be consulted on applications for planning
permission relating to or involving the erection of buildings or installation of plant for the compounding, manufacture, storage, or significant use of toxic chemicals and on proposals to change the use of
existing buildings to use for that purpose being received. Authorities
are asked to let water authorities know of any proposals which appear
to them likely to give rise to pollution.

    Another circular dealing with water pollution advises that local
planning authorities should consult water undertakers when the construction of pipelines is proposed which (if they were to leak toxic or
other polluting liquids) might endanger water supplies.[25] Although
the consultation arrangements have now changed, potential pollution
is still considered important since promoters of cross-country
pipelines are required 'to serve notice of their applications at the
appropriate time on every local planning authority, regional water
authority, statutory water company and other statutory water undertakers through whose area a proposed pipeline would pass'.[26] In the
case of local pipelines, 'the relevant planning authority should consult
regional water authorities, statutory water companies and other
statutory water undertakers through whose area a proposed pipeline
would pass'.[26]

    There are three circulars concerned with development control
planning and noise pollution. Noise can properly be taken into

account when dealing with applications for planning permission for industrial development and for development likely to be affected by aircraft noise.[20] In some cases it may be appropriate to grant permission subject to a condition requiring the incorporation of reasonable soundproofing in the buildings. A circular dealing with planning conditions generally[27] indicates that conditions relating to the use of certain types of machinery, to the times when machinery may not be used and to soundproofing, may be attached to planning permissions for certain types of development, in order to limit the effects of noise.

The circular on planning and noise[22] deals with noise from roads, aircraft and industrial development, and provides a large number of detailed guidelines. In planning new roads, an important factor to be taken into account is whether predicted noise levels are acceptable in relation to existing development. Similarly, policies should be adopted which will ensure that the effects of traffic noise are given full weight when decisions are being reached on planning applications for new housing development. It suggests that development on comprehensive lines may be necessary adjacent to major roads so that continuous noise barriers can be constructed or layouts devised to reduce noise in hospitals, schools and other noise sensitive developments. Local planning authorities are requested to work closely with highway authorities to ensure that noise levels to which residential development is exposed do not exceed 70 dB(A) on the L_{10}(eighteen-hour) scale now or during the next fifteen years.

In the case of aircraft noise, the circular lays down principles relating to development of various types within certain noise contours. It is extremely important to ensure that land which is (or is likely to be) subject to significant aircraft noise nuisance is not used for noise sensitive development. Aircraft noise is taken not to present a problem at levels below 40 NNI, whereas housing should not normally be permitted at levels in excess of 50 NNI. The circular urges local planning authorities to co-operate closely with airport owners to ensure that policies take into account noise levels projected to apply in fifteen years' time.

The circular stresses that local planning authorities should seek to avoid the creation of situations in which new commerce or industry might inflict noise annoyance on existing development in the vicinity, or in which new residential or other noise sensitive development might be subject to noise annoyance from existing industrial or other premises. Authorities are urged to co-operate closely with the appropriate public health authority to ensure that increases in ambient noise levels affecting residential and other noise sensitive development are avoided. It suggests that ambient levels affecting such development should not be allowed to rise above a Corrected Noise Level of 75 dB(A) by day or 65 dB(A) by night.[22]

In the case of air pollution, local planning authorities have been reminded of the need to give especially careful consideration to proposals for the erection of very tall new buildings in situations where they might be affected by emissions from existing chimney stacks serving large industrial installations.[28] The draft circular,[23] which will incorporate this advice when released, suggests that the need to consider questions of atmospheric pollution will arise both in relation to proposals to erect industrial plant or buildings and proposals for residential or other sensitive development in the vicinity of existing industrial buildings. It recommends that medical officers of health or environmental health inspectors be consulted in deciding applications. In some cases, not necessarily confined to pollution from registered works, Her Majesty's Alkali and Clean Air Inspectorate should be consulted. Local planning authorities concerned with proposals for registrable works or development in the vicinity of such works should always consult the Inspectorate. The circular stresses that where the best practicable means are unlikely to secure a suitable environment for surrounding development planning conditions designed to secure greater control of the processes themselves will generally be difficult to justify and the issue to be decided will be whether to grant or refuse permission for the industrial development.[23]

A circular dealing with refuse disposal[29] states that when considering applications for permission to use land for the tipping of refuse, local authorities will have regard to the recommended code of practice (reproduced in the circular), much of which will often be appropriate for incorporation in conditions attached to planning consents. As mentioned earlier, it is now a statutory duty to consult the regional water authority (previously the river authority) when such an application is received. The circular draws attention to a report on refuse disposal which pointed out the limitations of planning control over solid and liquid waste disposals.[30]

AUTHORITY TO CONTROL POLLUTION

This review has demonstrated that local planning authorities do, in fact, possess very considerable powers and responsibilities in the field of pollution control. However, this authority to control pollution has not always been fully recognised. Thus, two excellent reviews of the various powers to control pollution in Britain have appeared in the planning literature, neither of which has sufficiently emphasised the powers and responsibilities of the local planning authority in this respect. Indeed, one review mentions only the planning authority's power to redress injury to amenity by solid waste pollution.[31] The other, while listing rather wider responsibilities, states that the local planning authority's legal powers, other than in terms of development control, are very limited.[32]

This lack of recognition of the local planning authority's power to control pollution may well stem from the fact that official emphasis has only recently been granted to it. For example, there was much less weight attached to pollution in plan preparation prior to the advent of structure plans in the 1968 Town and Country Planning Act. Before that date a development plan was to be submitted 'indicating the manner in which a local planning authority propose that land in their area be used, whether by the carrying out thereon of development or otherwise, and the stages by which any such development should be carried out'.[33] Despite the power to serve discontinuance orders[6] mentioned earlier, pollution was certainly not stressed as a relevant consideration in drawing up this type of plan.

Statutory instruments have also shown increasing recognition of pollution. Only the most recent Use Classes Order[7] groups works controlled by the Alkali Inspectorate into classes which take account of the character of the offence likely to arise from the process, rather than relying wholly on the criterion whether the works are registrable,[34] and only the most recent General Development Order imposes a duty to consult the regional water authority.[15] As pointed out above this Order also widens the range of polluting activities about which the public can make representations. There has, too, been a marked change in emphasis in official circulars, as the earlier discussion of the planning and noise[22] and the draft planning and clean air[23] circulars demonstrated. It is apparent that a real shift in thinking about the role of planning in the control of pollution is taking place and that the positive contribution that local planning authorities can make is beginning to be recognised.

There is obviously scope for considerable further development of this thinking, for example, in the further planning control of pollution from solid wastes, in the enforcement of planning conditions relating to pollution control and in ensuring that gradual increases in noise levels arising from intensification of use (rather than change in use) are controlled. There are also criticisms to be made of some of the requirements, for example, that instructing an authority to seek the advice of the Alkali Inspectorate, who also advise the industrial concern applying to them for planning permission. Nevertheless, it is clear that the very considerable powers of pollution control which are vested in planning authorities are increasing both in scope and in recognition.

REFERENCES
1   Cullingworth, J. B. (1972) *Town and country planning in Britain* Allen & Unwin, London.
2   Heap, D. — *Encyclopaedia of planning law and practice* Sweet & Maxwell, London.
3   *Town and Country Planning Act, 1971* s. 7 (3).
4   *Town and Country Planning Act, 1971* s. 11.
5   Department of the Environment (1971) *Memorandum on Part 1 of the Town and Country Planning Act, 1968* Circular 44/71, HMSO, London.
6   *Town and Country Planning Act, 1971* s. 51 (1).
7   *Town and Country Planning (Use Classes) Order, 1972* SI 1972, No. 1385.
8   *Town and Country Planning Act, 1971* s. 147 (4).
9   *Town and Country Planning Act, 1971* s. 65 (1).
10 *Town and Country Planning Act, 1971* s. 22 (3).
11 *National Parks and Access to the Countryside Act, 1949* s. 89 (2).
12 *Countryside Act, 1968* s. 11.
13 *Countryside Act, 1968* s. 38.
14 *Land Compensation Act, 1973* s. 1 (2).
15 *Town and Country Planning General Development Order, 1973* SI 1973, No. 31.
16 *Town and Country Planning Act, 1971* sched. 8 (1).
17 Department of the Environment (1972) *Implementing the report of the Urban Motorways Committee* Circular Roads 56/72, DoE, London.
18 Department of the Environment (1972) *Third report of the Royal Commission on Environmental Pollution* Circular 118/72, HMSO, London.
19 Royal Commission on Environmental Pollution (1972) *Third report* Cmnd 5054, HMSO, London.

20 Ministry of Housing and Local Government (1967) *Noise, industrial noise* Circular 22/67, HMSO, London.
21 Committee on the problem of noise (Wilson Committee) (1963) *Final report* Cmnd 2056, HMSO, London.
22 Department of the Environment (1973) *Planning and noise* Circular 10/73, HMSO, London.
23 Department of the Environment (1972) *Planning and clean air* Draft circular, DoE, London.
24 Department of the Environment (1973) *Town and Country Planning General Development Order, 1973* Circular 12/73, HMSO, London.
25 Ministry of Housing and Local Government (1962) *Pipelines Act, 1962* Circular 69/62, HMSO, London.
26 Department of the Environment (1974) *Pipelines Act, 1962* Circular 25/74, HMSO, London.
27 Ministry of Housing and Local Government (1968) *The use of conditions in planning permissions* Circular 5/68, HMSO, London.
28 Ministry of Housing and Local Government (1965) *Clean air: tall buildings and industrial emissions* Circular 69/65, HMSO, London.
29 Department of the Environment (1971) *Report of the working party on refuse disposal* Circular 26/71, HMSO, London.
30 Department of the Environment (1971) *Report of the working party on refuse disposal* HMSO, London.
31 Layfield, F. H. B. (1971) Powers for conservation *JTPI, 57* 142–51.
32 Williams, A. J. (1973) The role of the local planning authority in regard to waste and pollution *JPL (1973)* 14–22.
33 *Town and Country Planning Act, 1971* sched. 5 (1 (2)).
34 Department of the Environment (1972) *The Town and Country Planning (Use Classes) Order, 1972* Circular 97/72, HMSO, London.

Apart from limiting new residential development within certain noise contours around airports, the local planning authority may insist that soundproofing conditions are appended to planning conditions. Such planning control requires the use of pollution standards.

CHAPTER 4

Planning as a method of pollution control

It has been established that planning possesses the potential to contribute to pollution control at various stages in the pollution process and that the local planning authority, whether by intention or not, actually does play a considerable part in determining pollution levels. It has also been shown that planning authorities have at their disposal very substantial powers to control pollution. It now remains to analyse the nature of this potentially powerful method of pollution control in more detail.

The first stage in such an analysis must be to discuss the level of pollution control which is appropriate. Only then is it realistic to consider the role of planning in implementing that control. This chapter accordingly commences by examining the criteria which planning authorities might follow in controlling pollution and the extent to which the exercise of planning powers is compatible with the general principles of pollution control, of which the most basic is the attainment of an optimum level of control. After discussing the use of pollution standards the chapter delineates the various contributions that local planning authorities could make to the implementation of pollution control and raises the question of planning control in the absence of agreed criteria. Finally, it discusses briefly the extent to which the exercise of planning powers is complementary to or conflicts with the activities of other pollution control authorities and the reconciliation of pollution control objectives with the numerous other planning objectives.

OPTIMUM LEVEL OF POLLUTION CONTROL

There exists, in principle at least, an optimum level of pollution control at which the additional (or marginal) costs of controlling pollution equal the additional benefits arising from it. Suppose that a firm manufactures some product by a process generating a certain amount of waste which, when released to the environment, causes a certain level of pollution damage. This level of damage can be reduced by controlling the release of waste. In Figure 2 the function AB indicates the level of pollution damage caused, varying according to the degree

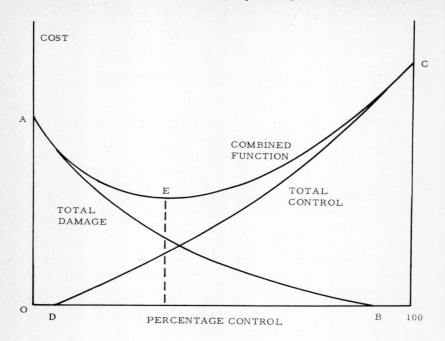

FIGURE 2   Damage and control costs

of control exercised. An incremental increase in control will lead to a
corresponding reduction in pollution damage of all kinds. Similarly
CD indicates the corresponding control costs associated with different degrees of control. These costs include the capital and operating
costs of control equipment, the administrative costs of control and the
broader social costs (including effects on local unemployment, regional development, etc) associated with stricter control.

Which is the 'best' level of pollution control among the alternatives
shown? The point of nearly 100 per cent control eliminates pollution
damage but entails high control costs: the point of zero control avoids
all control costs, but entails high damage. An intermediate view is
that the 'best' level of control occurs where the combined damage
and control costs (AB and CD) are at a minimum, corresponding to a
control level of E in Figure 2.[1] That this is the optimum level of
control can be shown by equating the marginal costs of damage and
control.[2] If this argument is accepted, then the 'best' solution to the

pollution problem may mean that some pollution damage is still caused, the elimination of which could cost society more than the additional benefit to which it would give rise.

The 'polluter pays' principle
The objective of an optimal level of pollution control is related to the question of who should pay the costs of controlling pollution. It is generally regarded as equitable to make the polluter pay; ie, the costs associated with pollution should be fully borne by the polluter responsible. In Britain the polluter normally bears the full cost of implementing whatever level of control is decided upon. There are exceptions to this generalisation: the government makes grants to householders for approved capital costs of conversion to smokeless fuel systems, for example. On the whole, however, the polluter pays for the control of pollution, but makes little or no contribution towards the cost of the damage caused by the pollution arising from the uncontrolled proportion of the wastes.

Two ways of ensuring that the polluter bears the cost of damage or of additional control by others are to allow third parties the right to claim compensation for damage and the imposition of a system of charges. The legal right to compensation for the effects of pollution is restricted in Britain, being limited to riparian owners, certain property owners and those seriously affected by a public nuisance.[3] Nevertheless there have been circumstances in which actions have been successfully brought (for example, riparian rights to fish and claims under the Land Compensation Act, 1973). Charges are not widely levied upon polluters in Britain, although sewage disposal authorities normally demand payment for the treatment of industrial wastes according to volume and content, quite apart from the normal rate charge. Both methods of enforcing the 'polluter pays' principle are capable of extension to other situations.

Problems inherent in the objective
of optimum pollution control
In most pollution control situations it is, at present, unrealistic to attempt comprehensive cost-benefit comparisons of a nature similar to that outlined above because of both conceptual and empirical measurement problems in identifying the determinants of the optimum level of pollution control. There are very considerable

difficulties associated with the establishment of dose/response (damage) functions. In other words, it is not generally known what degree of damage to a particular receptor is associated with a given level of pollution. Although numerous laboratory experiments on materials, animals and plants have been conducted to determine responses, the translation of these experiments into situations where more than one pollutant, weather, exposure and other factors constitute the relevant variables is fraught with difficulty. The accurate identification of the source or sources of a particular pollutant is also very hazardous.

Because of the difficulties involved in establishing the extent of damage actually associated with pollution concentrations in a particular area, the estimation of these effects in terms of measurable parameters (number of days off work, percentage drop in crop yield, number of hours sunshine lost, etc.) is obviously hazardous. Similarly the next stage, the fixing of money values to these parameters, involves additional uncertainties and controversy.[4]

In principle, it should be less difficult to obtain estimates of expenditure on pollution control than it is to put a monetary value upon damage. In practice, figures are by no means readily available. Although it is extremely difficult to operate a system designed to attain the optimum level of pollution control, the cost-benefit rationale is valuable in establishing, on a systematic basis, all the categories of cost and benefit which are relevant when formulating objectives in any pollution control situation. The use of environmental impact statements (discussed in Appendix 1) involves inventories of pollution and other environmental damage prior to the granting of permission for construction to proceed and can be viewed as an intermediate step towards this cost-benefit approach.

Difficulties in achieving the optimum level
by planning controls
It is clearly necessary that a set of principles should guide the control of pollution by planning. Planning control can, in theory at least, be compatible with the attainment of the optimum level of pollution control and so, in principle, it should be possible to establish planning criteria which are consistent with this objective. However, apart from the problem of actually identifying the optimum level, there are additional obstacles to the use of planning to achieve the optimum level of pollution control.

First, planning is not a particularly sensitive method of controlling pollution. Unlike the systems of control which it complements, planning does not have a continuing interest in and control over the pollution from a particular activity. Once the planning decision has been made, it can only be altered by the serving of a discontinuance order, the revocation of permission or the modification of conditions attached to the permission. These procedures involve confirmation by the Secretary of State for the Environment and the payment of compensation. Pollution control requirements can thus only realistically be set at the particular point in time when the planning authority can reach their initial decision on an application without having to pay compensation to the parties affected. These requirements may, of course, be met for a considerable period. (The approval of a discontinuance order made on pollution grounds is cited in Chapter 10 but this appears to be one of very few such actions.) An additional element of insensitivity is provided by technological change affecting the pollution arising from a development over the years—such change obviously cannot be accurately forecast at the time the decision is made (some alterations may be deemed to represent changes of use and hence be subject to planning controls but these would be exceptional). Even at this time, pollution is weighed against other planning criteria and the ultimate design solution may naturally not be that which would result from considering pollution alone. However, if the determinants of the optimum level are sufficiently broadly defined, this type of conflict might not be important.

Second, the control of pollution through the use of planning conditions has not always been effective partly because of enforcement difficulties and partly because of the problem of their duplicating the requirements of other pollution control authorities (discussed later). Once a development has been sanctioned, local authorities are often loath to take legal action to ensure the complete fulfilment of conditions. In addition, the small fines payable under enforcement orders do not provide an adequate incentive to adhere to planning conditions. For example, it has sometimes been difficult to ensure that land used for tipping is fully restored in accord with the conditions attached to the permission once the activity has ceased.[5][6] However, planning conditions are now being expressed in much more specific terms than previously[7][8] and enforcement may become less difficult.

Third, it is essential that pollution control objectives be defined

very clearly, since objectives which simply refer to 'reducing pollution' are not particularly helpful in attempting to attain the optimum
level of pollution control. Ideally, recognition of the costs and
benefits inherent in controlling pollution would need to be taken into
account in the formulation of planning objectives designed to achieve
the optimum level. This would necessarily present local planning
authorities with considerable difficulties since the necessary cost-
benefit information would seldom be available and, in any case, planning objectives are normally framed in much more general terms.

The multiplicity of planning objectives presents a fourth fundamental difficulty in achieving the optimum level of pollution control.
The central government circulars discussed in Chapter 3 clearly state
that the pollution control responsibilities of local planning authorities
are to be exercised along with their other planning duties. Even
where noise standards are indicated, it is apparent that these may be
exceeded if other planning considerations outweigh noise pollution.
The powers and responsibilities of local planning authorities in controlling pollution, while considerable, are obviously intended to be
exercised according to local circumstances and to be weighed against
other criteria. For these reasons, it is apparent that the control of
pollution through the exercise of planning powers cannot be administered in such a way as to attain the theoretically ideal objective of an
optimum level of pollution.

STANDARDS

The difficulties inherent in operating a system of control based upon
the 'optimum level' lead to the examination of an alternative but
complementary system, that of standard setting. Standards, which
may be set either to achieve the optimum level of control or to attain
some more empirical objective, may relate to the effluent and emissions of an individual waste discharger, to the quality of the air, water
or land environment or to the quality of products.

Pollution control standards are set by the appropriate pollution
control authority in the light of the relevant circumstances and generally take some account of the relationship between the costs and
benefits of control. However, they tend, of necessity, to be generally
somewhat arbitrary since numerical levels have to be fixed in the
absence of a complete knowledge of the facts. In Britain standards
are brought to bear on several types of waste discharge. The Alkali

Inspectorate imposes numerical standards on certain emissions in administering the 'best practicable means' method of control (below).[9] Environmental Health Inspectors' use of 'approved appliances' involves observing a standard[10][11] and the regulations limiting emissions from motor vehicles[12] represent a third set of standards over air-borne wastes. There are no true standards applied to land pollution, although a recommended code of practice applies to waste tipping (Chapter 3), but the regional water authorities' consent conditions are another example of effluent standards.[13] There are also standards set for motor vehicle noise.[12]

It is much less common to impose standards on pollutant concentrations in this country, although smoke control areas (which involve the virtual prohibition of smoke emissions [10][11]) and the recent noise control areas[14] are examples of this type of environmental quality standard. They are more usual in the United States.[15] Discharge standards are, however, related to pollution concentrations in the air or in water or to noise levels; in other words, to pollution standards.

Where precise numerical environmental standards have not been set, the pollution control authorities normally exert control on the basis of a general set of objectives, often related to the 'best practicable means' of control. This is a somewhat empirical approach to control in which standards for a particular discharge are gradually raised in accordance with the best means of control available at a realistic cost. The control authority are thus able to exert better performance by comparison with that achieved elsewhere and poor temporary emissions may be tolerated provided that overall improvements are being made.[16] This method of control, which relies on co-operation—and on a degree of compromise—between controller and polluter, is widely employed in Britain.

Standards as planning criteria
The exercise of planning powers to assist in the implementation of independently determined standards is a much more practicable proposition than employing such powers to promote the more nebulous objective of the optimum level of pollution control. The local planning authority could assist in the attainment of standards relating to air, land, water or noise pollution at the plan-making stage and by limiting or imposing conditions on new development at the development control stage. For example, a standard requiring no increase in

the existing noise level could be maintained by ensuring that no new commercial or industrial development is permitted in the relevant area. Again, an air quality standard could be attained by limiting development to that which will emit no smoke or only a given quantity of, say, sulphur dioxide. Similarly, the rejection of applications for development which would occasion direct discharges to a water course could be used to attain an existing water quality standard.

Standards may be fixed either nationally or locally. They can also, of course, be fixed quite independently of the activities of local planning authorities. Although feasible, the enforcement of national standards by planning does not appear to be very appropriate. The very flexibility of planning as a method of pollution control tends to militate against the uniform adoption of national standards. Nevertheless, appropriately defined general standards, which were capable of being met by a variety of planning strategies, could often be achieved by planning authorities.

The essence of planning is the adaptation of national policy and general precepts to local circumstances. This extends to pollution standards, since pollution which may be intolerable in one area may be acceptable in another. For example, a certain noise level may be allowable in an industrial estate but be far too high in a residential area. The conflict between concern for amenity and pollution presented by a tall chimney (visual intrusion versus pollutant dispersion) will be resolved differently by different local planning authorities because the local circumstances will vary. Again, the zoning of land close to pollution sources as open space (because sensitive users would be damaged by the pollution) is a matter to be decided in the light of local conditions. To be most appropriate, therefore, pollution standards enforceable by planning measures need to be agreed locally between the pollution control authorities and the planning authority. (The Land Compensation Act, 1973, is likely to have an increasing effect in determining more general standards, however.)

IMPLEMENTATION OF PLANNING CONTROL OVER POLLUTION

At present very few such agreements are reached between pollution control and planning authorities and few precise standards are agreed by the individual pollution control authorities. In these circumstances it is obviously difficult for planning authorities to exert control over pollution in accord with clear and precise pollution control targets. However, in the absence of accurate knowledge about the optimum level of pollution control and of working standards, it is still essential that planning authorities formulate a strategy for pollution control since, whether they are aware of it or not, many of their decisions directly affect pollution levels. Indeed, the number of points in the pollution process at which it is possible to exert planning control and the range of planning powers available to impose such control suggest that there is a wide range of ways in which planning could contribute to pollution control.

Planning decisions relating to the location of waste product generation should be determined in the light of pollution considerations. For example, when a local planning authority takes a decision whether or not to allow a cement works to be built in a particular location, it also decides whether or not the dust which inevitably results from cement manufacture will affect the area surrounding the proposed site. It is apparent that this pollution and the associated damage ought to be considered in reaching the planning permission decision. It has been mentioned that, in addition to their control over the location of waste product generation, the local planning authority also allocate land specifically for waste treatment and disposal. The location of these activities should clearly be decided in relation to the possible pollution arising from the waste treatment.

Although the most potent contribution of planning control would normally be expected to relate to the location of waste products generated by land use activities, it could affect the release of wastes generated by an activity in certain circumstances. In the case of noise, for example, the local planning authority could require adequate soundproofing, thus altering the level of noise emitted from a site. Similarly, they could affect the hours of operation of an activity, thus limiting the time period during which others were damaged by pollution. Again, the authority could lay down conditions specifying the manner of disposition of solid wastes from mineral working in order to control pollution damage to amenity.

The location of receptors with respect to pollution sources could also be influenced by planning control. For example, the allocation of residential land close to sources of air pollution such as steel or chemical works will determine the number of people who suffer annoyance from them. Similarly the decision whether or not to allow housing to be built in close proximity to airports or motorways should be made with noise pollution as a prominent consideration.

In general, as in the case of waste generation, planning can only affect the location of receptors. However, there are occasions where the degree of pollution experienced could be altered. To use the examples of aircraft or road traffic noise, the local planning authority could demand double glazing, sound insulation and other protective measures as a condition of planning permission in order to limit the effects of the noise.

Plan making

The general relationship between the locations of waste producers and of the various types of receptor is established at the plan making stage when the broad allocation of land uses (the areas designated for industrial and residential uses, for recreational pursuits, for waste disposal and for other activities) is laid down. For example, the general location of industry and of major roads with respect to existing and future residential land uses is decided at this stage. Similarly, the type of development to be permitted alongside a river may be planned. It is apparent that the broad land use pattern could be determined in such a way that a considerable contribution was made to pollution control.

Apart from their direct control over land use, the local planning authority are required, in preparing a structure plan, to put forward general policies and specific proposals relating to various matters of environmental concern. The authority must bring the relevant issues before the public, spell out the implications for public investment and provide a co-ordinated basis for the work of the local planning authority and other authorities.[17] It follows that if pollution is to be a relevant issue in the preparation of this type of plan, the authority could have a central co-ordinating role to play in the control of pollution. They could, for example, quite properly arrange for the preparation of a broad ranging review of pollution problems and then encourage the other pollution control authorities to act in a concerted manner in solving them. Although this proposal stems logically from the nature of the structure plan, it is arguable whether such a planning role would be recognised by these authorities without considerable discussion.

In plan preparation at a local level, the planning authority could also make a considerable contribution to pollution control. Apart from the effect of the location of different uses with respect to each other, it is possible that the authority could encourage the drawing up of detailed designs to mitigate the effects of, for example, air and noise pollution.

Similarly, the planning authority could stimulate others to control pollution. For example, the establishment of an urban 'general improvement area' (within which the aim is to help and persuade owners to improve their houses not only by grants and advice but also by improving the environment)[18] will normally be accompanied by a smoke control order, leading to a fall in smoke pollution. The tidying up of the area will remove much solid waste pollution (litter and large dumped items) and tend to prevent its reappearance.

Again, in central area redevelopment schemes, the opening up to a view of a river and the creation of riverside walks may cause the improvement of its condition to be given greater priority. The creation of country parks[19] could encourage water authorities to apply more stringent controls in order to improve water quality where water sports are important. Even without applying these direct stimuli, the local planning authority could use their influence to achieve a good deal in encouraging the control of pollution by the polluters themselves.[17]

Development control

The detailed decisions about the use of land and buildings made at the development control stage can often be of considerable importance in determining the pollution levels in a particular locality. For example, permission to develop a site in an area designated for industry as, say, an iron foundry will give rise to a certain amount of metallurgical fume pollution around the works. Again, the change of use of a cellar from warehouse to a night club will create night-time noise. Pollution control could be an important consideration in making decisions about the granting of planning permission or in imposing conditions upon it.

Planning could have a further pollution control management function during the administration of development control. The authority could inform the relevant pollution control authorities when an application to develop is received and the control authority could then recommend that the development be permitted or refused on pollution grounds or that conditions be attached. On receiving notification, the control authority could advise the developer about pollution control requirements directly, thus ensuring that the necessary steps to meet them are taken at the outset. This is generally a more satisfactory procedure from every point of view than attempting to impose control measures once the design stage has been completed.

Planning control in the absence of agreed objectives
It is clear that certain planning decisions can affect pollution levels at both the plan-making and the development control stages of the planning process. It is also clear that pollution can be taken into account in the decision or it can be ignored. It is more likely that planning authorities will consider pollution if precise pollution control targets have been communicated to them by the other pollution control authorities. However, even in their absence, it is essential that the planning authority adopts a positive attitude to control if pollution levels are not to be unnecessarily increased. Indeed, the local planning authority can give the lead to the other control authorities as the examples of general improvement areas and riverside walks (above) suggest.

Planning authorities should, therefore, while pressing the other control authorities to set quantitative standards where appropriate, proceed on the basis of qualitative objectives formulated on the best advice available from the control authorities in the interim. Even an objective like 'minimise pollution' would be better than none in a situation where it enabled the planning authority to make a decision in which other considerations were evenly balanced. In general, however, they would be more precise than this and might be stated in such terms as, for example, 'reduce the effect of industrial air pollution and noise on nearby dwellings by reallocation of land whenever the opportunity arises'.

Reconciliation of planning and other types of pollution control
It is apparent that planning could play a very constructive role in the implementation of pollution control objectives, whether these are set by pollution control authorities or by the local planning authority. The opportunities to exercise planning powers to control pollution will depend upon the type and age of the settlement administered. New development and the redevelopment of older areas obviously

afford more opportunities for intervention in pollution control than heavily developed areas with a substantial life. The degree to which planning powers are exercised to control pollution will depend not only upon the existence of objectives but on the motivation of the local planning authority, which will turn, to some extent, upon conflicts with the other authorities.

It will seldom be the function of the local planning authority to formulate objectives in isolation (except, for example, in the case of derelict land reclamation targets) but it is obviously appropriate that they be closely involved in the process of formulation of agreed policies. In an ideal arrangement, control standards could be implemented by reference to a land use planning/pollution model, although such a methodology is unlikely to be of practical value for some years (Chapter 5). In the absence of the guidance which such a model might provide, it is essential that a very close working liaison exist between the local planning authority and other pollution control authorities to avoid conflicts during the implementation of objectives.

Any conflict with the authorities responsible for controlling pollution of the air, of the land, of water and by noise would arise over decisions relating to the location of polluting activities or sensitive receptors and over the appending of conditions intended to control pollution to the planning permission. There appear to be three reasons for potential disagreement. First, there is the question of who should implement an agreed standard of pollution control. Second, the authorities may disagree about whether a particular discharge is consistent with an agreed standard. Third, the planning authority may not be aware of a standard or may face a choice between implementation of a pollution control objective and other planning objectives.

In the case of air pollution it is quite possible that a conflict with either the local environmental health officer or the Alkali Inspector could arise if the planning authority disregarded their advice and refused permission for development on the grounds that it was likely to give rise to air pollution. It is perhaps more likely, however, that the authority would disregard their advice that pollution would result and grant permission. A very real problem could occur if the planning authority attempted to impose conditions to the permission to limit pollution (for example, by restricting the sulphur content of fuel). Both air pollution control authorities have powers to impose control on emissions and any attempt to duplicate these by the use of plan-

ning conditions would be fiercely resisted by the Department of the
Environment (see Chapter 10).

There is unlikely to be significant conflict in the control of land
pollution, since the local planning authority is the agency principally
responsible. (The environmental health officer does possess some
powers over nuisance from tipping operations but few disagreements
seem likely to arise.)

Conflict with the regional water authority or sea fisheries committee could be precipitated by a decision about the location of new
development likely to generate water-borne wastes, in much the
same way as with the air pollution control authorities. There is, however, a statutory requirement in the case of certain types of development control to consult regional water authorities (see Chapter 3),
whose views must be considered and reported in the decision. It
appears that planning authorities have not frequently tried to impose
conditions relating to effluent discharges and any attempt to do so
would no doubt be resisted as a needless and complicating duplication of existing powers.

In the case of noise, the environmental health officer possesses only
limited powers but conflicts could arise if his advice about whether or
not to grant permission to a noisy development was disregarded.
Because no parallel powers exist, some planning authorities have
attached conditions relating to noise levels to planning permissions,
conflicts only arising from the nature of the conditions and not from
their use.

Conflicts can also occur between the local planning authority and
the various pollution control authorities about the location of sensitive pollution receptors, particularly housing developments. The
planning authority may feel an area is too polluted and refuse permission despite advice from, say, the environmental health officer. However, it is again probably more likely that permission will be granted
against the advice of the control authority. Conflicts about conditions
might arise if, for example, the planning authority insisted upon
soundproofing or planting (to reduce air pollution) before permitting
a development.

The planning authority's decision in any land use conflicts is generally final since they hold the power to grant or refuse planning permissions, subject to appeal. However, the number of serious conflicts
should be reduced to those where pollution control is overridden by

other objectives, provided the local planning authority are careful to carry out full and meaningful consultations. Indeed, in general, planning powers are complementary to those of other pollution control authorities and could be employed to reinforce them. The number of areas where the responsibilities of planning authorities conflict directly with the powers of other agencies is very small, and disagreement is only likely to arise over the way in which planning powers are exercised, not over whether they are exercised.

In effect, the local planning authority are generally free to exercise their statutory powers to control pollution to the degree they feel appropriate. It is, in the last resort, open to the authority to decide either to contribute to the control of pollution or not to contribute. The one exception is the statutory requirement to consult regional water authorities mentioned earlier, though the weight to be given to the opinions expressed is discretionary. Similarly the circulars, while being much more specific than the statutes about the role of local planning authorities in controlling air, land, water and noise pollution, make it plain that their pollution control responsibilities should be exercised according to local circumstances and to the extent the authority feel to be appropriate.

Reconciliation of conflicts with other planning criteria
The exercise of the numerous planning roles in the control of pollution is thus seen to be almost totally at the discretion of the local planning authority, despite the fact that planning powers are mainly complementary to those of other pollution control authorities and despite the undoubted potential effectiveness of the powers. Apart from possible conflicts with these authorities, one of the most important factors influencing the local planning authority in the discharge of their responsibilities (which has already been mentioned briefly) is the reconciliation of pollution control criteria with the numerous other planning objectives.

The large number of objectives which must be considered in the planning process is apparent from the description of town and country planning as 'the art and science of ordering the use of land and the character and siting of buildings and communication routes so as to secure the maximum practicable degree of economy, convenience and beauty'.[20] This implies that the reconciliation of all the various objectives (whether expressly formulated or not) will inevitably involve compromise in arriving at the final land use pattern or in deciding to grant permission to a particular development. Because many planning objectives conflict directly with others (for example, the objectives of controlling noise from roads by using barriers and of maintaining visual amenity by limiting the height of barriers), it is taken for granted that some will not be achieved and that others will be only partially achieved. This certainly applies in the case of the general type of pollution control objective explicitly or implicitly adopted by many local planning authorities.

There is a large literature relating to the formulation[21] and reconciliation[22] of planning objectives. Although there may be a case for defining objectives to be mutually compatible, there are considerable difficulties where large numbers of aims are involved. Planning objectives are generally stated in terms which do not take account of the contingent or conflicting objectives. The weighting of pollution and other objectives (whether explicit or not) is thus an essential part of the planning process. One method of formalising the procedure, heavily employed in structure planning,[23] is the goals achievement matrix,[24] which maximises the satisfaction of weighted objectives by ensuring that alternative planning solutions are evaluated with respect to these objectives and selecting that attaining the highest score.

The incorporation of pollution control into the planning process in any meaningful way implies that pollution control objectives be defined, that they be weighted against other objectives and that planning solutions be based upon these objectives. The difficulties of following such a procedure where the objective is as nebulous as the achievement of the optimal level of pollution control are obvious. However, it would appear that local planning authorities could have an important contribution to make in the implementation of measures (in conjunction with other pollution control authorities) to achieve pollution standards. It would also seem that the wider use of standards might represent a method of enabling planners to specify objectives more precisely and therefore to make a more effective contribution, through plan making and development control, to the attainment of pollution control targets.

Unfortunately, the local planning authority are regularly faced with decisions having pollution implications which have to be made in the absence of definite information about the optimum level of control and of precise environmental standards. The implementation of pollution control by planning in the absence of agreed criteria is therefore an important issue. A set of principles should underlie not only the implementation of such criteria but the taking of decisions in their absence. Because certain actions will inevitably affect pollution levels, the local planning authority should formulate clearly defined objectives as a basis for controlling pollution, even if these are more closely related to the empirical 'best practicable means' approach than to more precise criteria. In other words, the planning authority may have to formulate pollution control objectives in such terms as 'reduce pollution to the maximum degree in the light of all the relevant planning circumstances'. Such objectives may, in practice, not be explicitly formulated in every case, provided they are implicitly accepted.

It is not, however, sufficient for local planning authorities to create a 'shop window effect' by paying lip service to the problem of pollution in their plans, while omitting to make any positive planning proposals to control it. On the contrary, it is imperative that local planning authorities recognise the consequences of their decisions on pollution levels and that the decisions reflect this knowledge in a constructive manner.

REFERENCES

1   Ridker, R. G. (1967) *The economic costs of air pollution* Praeger, London.
2   Lee, N., and Luker, J. A. (1971) An introduction to the economics of pollution *Economics*, 9 19–31.
3   McLoughlin, J. (1972) *The law relating to pollution* Manchester University Press, Manchester.
4   Programmes Analysis Unit (1972) *An economic and technical assessment of air pollution in the United Kingdom* Report PAU M20, HMSO, London.
5   Department of the Environment (1971) *Report of the working party on refuse disposal* HMSO, London.
6   Royal Town Planning Institute (1972) *Memorandum of evidence to the Committee on Minerals Planning Control* RTPI, London.
7   Ministry of Housing and Local Government (1968) *The use of conditions in planning permissions* Circular 5/68, HMSO, London.
8   Department of the Environment (1973) *Planning and noise* Circular 10/73, HMSO, London.

9   *Alkali, etc, works Regulation Act, 1906* as extended by the 1966 and 1971 Orders.
10 *Clean Air Act, 1956.*
11 *Clean Air Act, 1968.*
12 *Motor Vehicles (Construction and Use) Regulations, 1973* SI 1973, No. 24.
13 *Water Act, 1973.*
14 *Control of Pollution Act, 1974.*
15 For example, Environmental Protection Agency (1970) *Air quality criteria for sulphur oxides* Publication AP–050, US Government Printing Office, Washington.
16 Department of the Environment (1974) *110th annual report on Alkali, etc, works 1973* HMSO, London.
17 Williams, A. J. (1973) The role of the local planning authority in regard to waste and pollution *JPL (1973)* 14–22.
18 *Housing Act, 1969* Part II.
19 *Countryside Act, 1968* s. 7 (1).
20 Keeble, L. (1969) *Principles and practice of town and country planning* Estates Gazette, London.
21 Chadwick, G. (1971) *A systems view of planning* Pergamon, Oxford.
22 See, for example, Alexander, C. (1970) *Notes on the synthesis of form* Harvard University Press, Cambridge, Mass.
23 McLoughlin, J. B. (1973) Structure planning in Britain *JRTPI, 59* 115–24.
24 Hill, M. (1968) A goals–achievement matrix for evaluating alternative plans *JAIP, 34* 19–28.

CHAPTER 5

Planning techniques for controlling pollution

Dove Holes, Derbyshire, 1972. Local planning authorities can limit motor vehicle noise and air pollution by a variety of traffic management and design techniques. They can also control land pollution by reclaiming derelict land for attractive and constructive uses.

It has been demonstrated that planning could play a variety of roles in contributing to pollution control and that planning authorities possess considerable powers and responsibilities in this field. It is now necessary to examine the techniques available to planners in controlling pollution. However, before analysing the range of techniques for controlling air, land, water and noise pollution, it is instructive to consider the treatment of pollution in planning textbooks and in the planning journals.

POLLUTION IN PLANNING TEXTBOOKS
Both pollution and the planner's role in its control have received

scant attention in the large number of general planning textbooks published during the last fifty years. Without mentioning the word pollution, the need to locate certain industries away from housing because of the noise, dust and smell generated was recognised by 1923.[1] A few years later, planners were encouraged to consider the effect of industry and the design of sewage disposal systems so as to minimise water pollution.[2] Another, later, book commences with a quotation about noise and foul air, but makes no further reference to pollution.[3] Despite these minor exceptions most planning textbooks published before 1945 made little or no mention of pollution or its control.[4-7]

The problem was better recognised after the war. As well as mentioning noise and water pollution, a book published in 1948 urged the use of planning conditions as a method of controlling smoke emissions.[8] A slightly later book devoted a section to air pollution, emphasising its importance in siting such industries as gas production.[9] The desirability of separating airports and industry from housing on noise grounds was also stressed. In 1952 Logie reviewed the noise, the smell, dust and other atmospheric pollutants and the water pollution arising from different industries and produced a table of nuisances.[10] The dangers of siting factories in valleys, the need for control of grit emissions and the need to locate industries with regard to the prevailing wind were stated but the necessity of examining each firm individually, whether a 'special' industry or not, was also emphasised.[10]

Vibration, noise and smell were recognised as affecting the 'environment' in 1961.[11] The importance of atmospheric pollution in planning surveys has been stressed elsewhere,[12] the siting of land uses with respect to pollution being seen as a planning function. Noise and smoke were regarded as matters requiring (unspecified) planning action in 1967[13] and the importance of aircraft noise in airport site selection was re-emphasised in 1969.[14] Many books, however, continued to neglect pollution.[15-18]

Probably the best British treatment of pollution is presented by Cullingworth,[19] whose earlier edition[20] made little mention of the problem. Well referenced sections cover the control of mineral workings, domestic smoke, industrial emissions, vehicle emissions and noise but there is no recognition of the planner's role in controlling pollutants other than solid waste dereliction.[19] A useful pollution bibliography can also be found in a recent guide to planning information[21] which, however, gives little indication that the planner might be able to contribute to pollution control.

A recent book on policy planning (rather than on specifically land use planning) places the greatest emphasis on pollution control measures.[22] It suggests an environmental protection programme which would take its context from the structure plan and involve several agencies in implementation: the various local authority departments, county and district authorities and the water authorities, for example. The programme, which would involve the commitment of capital, would find further expression in local plans, and would consist of sub-programmes for air, water and land. The air sub-programme would set air quality and noise standards and define policies for attaining them (for example, zoning, smoke control, direct actions) where conditions currently fall short and for maintaining them once they have been achieved. The water sub-programme would set water supply and quality standards. Planning policies would then be designed to regulate the location and growth of development as it affects water gathering grounds or overloaded water-courses. The land sub-programme would be concerned with the location and management of domestic refuse and industrial waste disposal and of mineral working, and with the reclamation of derelict land.[22] This approach to pollution control is similar to that proposed as desirable in Chapter 4 and demonstrates a very real awareness of the potential contribution of planning. The difficulties involved in gaining acceptance of the policies, in setting standards and in implementation are not stressed in the book, however.

American planning textbooks generally appear to be marginally more concerned with pollution and its control than their British counterparts. As with Cullingworth,[19] [20] the second edition of Lynch's book[23]—which discusses the reduction of noise by spatial separation, the use of barriers and the sealing of buildings—reflects much more concern with pollution than the first, published eight years earlier. Probably the fullest appreciation of the planner's role in controlling pollution is shown by Chapin,[24] who suggests that land use planning can control exposure to noise and air pollution from road traffic and industry by separation, orientation and internal design of land use areas (for example, by the alignment of roads and use of buffer strips).

L. I. H. E.
THE MARKLAND LIBRARY
STAND PARK RD., LIVERPOOL, L16 9JD

POLLUTION IN PLANNING JOURNALS

A significant number of articles have appeared in those journals British town planners normally take to constitute the planning literature, particularly in more recent years. However, from the planning practitioner's point of view, many of them must be regarded as being of only peripheral academic interest since they are often not directly concerned with planning issues.

Thus one article is devoted to a criticism of the economist's concept of pollution[25] and another to constructing a mathematical model of the process involved in deciding whether or not to pollute the environment.[26] Pollution is one of the considerations in a case study of the costs and benefits involved in constructing a new urban road presented in another journal.[27] Another case study prepared for the same government committee (the Urban Motorways Committee) is reported elsewhere.[28]

In the field of air pollution the use of a regional economic model to assess the economic effects of different (non-planning) control strategies is described[29] in one journal. A later issue carries an account of the calculation of price effects of alternative abatement proposals.[30] Another article describes the calculations of the effects of air pollution on residential property values, concluding that pollution has a very real negative influence.[31] One article which does mention the planner's role briefly (to state that planning should not rely on remote siting, high stacks and atmospheric pollution as effective 'control' techniques) describes air pollution in west central Scotland.[32]

Although numerous articles on dereliction have been published in the planning journals, none appear to have dealt with other land pollution problems. A paper describing the disposal of waste to rivers has appeared in the planning literature[33] together with others which make no mention of the planners' potential contribution to water pollution control.[34-36] An article describing the incorporation of noise into a Lowry-type model assessing the effects of alternative airport sites has appeared.[37] Only a single mainstream planning journal[38] appears not to have printed any articles on pollution.

One journal devoted an issue to noise and its control by planning,[39] another included a useful article on the control of noise[40] and another published two articles on the role of the planning authority in the control of pollution[41,42] (both mentioned earlier), but it is perhaps unsurprising that the journal of the Royal Town Planning Institute

(*The Planner*) has tended to print articles about pollution which are probably of the greatest relevance to the planner. This journal has carried a general review of the subject of pollution and its control by planning.[43] It also printed an early article on special industries[44] stressing the need for the intelligent application of development control by segregation of industries necessarily giving rise to pollution and by the application of planning conditions. The local planning authority's powers of persuasion to implement improvements was also emphasised.[44] Another early paper discussed the relationship between land use planning and air pollution and called for close co-operation between public health and planning officers in taking positive action.[45] An article on planning for clean air, which discussed the siting of new towns, industry and the use of district heating to reduce air pollution, has also appeared.[46]

This journal has, in addition, published a number of articles dealing with noise, the first treatment in depth being contained in a discussion of the planning effects of a new rapid transit system.[47] Three articles on noise[48-50] appeared in a single issue. Together they explain the problem of noise and stress the planner's contribution to its control. A further article demonstrates that urban motorways do not necessarily create a noise nuisance, if appropriate planning action is taken in conjunction with the opening of the new road.[51]

Pollution has not been neglected in the Royal Town Planning Institute's annual Town and Country Planning Summer School either, one contribution[52] being very pessimistic about the planner's ability to control pollution and the next[53] more optimistic. In addition, seminars on noise[54] and papers on international environmental problems[55] and the recycling of urban wastes[56] have been reported.

Pollution has also been a significant subject in the leading American planning journal, that of the American Institute of Planners. Indeed, it has devoted the whole of one issue to the planning of the natural environment[57] and has subsequently published three articles in which pollution has been of general importance.[58-60] A recent article questioned the use of environmental impact statements, suggesting that they might be giving decisions false justification.[61]

Four articles of considerable value to planners seeking to play a role in air pollution control have appeared in the journal. The first deals with the optimum shape of urban areas given widespread use of the automobile.[62] The second presents an excellent summary of the control techniques available to the planner, stressing that the urban form should be designed to clean the air its inhabitants breathe.[63] The next reviews current American research designed to help the planner in controlling air pollution[64] and the last deals with the danger of planning recreational land uses close to roads generating high levels of pollution.[65] An article on the monitoring of noise has also appeared.[66]

From this limited review of the planning literature it would appear that, until recently, pollution was largely ignored. Even now only a proportion of the infrequent articles on the subject are concerned with the potential contribution of planning to pollution control, and these deal mainly with air and noise pollution. It is clear from the handful of articles dealing with air pollution that planning concern has moved from sanitary control (for example, the location of industry with respect to wind direction) to a greater realisation of the urban pollution problem. The relevant papers do contain a considerable amount of information about techniques of pollution control and these, together with the much more numerous items dealing with the contribution of planning control appearing in the pollution literature, form the basis of the following sections.

AIR POLLUTION

Most of the voluminous air pollution literature dealing with the contribution of planning to controlling the problem is American. One book devoted to this subject has been published[67] and a number of the major US textbooks on air pollution contain a chapter on the role of land use planning.[68][69] In addition, three American reviews of the literature on this topic have appeared.[63][70][71] There are several ways in which planning techniques can be applied to air pollution control and many of these may conflict with planning measures against other types of pollution, as well as with other planning aims.

The siting of new development is an important technique for controlling air pollution. An exposed, windy site will allow maximum dispersion of air pollutants to occur and may be chosen in preference to valleys and basins where pollution is liable to be trapped by temperature inversions. [46][72][73] Windward slopes of hills are subject to less air pollution than leeward slopes, which have the better climate.[63] The pollution drifting from other towns separated from the development by open country is unimportant under most conditions.[72]

The separation of industry from residential and other sensitive areas is another effective technique, since the particulate pollutants generated tend to fall out in a localised manner and high chimneys for the dispersal of gaseous pollutants may be employed with less aesthetic difficulty. There are obvious advantages in siting an offending industry at the centre of a large tract of ground to minimise concentrations at the periphery. The location of industrial pollution sources to the leeward side of a town is only really satisfactory when considering tall chimneys emitting large quantities of pollutants. [46] [72] For lower-level emissions wind speed is of more significance than wind direction, and the worst pollution conditions often accompany light non-prevailing winds.[74] The selection of industrial sites to minimise pollution concentrations is thus a matter for detailed analysis.[63] [75] [76] However, valley sites should be avoided wherever possible and, if development of such sites is essential, very high chimneys discharging pollutants above the level of inversions are advisable.[77]

A buffer zone may be placed between industrial uses and sensitive receptors, no matter what their respective orientations are to the wind.[46] Such buffers, of course, are not intended to be a substitute for adequate air pollution control at the source, but rather to supplement control and provide some protection in the event of equipment breakdowns or adverse meteorological conditions. It is difficult to gauge how wide 'sanitary clearance zones' need to be but it is possible to state that they should be planted. Such green buffer zones may well become subject to the same pressures for development as urban green belts (which serve a similar pollution control function) and might best be dedicated to recreational use.

The design and arrangement of buildings may have a considerable effect upon pollution since local temperatures and winds, the two principal determinants of atmospheric diffusion, are affected. The orientation of a single building with respect to topography or local winds can influence dispersion, since eddies may be generated which cause pollution from one building to affect another.[78] The intermixing of high and low buildings should be handled with care since emissions from the lower buildings can cause high pollutant concentrations to affect the upper floors of the taller ones. Wind tunnel experiments to test alternative arrangements may be advisable.[74]

Pollution from residential areas may be reduced by two methods. The first involves reducing the density of dwellings and the second requires the use of district heating. Low-density areas emit less pollution than the equivalent higher-density areas and district heating eliminates individual emissions altogether, centralising fuel-burning into a single easily controlled unit. (The arguments for district heating are less convincing if 'clean' fuels are burned in individual dwellings.[79]) Although the implementation of smoke control areas is not a planning function, planners may encourage the designation of particular areas to reduce air pollution.

Air pollution from road traffic can be abated in a number of ways.[80] The creation of corridors of dense development encourages the use of public transport, which considerably reduces emissions.[81] Vehicular pollution can also be reduced by means of segregating highways from adjoining structures either by vertical or horizontal distance (including green spaces), improving traffic flow by synchronised traffic signals, longer blocks, limited access roads and higher traffic speeds.[82] The optimum speed appears to be about 40 mph, and grade separation and by-passes can be designed to obtain smooth flows to minimise pollutant emissions. Traffic congestion and through traffic in residential areas should be avoided and city-centre pedestrianisation encouraged on air pollution grounds. The zoning of land uses to minimise trip journeys and lengths and the use of car restraint policies to encourage the patronage of public transport are also important in reducing vehicular pollutant emissions.[76]

Pollution concentrations can be reduced by appropriate road and street design. Other things being equal, the more open the roadway configuration, the lower the resultant concentrations of pollutants.[64] Canyon-like city streets inhibit the diffusion of exhaust gases, high buildings and narrow streets retaining pollutants (the leeward side of the street exhibiting the highest pollutant concentrations). Wind velocity, however, is the most important factor in dispersion and this can be increased by city streets under appropriate conditions.[78] Redevelopment may help to disperse pollutants by widening roads and increasing ventilation. Conflicts with noise and amenity objectives are apparent in following some of these road traffic air pollution control procedures and it is often felt in Britain that control of vehicular emissions is preferable to planning control.[83]

Apart from producing a distancing effect, open spaces with trees, shrubs and grasses alter local climate, thus increasing dispersion of pollutants, and directly absorb pollutants on their foliage, thus reducing air pollution.[84] The average concentration of a pollutant declines with increasing proportions of planted urban open space. Beneath tree canopies the air contains a fraction of the pollution found above and in surrounding built-up areas. Tree barriers between industrial and residential areas can thus reduce air pollution considerably, a plantation 30 m deep giving almost complete dust interception and significant reductions in gaseous concentrations. Even one row of trees can reduce air pollution significantly, if planted on a green verge.[85] The danger of encouraging violent physical exercise close to major pollution sources (especially roads), by the provision of planted spaces, should not be overlooked.[65]

The greatest impact on air pollution can obviously be made in the overall design of a town, when all these control techniques are brought together.[76] It is at this stage that the very sensitive: the old, the sick and the young, can be protected best by land use arrangement. One fundamental approach would be to lower population density, causing a city of a given size to spread out under a larger air shed and thus reducing pollutant concentrations.[63] A balance must be struck between stationary and moving source pollution, but there is no evidence that pollution concentrations rise with urban size.[63 72] It appears that the three most important determinants of pollution concentrations are the effect of background air quality, the effect of topography and meteorology and, of course, the effect of the mix, location and intensity of land use activities. Indeed, very high reductions in concentrations of certain pollutants have been claimed as a result of land use planning contributions to pollution control. It is quite possible to test the air pollution consequences of different regional planning strategies on this city-wide basis.[86]

Recognition that the most effective control of air pollution results from comprehensive action on the urban scale leads to a consideration of air use planning. The amount of air within an area (air shed) available to absorb pollutants and effect dilution is limited, at any one time, by wind speed and inversion layers. The air may therefore be treated as a resource to be used by emitters, on the one hand, and by receptors, on the other. The function of the air use plan is to optimise the use of air by limiting emissions from particular individual sources, by curtailing emissions from existing sources in certain areas, or even by refusing to allow new pollution sources in overburdened areas. (Limiting emissions at times of adverse dispersion—meteorological

LIVERPOOL INSTITUTE OF HIGHER EDUCATION
THE MARKLAND LIBRARY

control—is a natural corollary to the air use plan.) Such a plan normally requires the use of a mathematical diffusion model, so that land use data may be converted to emission data and emission data to air quality data. There are a number of operational models in the process of development in the United States, and it is intended that major new planning proposals be judged against air quality standards before they are approved,[87-9] emission rights perhaps being applied to land use rights.[90] However, there are a number of inherent problems[91] and it will probably be some time before the British planner is able to evaluate plans in this way. Even then, it will almost certainly be the function of the air pollution control authority, and not the planning authority, to initiate and operate the model. The fundamental concept of the air use plan—that the air can only disperse a certain amount of pollution—could nevertheless be applied with benefit to planning practice in this country.

LAND POLLUTION
Planning has little control over land which is polluted by pesticides or heavy metals, except when such land is reallocated. However, local planning authorities have considerable control over land polluted by solid wastes. They can employ a number of techniques to reclaim land made derelict by spoil heaps and tips (i.e. they can control existing land pollution) and they can help to prevent additional pollution arising.

New development can be carefully utilised to restore derelict land. For example, industrial sites may be located on regraded colliery spoil heaps. Similarly, waste disposal from new mineral workings can be utilised to reclaim existing deposited solid wastes. Wastes from open-cast coal extraction, new collieries, ironstone workings and sand and gravel sites may all be employed to restore polluted land. Again, wastes from power stations or other large scale industry may be diverted to control pollution from other solid wastes.

Quite apart from reclaiming polluted land by the location of new development, local planning authorities are often responsible for implementing programmes to clear old waste disposal sites, now derelict. The techniques for reclaiming waste heaps and tips and other forms of derelict land are well documented and planning activity in this field is intensifying.[92-4]

The techniques available in dealing with new waste disposal sites relate to location and the imposition of conditions. The location of the disposal of waste (whether it is part of a larger industrial or mineral site or is a separate activity) can be chosen to avoid damage by virtue of air pollution, water pollution, noise or appearance. Unobtrusive, shielded sites remote from water courses and dwellings are clearly preferable. Conditions relating to the control of pollution from waste disposal can be attached to planning permissions (although, as mentioned in Chapter 4, it is sometimes difficult to ensure compliance).

In granting permission for refuse disposal sites, conditions designed to meet the recommended controlled tipping requirements can be imposed.[95] In dealing with mineral working applications, conditions may be designed to restore land to its previous use or to ensure that some other beneficial after-use is possible.[96] In either case conditions need to be phrased very precisely and should be capable of enforcement. (A large number of unsatisfactory sites with existing land use rights remain to point to the need to award planning permission and to frame conditions judiciously.)

The importance of paying careful regard to waste disposal in the planning process is clear from the enormous quantities of solids generated each year (around 160 million tons)[97] and solid waste plans can be devised. On the one hand, as the population and level of industrial activity of an area increase, so the quantity of wastes requiring disposal increases. On the other hand, it may well be difficult to ensure that the capacity of available disposal sites increases commensurately. Solid waste plans can relate the generation of various types of solid waste to the present and future pattern of economic activity and land use and can formulate appropriate disposal solutions (for example, the use of demolition waste to reclaim marginal land or the construction of incineration plants). Such plans, embodying criteria for the evaluation of alternative waste management systems by means of models, are under development in the United States.[98] Rather less sophisticated solid waste plans are also to be instituted in Britain.[99]

WATER POLLUTION

A number of planning techniques may be utilised to influence the control of water pollution. At the development control stage, the locational decision and the use of planning conditions can both be employed to control pollution. At the plan making stage, water cycle planning and the various constituent parts of this type of resource planning[100] are appropriate control techniques.

Planning can seek to reduce the risk of contamination of the public water supply through limitations on development in gathering grounds or close to points where underground water is pumped. This strategy can be effected either through the prohibition of certain types of development; for example, septic tanks or refuse disposal sites,[101] or through the imposition of rigid conditions relating to sewage disposal.

A number of techniques affect river water quality. Planning can restrict large scale industrial development which will discharge effluents direct to rivers, since even extensively treated effluents will normally add a polluting load to the river. In addition, by controlling development by making it conditional upon the provision of adequate sewerage and sewage treatment facilities, local planning authorities can influence the quality of sewage effluent discharged to rivers. At present, the overloading of existing treatment works by sewage from new development is one of the major causes of river pollution.[102] Similarly, because the pollution of rivers and canals by effluents from pleasure craft is sometimes a serious problem,[103] planners can control pollution by limiting the growth of shore facilities which encourage the development of water recreation or by insisting upon the provision of appropriate services.

The planning control of industrial and sewage works effluents (and, to a lesser extent, sewage from boats) also applies to estuaries and the sea. In fact, since a high proportion of industry requiring large quantities of water for process treatment (for example, pulp mills, refineries, steel works) tend to seek coastal sites, the exercise of the power of granting planning permission can be a critical pollution control measure. (Needless to say, other planning criteria may well conflict with this strategy.)

The creation of the regional water authorities afforded recognition to the need to achieve consistency between the discharge of effluents, river quality and water supply requirements. The town planner can make an effective contribution to water pollution control by insisting upon separate sewage systems (as being the only practical way of eliminating overflows of dilute untreated sewage to water courses), by postponing development until sewage treatment facilities are available and by other measures. Because land use and development

policy affect both future water requirements and future effluent discharges, such measures could form part of a comprehensive planning
approach to the river basin water cycle, in which planners could also
site new activities to tie in with predicted water resources.[100]

NOISE POLLUTION

Unlike land and water pollution, there is a considerable literature
devoted to planning techniques for reducing noise pollution and,
unlike the air pollution literature, most of it is British and has
appeared in planning publications. Great progress has been made in
this area since the Wilson report advocated planning control of
neighbourhood, motor vehicle and traffic noise.[104] There are several
books on noise control which include planning measures.[104–107]

The siting of new roads or other noise sources in relation to local
topography is important, since valleys and basins which are affected
by temperature inversions tend to spread noise over a wide area,
sound attenuation by distance not being very effective in such conditions.[50] Because sound is wind-borne local climate is also significant
in determining noise levels: noise can be both reduced and increased
by the wind.[108]

Noise from industrial activity can be countered to some extent by
sufficiently separating noisy processes from residential and other
noise sensitive areas. The width of the belt will depend upon the noise
emitted, upon the noise standard deemed desirable in a residential
area and upon whether dwellings are situated to the leeward or
windward of the factory.[109] Buffer zones should preferably be
planted. The use of planning conditions to limit noise levels at the
perimeter of the site is a powerful technique at the disposal of the
planner,[48] which needs to be exercised with care.[104]

There has been a considerable amount of work on the reduction of
road traffic noise by planning techniques. The basic methods are
separation, traffic management, the use of barriers and the design and
insulation of buildings. Separation of motor vehicles from receptors
can be achieved by such methods as the construction of ring roads,
the creation of pedestrian-only shopping areas, the limitation of
heavy vehicles to restricted routes[110] and the establishment of
minimum distances between new residential developments and traffic
flows of prescribed volumes.[111]

Traffic management to achieve smooth flows can be effective[112] and there may be less noise on an urban motorway where there is little acceleration or gear changing than on a busy urban road. The control of traffic flow is not normally of great value since, although the level of noise may be raised, the type of noise is rendered less annoying because it is less fluctuating.[54] In fact, if the development of a motorway system is combined with measures to ensure that traffic is channelled onto the motorways off existing roads, then it can bring about an improvement in the urban noise environment.[51] Traffic restraint and the encouragement of public transport are also extremely effective management techniques for noise control.

Several types of noise barrier can be erected to protect sensitive development from traffic noise. A wall may be effective if it is close to either source or receiver and if it is high and long enough.[108] However, it may present amenity problems and the use of vegetation to screen the screen is often very valuable. Alternatively one side of the wall can be banked and planted. Another alternative—requiring more land—is the mound, which gives good noise reduction and can be attractively landscaped.[110] The configuration of the road is obviously very important, the tunnel being a most effective control device.[113] Cuttings can be quite useful in limiting noise but they have a tendency to reflect sound, which can cause problems when the ground form slopes up from the road.[110] The structure of an elevated road can be an effective acoustic barrier.

Insulation of receptor buildings can be achieved by the arrangement of dwellings to provide barrier blocks,[39] by the arrangement of rooms within dwellings,[40 111] and by the use of double glazing and reduced window size. These techniques can be very effective but ventilation difficulties may arise and housing design and layout may not be satisfactory on other criteria. The use of long continuous housing blocks can completely shield lower dwellings and play spaces located in their 'noise shadow'.[39 50 113]

Open spaces are mainly effective in distancing. Grassland produces some absorption of the sound while hard surfaces such as paved areas or concrete reflect noise to some extent.[49] Trees do not absorb noise effectively, a dense belt of evergreen trees and shrubs needing to be 50 m wide to achieve a reduction in noise exposure of 10 dB(A).[108] Nevertheless, trees provide an important perceptual barrier, since a source which is not visible does not appear to sound as loud as one which is.

As with air pollution, the most effective way of dealing with noise pollution is to bring all the various control techniques together. In addition to the methods already mentioned, non-sensitive uses, such as warehousing or multi-storey car parks, can then be used to protect sensitive land uses (schools or hospitals, for example). Zoning policies for areas affected by aircraft noise can be applied, perhaps by limiting the noisiest areas to industry, the next area to insulated housing and only allowing schools and uninsulated dwellings in the least noisy zone.

As in the case of the other types of pollution, 'noise planning' can be an effective technique. Each urban area may be divided into a number of zones for which noise emissions and noise levels are estimated on the basis of the activities undertaken. Noise standards can then be set for each zone[48] and land uses planned to attain them in accord with the predictions of a simple model. Apart from contour maps of aircraft noise, much is known about the noise contours resulting from road traffic flows of differing characteristics[108] and, to a lesser extent, about the kinds of industrial process which give rise to the greatest noise problems. The information from which standards can be calculated and applied is thus largely available. Noise abatement zones can clearly be chosen having regard to planning policies for other types of environmental improvement in the area.

It is apparent that, despite the limited treatment of pollution in planning textbooks and, with some exceptions, in planning journals, a range of planning techniques do exist to control air, land, water and noise pollution which can be administered within the British planning system. Although many of these techniques can be utilised only at the plan-making stage, others can be employed by planners responsible for development control. Some of these techniques conflict with each other, but many are quite compatible. It has already been shown that the local planning authority possess the powers to play a number of roles in the control of pollution. It now appears that planning authorities also have the techniques to place them in a position, in dealing with the planning process generally,[114] or in dealing with, for example, industrial location, [115] to make a very significant contribution to pollution control.

REFERENCES

1   Adshead, S.D. (1923) *Town planning and town development* Methuen, London.
2   Adams, T. (1932) *Recent advances in town planning* Churchill, London.
3   McAllister, G., and McAllister, E. G. (1941) *Town and country planning* Faber & Faber, London.
4   Lanchester, H. V. (1932) *The art of town planning* Chapman & Hall, London.
5   Lloyd, T. A. (1935) *Planning in town and country* Routledge, London.
6   Gibbon, G. (1937) *Problems of town and country planning* Allen & Unwin, London.
7   Brumphrey, G. (1940) *Town and country tomorrow* Nelson, London.
8   Wright H. M. (1948) *The planner's notebook* Architectural Press, London.
9   Association for Planning and Regional Reconstruction (ed.) (1950) *Town and country planning textbook* Architectural Press, London.
10 Logie, G. (1952) *Industry in towns* Allen & Unwin, London.
11 Powdrill, E. A. (1961) *Vocabulary of land planning* Estates Gazette, London.
12 Jackson, J. N. (1963) *Surveys for town and country planning* Hutchinson, London.
13 Abercrombie, P. (1967) *Town and country planning* Oxford University Press, London.
14 Brown, A. J. , and Sherrard, H. M. (1969) *An introduction to town and country planning* Angus & Robertson, London.
15 Fogarty, M. P. (1948) *Town and country planning* Hutchinson, London.
16 Gillie, F. B., and Hughes, P. L. (1950) *Some principles of land planning* University Press, Liverpool.
17 Adams, J. W. R. (1952) *Modern town and country planning* Churchill, London.
18 Keeble, L. (1969) *Principles and practice of town and country planning* Estates Gazette, London.
19 Cullingworth, J. B. (1972) *Town and country planning in Britain* Allen & Unwin, London.
20 Cullingworth, J. B. (1964) *Town and country planning in England and Wales* Allen & Unwin, London.
21 White, B. (1971) *Sourcebook of planning information* Clive Bingley, London.
22 Solesbury, W. (1974) *Policy in urban planning* Pergamon, Oxford.
23 Lynch, K. (1971) *Site planning* MIT Press, London.
24 Chapin, F. S., Jnr. (1965) *Urban land use planning* University of Illinois Press, Urbana.
25 Norton, G. A., and Parlour, J. W. (1972) The economic philosophy of pollution: a critique *Environment & Planning, 4* 3–11.

26 Dawes, R. M., Delay, J., and Chaplin, W. (1974) The decision to pollute *Environment & Planning, 6* 3–10.

27 Flowerdew, A. D. J., and Hammond, A. (1973) City roads and the environment *Regional Studies, 7* 123–6.

28 Bor, W., and Roberts, J. (1972) Urban motorway impact *Town Planning Review, 43* 299–321.

29 Lakshmanan, T. R., and Fu-chen, L. (1972) A regional economic model for the assessment of effects of air pollution abatement *Environment and Planning, 4* 73–97.

30 Fiarratani, F. (1974) Air pollution abatement: output and relative price effects, a regional input-output simulation *Environment and Planning, 6* 307–12.

31 Anderson, R. J., and Crocker, T. D. (1971) Air pollution and residential property values *Urban Studies, 8* 171–80.

32 Ollswang, J. (1972) Air pollution in west central Scotland *Built Environment, 35* 331–4.

33 Fish, H. (1972) Disposal of waste *Town and Country Planning (1972)* 429–32. ₁

34 Trice, J. E., and Godwin, H. (1974) The control of river pollution in Wales (1963–73): an assessment of the working of the Water Resources Act, 1963, in Wales *JPL (1974)* 314–32.

35 Robertshaw, P. (1974) Water pollution control—problems of harmonisation in EEC States *JPL (1974)* 642–5.

36 McLoughlin, J. (1973) Control of pollution in inland waters *JPL (1973)* 355–61 and 414–21.

37 Cripps, E. L., and Foot, D. H. S. (1970) The urbanisation effects of a third London airport *Environment and Planning, 2* 153–92.

38 *Planning Outlook.*

39 (1967) Planning against noise *Official Architecture and Planning, 30* May.

40 Foster, C. D., and Mackie, P. J. (1970) Noise: economic aspects of choice *Urban Studies, 7* 123–35.

41 Williams, A. J. (1973) The role of the local planning authority in regard to waste and pollution *JPL (1973)* 14–22.

42 Wood, C. M. (1973) Powers and responsibilities of local planning authorities in controlling pollution *JPL (1973)* 635–41.

43 Lee, N., and Wood, C. M. (1972) Planning and pollution *JRTPI, 58* 153–8.

44 Watkin, B. (1951) Special industry: definition and control *JTPI, 37* 137–42.

45 Graham, J. (1957) Clean air: the relation between land use planning and air pollution *JTPI, 43* 166–73.

46 Craxford, S. R., and Weatherley, M-L. P. M. (1966) Planning for clean air *JTPI, 52* 144–5.

47 Millar, J., and Dean, J. (1968) Practical consideration of rapid transit *JTPI, 54* 158–71.

48   Williams, H. (1973) Noise measurement in planning *JRTPI, 59* 7–9.
49   Rowlands, E. (1973) Noise from urban roads *JRTPI, 59* 10–13.
50   Allen, W., and Ginsburg, L. B. (1973) Traffic noise: some practical implications *JRTPI, 59* 14–16.
51   Waller, R. A. (1973) Do urban motorways create a noise nuisance? *JRTPI, 59* 278–83.
52   Kirby, C. P., Garnett, A., and Medhurst, F. (1970) Environmental pollution *Proc. Town and Country Planning Summer School, Swansea* 39.
53   Lee, N., and Wood, C. M. (1971) Economics of pollution in relation to planning *Proc. Town and Country Planning Summer School, Southampton* 43–4.
54   Waller, R. A., and Willson, T. K. (1971) Noise *Proc. Town and Country Planning Summer School, Southampton* 49–51.
55   Holdgate, M. (1972) International environmental problems *Proc. Town and Country Planning Summer School, St Andrews* 66–70.
56   Cook, D. B. (1972) Recycling of urban wastes *Proc. Town and Country Planning Summer School, St Andrews* 24–7.
57   (1971) The greening of public policy *JAIP, 37* July.
58   Humphrey, M. J., Seley, J. E., and Wolpert, J. (1971) A decision model for locating controversial facilities *JAIP, 37* 397–402.
59   Krueckeberg, D. A. (1972) State environmental planning: requirements *v.* behaviour *JAIP, 38* 392–6.
60   Commoner, B. (1973) Alternative approaches to the environmental crisis *JAIP, 39* 147–62.
61   Greenberg, M. R., and Hordon, R. M. (1974) Environmental impact statements: some annoying questions *JAIP, 40* 164–75.
62   Rydell, C. P., and Stevens, B. H. (1968) Air pollution and the shape of urban areas *JAIP, 34* 50–1.
63   Rydell, C. P., and Schwarz, G. (1968) Air pollution and urban form: a review of current literature *JAIP, 34* 115–20.
64   Kurtzweg, J. A. (1973) Urban planning and air pollution control: a review of selected recent research *JAIP, 39* 82–92.
65   Everett, M. D. (1974) Roadside air pollution hazards in recreational land use planning *JAIP, 40* 83–9.
66   Branch, M. C., Gilman, S., and Weber, C. (1974) Monitoring community noise *JAIP, 40* 266–73.
67   Hagevik, G., Mandelker, D., and Brail, R. (1974) *Air quality management and land use planning* Praeger, London.
68   Schueneman, E. (1962) Planning and zoning in air pollution control. In Stern, A. C. (ed.) *Air pollution, 2* Academic Press, London.
69   Taylor, J. R., Hasegawa, A., and Chambers, L. A. (1961) Control of air pollution by site selection and zoning. In *Air pollution* World Health Organisation, Monograph 46, Geneva.
70   Pelle, W. J. (1964) *Bibliography on the planning aspects of air pollution control, summary and evaluation* Public Health Service, US Government Printing Office, Washington.

71   Burns, L. S. (1970) *Urban planning aspects of air pollution abatement.* Task Force 3, Project Clean Air II, University of California, Berkeley.

72   Craxford, S. R. and Weatherley, M-L. P. M. (1964) Air pollution and town planning *Proc. Clean Air Conf. Harrogate* 54–70, National Society for Clean Air, Brighton.

73   Arnold, G., and Edgerley, E. (1967) Urban development in air pollution basins – an appeal to the planners for help *J. Air Poll. Cont. Ass., 17* 235–7.

74   Page, J. K. (1964) Air pollution and town planning *Proc. Clean Air Conf. Harrogate* 71–8, National Society for Clean Air, Brighton.

75   Ministry of Housing and Local Government (1955) *The use of land for industry* Technical memorandum 2, HMSO, London.

76   Branch, M. C., and Leong, E. Y. (1972) *Air pollution and city planning* Department of Science and Engineering, University of California, Los Angeles.

77   Scorer, R. S. (1972) *Air pollution* Pergamon Press, London.

78   McCormick, R. A. (1971) Air pollution in the locality of buildings *Phil. Trans. Roy. Soc. Lond. A, 269* 515–26.

79   Craxford, S. R., and Weatherley, M-L. P. M. (1971) Air pollution in towns in the United Kingdom *Phil. Trans. Roy. Soc. Lond. A, 269* 503–13.

80   Hauser, E. W., West, L. B., and Schleicher, A. R. (1972) Fundamental air pollution considerations for urban and transportation planners *Traf. Quart., 26* 71–84.

81   Mukherji, A. (1968) Abatement of atmospheric pollution by urban planning *Traf. Quart., 22* 433–50.

82   Bellomo, S. J. (1971) *Air pollution reductions through comprehensive urban planning and transportation* Preprint, Air Pollution Control Office, New York.

83   Department of the Environment (1972) *New roads in towns* HMSO, London.

84   Hill, A. C. (1971) Vegetation: a sink for atmospheric pollutants *J. Air Poll. Cont. Ass., 21* 341–6.

85   Saunders, P. J. W., and Wood, C. M. (1974) Plants and air pollution *Landscape Design, No. 105* 28–30.

86   Zupan, J. M. (1973) *The distribution of air quality in the New York region* Resources for the Future, Johns Hopkins Press, London.

87   Williams, J. D., Farmer, J. R., Stephenson, R. B., Evans, G. G., and Dalton, R. B. (1968) *Air pollutant emissions related to land area—a basis for a preventive air pollution control program* National Pollution Control Administration Publication APTD 68–11, US Government Printing Office, Washington.

88   Fensterstock, J. C., Kurtzweg, J. A., and Ozolins, G. (1970) *Reduction of air pollution potential through environmental planning* Paper 70–14, Air Pollution Control Association, Pittsburgh.

89   Willis, B. M., Gaut, N. E., and Newman, E. (1971) *AQUIP—an air quality evaluation system for the planning community* Paper 71–142,

Air Pollution Control Association, Pittsburgh.

90   Roberts, J. J., and Croke, E. J. (1970) *Land use as an organisational basis for urban and regional air resource management* Paper 70–140, Air Pollution Control Association, Pittsburgh.

91   Scorer, R. S. (1970) Air pollution, its implications for industrial planning *Long Range Planning, 3(2)* 46–54.

92   Oxenham, J. R. (1966) *Reclaiming derelict land* Faber & Faber, London.

93   University of Newcastle (1971) *Landscape reclamation* (two vols) IPC Science and Technology Press, Guildford.

94   Hutnik, R. J., and Davis, G. (1969) *Ecology and reclamation of devastated land* (two vols) Gordon & Breach, London.

95   Department of the Environment (1971) *Report of the working party on refuse disposal* HMSO, London.

96   Royal Town Planning Institute (1972) *Memorandum of evidence to Committee on Minerals Planning Control* RTPI, London.

97   Royal Commission on Environmental Pollution (1974) *Fourth report* Cmnd. 5780, HMSO, London.

98   US Environmental Protection Agency (1970–71) *Comprehensive Studies of solid waste management* First, second and third annual reports, US Government Printing Office, Washington.

99   *Control of Pollution Act, 1974.*

100 Grava, S. (1969) *Urban planning aspects of water pollution control* Columbia University Press, New York.

101 McLoughlin, J. (1972) *The law relating to pollution* Manchester University Press, Manchester.

102 Working Party on Sewage Disposal (1970) *Taken for granted* Ministry of Housing and Local Government HMSO, London.

103 Nature Conservancy (1965) *Report on Broadland* NC, London.

104 Committee on the Problem of Noise (Wilson Committee) (1963) *Final report* Cmnd. 2056, HMSO, London.

105 Parkin, P. H., and Humphreys, H. R. (1969) *Acoustics, noise and buildings* Faber & Faber, London.

106 Beranek, L. L. (ed.) (1960) *Noise reduction* McGraw-Hill, London.

107 Moore, J. E. (1966) *Design for noise reduction* Architectural Press, London.

108 Scholes, W. E., and Sargent, J. W. (1971) Designing against noise from road traffic *Applied Acoustics, 4* 203–34.

109 Bell, A. (1966) *Noise* Public Health Paper 30, World Health Organisation, Geneva.

110 Telford Development Corporation (1971) *Traffic noise* Planning Policy Bulletin 4, TDC, Wellington.

111 Department of the Environment (1972) *New housing and road traffic noise* Design Bulletin 26, HMSO, London.

112 Road Research Laboratory (1970) *A review of road traffic noise* Report LR357, Department of the Environment, Crowthorne.

113 Greater London Council (1970) *Traffic noise: major urban roads* Urban Design Bulletin 1, GLC, London.
114 Wise, H. F. (1967) Pollution and planning: devices for guiding the planning process toward the resolution of environmental problems *Supplement to Trans. Kansas Acad. Sci., 70(3)* 19–24.
115 Fulton, W. (1971) New factors in plant location *Harvard Bus. Rev., 49(3)* 4–19, 166–8.

CHAPTER 6

Regional and sub-regional studies

Canals in urban areas in the North West are frequently much less polluted than adjacent rivers. The strategic plan for the North West identifies pollution as a major planning problem and makes numerous proposals for improving conditions.

It is convenient to commence an examination of the control of pollution in planning practice by reviewing regional planning studies. These non-statutory plans deal with planning problems at the regional scale and provide the necessary background for the formulation of smaller scale plans. Particular attention is paid in this chapter to the extent to which pollution has been considered in the recent strategic regional plan for the North West. The 'region' treated in these studies is the economic planning region[1] and, using this definition, many earlier 'regional' plans are, in fact, sub-regional in scope. The control of pollution in a sample of these is dealt with later in the chapter to provide an introduction to more recent plans at this scale.

REGIONAL PLANNING STUDIES

The economic planning region studies have tended to pay varying attention to the pollution problem, some completely ignoring it.[2-4] Perhaps because of the higher pollution levels prevailing in the north of the country, the northern councils have shown more concern than others. The North West study devoted several paragraphs to the problems of dereliction and smoke pollution, detailing the use of planning conditions to prevent the former and smoke control orders to control the latter.[5] In the fullest regional study treatment of the subject, the Yorkshire and Humberside report recognised derelict land, atmospheric pollution and water pollution as serious problems and described their incidence in a number of sections.[6] It advocated careful planning of new chemical industry to avoid polluting residential areas and the use of development control, including planning conditions, to control land pollution. The North regional study described the same problems but failed to mention planning control (other than in the reclamation of derelict land).[7]

The South West study dwelt on the mineral dereliction problem, without mentioning the use of development control powers.[8] The East Midlands report stressed the importance of reducing pollution to potential water supplies and the need to clear extensive areas of dereliction and it recognised the importance of planning conditions relating to reclamation.[9] The various West Midlands reports addressed some attention to pollution. The earliest dealt with derelict land alone of the pollution problems[10] but the effect of river pollution on water supplies was mentioned in a commentary upon it.[11] However, the effects of air pollution, noise and derelict land in discouraging incoming industry were briefly noted in a succeeding report.[12]

The later strategy reports again paid mixed regard to pollution. While those for the South East[13] and the West Midlands[14] ignored pollution and its control, that for the North West looked upon the disposal of waste, dereliction, water pollution and air pollution as serious regional problems.[15] It also mentioned motor vehicle emissions and made a number of non-planning pollution control recommendations. The Yorkshire and Humberside strategy report emphasised pollution problems and mapped environmental conditions in the region, air pollution and dereliction being determinants of these.[16]

The North West economic planning council has issued reports on

smoke control[17] and derelict land[18] which detail the regional situation
and legislative powers but make no mention of the planner's role in
controlling either type of pollution. However, one of the fullest regional analyses of pollution problems, to date, has been published by
the North region council.[19] It deals with air pollution, noise, fresh
water pollution, pollution of the sea and beaches and with derelict
land at greater length than any of the documents previously mentioned. The air pollution section covers smoke pollution, pollution
from chemical works (it mentions the notorious 'Teesside mist'),
from steel works, from power stations and from motor vehicles. The
contribution of the planner in locating potential sources of air pollution is recognised and this recognition is extended to the control of
noise pollution and to the reduction of land pollution caused by solid
wastes.[19]

Another extensive treatment of regional pollution problems[20] has
been prepared by the Yorkshire and Humberside economic planning
council whose publications have consistently shown considerable
concern about pollution. The report describes the river, air and land
pollution situations in the region, presenting numerous statistics and
emphasising the need for improvement. It mentions the need to site
intensive stock farming units carefully to prevent pollution. In the
case of air pollution it stresses the role of development control in
locating both polluters and receptors carefully to avoid pollution
problems. The report discusses the use of tall chimneys to disperse
sulphur dioxide and the need to avoid high local concentrations of
pollutants. It states that 'in the future, we believe that more account
should be taken of environmental factors—particularly of air pollution—in land use planning. Whenever new development is being considered in urban areas, the question should be asked whether pollutant levels will be offensive to people and the natural environment. If
there is a risk of nuisance, then it is better to ask the developer to
consider other sites. In rural areas the same question is relevant
where development, including intensive farm units near villages, is
proposed; but, generally, in country areas the main question will be
whether pollutant levels from new development will be acceptable for
agriculture and landscape conservation.'[20]

In the most recent series of regional reports the strategic plan for
the South East briefly mentions the effect of effluents on water supplies,[21] expanding on the theme in one of the supporting volumes.[22]

However, the plan does not mention the environmental consequences of water pollution and appears to neglect other pollution problems altogether. This cursory treatment of pollution is to be compared with that accorded in the North West strategic plan.

STRATEGIC PLAN FOR THE NORTH WEST

Pollution is mentioned at a very large number of points in the Strategic Plan for the North West (SPNW) report, and several sections of the document are devoted to the subject.[23] The reduction of pollution had been an objective of the joint planning team's work since its inception as, in 1971, the fundamental aim of the plan was to 'improve the quality of life for the people of the region, making best use of the resources available'.[24] One of the contributory aims was to 'improve the physical environment' and one of the twelve regional aspect objectives was 'to lower present levels of pollution and prevent future pollution and spoilation'.[24]

Five specific objectives were enunciated at this time:

1   To reduce air pollution.
2   To reduce pollution in water courses, estuaries and coastal waters.
3   To minimise noise pollution.
4   To provide for the disposal and re-use of waste of all kinds.
5   To restore spoiled land.

It is interesting to note that, in the commentary upon these objectives, it was stated that 'if a high-growth Mersey Belt strategy were adopted' (i.e. development was concentrated along the Liverpool–Manchester conurbation axis) 'an extra effort would be called for on objectives 1–4; for example, climate and topography make air pollution virtually endemic in South-Central Lancashire and the Manchester embayment'.[24]

By the end of 1971 the contributory aim had become a 'framework objective' and was rephrased to read 'to improve the quality of the environment and its performance as the physical setting for all other activities'.[25] The aspect objective was abandoned and the five specific objectives became six and were rephrased slightly:

1   To minimise air pollution.
2   To minimise pollution in watercourses, estuaries and coastal waters.
3   To minimise noise pollution.
4   To provide for the disposal and re-use of wastes of all kinds.
5   To restore spoiled land (including derelict, and other under-used land).
6   To prevent future pollution and spoilation.[25]

These are the provisional objectives quoted in the SPNW report.[26]

Environmental matters were always seen as crucial issues and in the 1971 SPNW 'issues report'[25] it was stated that any regional strategy needed to incorporate the latest thinking and policies in respect of:

1   Air pollution, whether by industrial or domestic emissions or by vehicles and aircraft
2   River and canal pollution
3   Coastal pollution
4   Litter control
5   Refuse disposal and the development of positive uses of waste
6   Noise in both town and country
7   The avoidance of further environmental pollution by good design and the full use of modern technology.

Both the team and the members of its consultative committee saw pollution abatement as the fourth most important objective, both in the short and the long term.[25]

Six alternative strategies for the location of population and employment were generated to take account of population growth and land availability,[27] [28] of which further development of the Mersey Belt was one. The evaluation of these strategies involved rephrasing the original objectives in more precise terms and weighting these so that they could be added together to give a total score.[29] [30] The objective relating to pollution became: 'to locate development so as to provide the most attractive living environment. Indicators (*a*) landscape features, (*b*) absence of pollution, noise, etc.,'[29] [31] This objective continued to receive the fourth highest weighting.[31]

Along with the other thirteen first cycle evaluation objectives, the effects on the environment objective were measured (on a 5 km grid square basis where appropriate) using a goals achievement matrix methodology. The factors taken into account in reaching a composite pollution score for 1981 and 1991 were the proximity of the location to a works registered under the Alkali Act, the likely level of road traffic noise as determined by traffic flow, the level of aircraft noise, based on noise and number contours, and the level of river pollution based upon expected river quality class. These factors were each given equal weight, except for river pollution, which was only deemed to be one quarter as important as each of the other three types of pollution, and the pollution part of the environment objective was then given a (negative) weight equal to that of the landscape features part before the two were added together.[32] Once the effects of alternative strategies on the fourteen objectives had been tested and qualitative assessments of feasibility, flexibility and costs had been made, second[33] and third[34] evaluation cycles were applied, relying on judgement rather than the goals achievement matrix, and the Mersey Belt strategy emerged as the preferred approach. The effects of this strategy upon the environment are not spelled out, beyond stating that the physical pattern, whatever its shape, must be fashioned so as best to help achieve the objective of environmental improvement[35] and that the introduction of new development will stimulate environmental improvement.[36]

The unique element of the SPNW report, apart from its treatment of pollution, is the recognition that the predominant issue in the North West is the improvement of living and working conditions in the towns and cities.[37] In other words, the main emphasis in the report is not on locating new development at all, but on endeavouring to alleviate the condition of existing development; not on a spatial strategy but on a policy strategy. Following this recognition, an assessment of pollution in 1981 had been made on the basis that current trends, policies and commitments would continue without any strategic planning input. The pollutants covered were smoke and sulphur dioxide, river quality class, noise from aircraft and traffic, and derelict land. For assessment purposes, fairly optimistic assumptions were made about improvements over present conditions taking place before 1981.[38] The report thus stresses that the 'prefixed physical pattern' must be complemented by environmental improvements.

Present pollution conditions, however, are poor by national standards.[39] The SPNW report demonstrates that the North West is the worst British region in respect of air pollution (smoke and sulphur dioxide combined) and proportion of total land derelict and nearly the worst in terms of the total numbers of premises in 'Black Areas' not subject to smoke control orders.[40] The advantages of specific grants in dealing with these derelict land and clean air problems are emphasised[41] and a whole chapter is devoted to public expenditure priorities, using pollution control as a prime example.

Estimates of expenditure necessary to improve the quality of the region's rivers, to reclaim its derelict land and to complete smoke control programmes in the main urban centres are presented. The total figure required (around £400 million) is frankly unattainable and the priorities selected are smoke control, derelict land reclamation and river pollution control, in that order. Apart from compiling a great deal of valuable information about these types of pollution, this chapter recommends that legislation be amended so that sewerage and sewage treatment schemes can be dealt with on the same grant-aided basis as derelict land schemes.[42]

The need to improve the conditions of the people now resident in towns and cities leads on to the calculation of an urban environment index as a basis for resource allocation. As a background to this calculation, a further section on pollution is presented[43] which deals with smoke and sulphur dioxide and their control, emissions from works registered under the Alkali, etc., Works Regulation Act, 1906, road traffic pollution, derelict land and refuse tips, river pollution and motor vehicle and aircraft noise. The review concludes with the need for local planning authorities to ensure that new urban development, especially housing, is located well away from sources of pollution.[44]

The urban environment index is based upon six measures, of which three relate to pollution (proportion of land derelict, a combined measure of smoke pollution and pollution from registered works and a road traffic noise measure).[45] The local authorities were, in fact, divided into four groups A, B, C and D.[46] The various strategic measures capable of remedying the extremely poor environmental condition of many North West local authorities are outlined and a constructive bid for greater resources is made. There are also a number of further references to pollution in the report, for example in the section on air transport.[47]

Commentary
It is not intended to offer a detailed criticism of the SPNW report here. Critiques have appeared elsewhere,[48 49] one of which states that fundamental criticisms can be levelled at the evaluation by goals-achievement matrix: 'even with careful analysis of the separate elements, the results often contradicted common sense judgement'. It suggested that the specification of the tools may have virtually determined the outcome by being heavily weighted in favour of the conurbation.[48] Rather, on the basis of the material presented in earlier chapters, it is appropriate to make a number of comments about the way in which pollution control is treated in the report. First, however,

it is essential to point out that the concern about the control of pollution and the level of presentation of this topic in the report demonstrate that it has made a very real contribution to regional planning thought in this regard.

The original provisional objectives relating to pollution used to choose the best strategy were frankly unsophisticated. As stressed in Chapter 4, it is necessary to formulate objectives with considerable precision if planning control of pollution is to be administered in any meaningful way and, say, 'to prevent future pollution and spoilation' is both unrealistic and incapable of evaluation. It might have been fairer to call this an 'aim'. Clearly the SPNW team saw that evaluation would be difficult and were careful to call the objective 'provisional' from the first. The more specific objective 'to locate development so as to provide the most attractive living environment' is certainly capable of evaluation but has perhaps swung too far away from the original pollution control objective. An intermediate statement such as 'to locate additional development so as to minimise pollution levels in areas of both new and existing development' might well have been more appropriate and some view about regional pollution standards could have been expressed.

The measures used in testing the first evaluation cycle objective could have been improved upon with benefit. It would have been quite possible to utilise smoke, sulphur dioxide, derelict spoil heaps and tips, canal quality, industrial density and population density as additional and useful measures of air, land, water and noise pollution.[50] To be fair, smoke and sulphur dioxide had been discounted as future problems[32] (a controversial assumption!). In view of the statement about the problems of pollution associated with the Mersey Belt strategy, quoted earlier, it is unsurprising (but nevertheless disappointing) to find that the impact of this strategy upon pollution levels is not dealt with. It might have been possible to show how pollution levels could be reduced although, as shown in Chapter 5, concentration tends to increase, not control, pollution. (In fairness, SPNW proposals for 'concentration' rely on elements of dispersal within the Mersey Belt, where there is, in fact, considerable elbow room.)

The same criticisms about the limited range of measures employed to define pollution conditions can be applied to the regional assessment to 1981 (assuming no intervention), to the regional comparison and to the local authority urban environment index. More elaborate

measures have been applied to the North West region and to some of
its constituent local authorities elsewhere.[50] It has to be said that, in
common with other regional initiatives, the implementation of the
report's recommendations based upon these and other measures may
prove extremely difficult.[49]

Finally, in view of the attention paid to the pollution problem, the
lack of specific recognition of the detailed local planning authority's
role in the control of pollution is somewhat disappointing. However,
one of the functions of the report is to provide a guide to the preparation of structure plans[51] and the Mersey Belt planning authorities
must be obliged to give pollution control a major place in their plans.
SPNW eschews the setting up of new agencies to improve living
conditions in favour of the local planning authorities, on whose behalf
central government is strongly petitioned to provide more funds for
environmental improvement. Despite the strategic nature of the
report, it is a matter of regret that the various planning methods
available to authorities in contributing to improving pollution in the
North West, at both plan-making and development control stages,
have not been elaborated.

SUB-REGIONAL PLANNING STUDIES
Certain early sub-regional studies, often called regional studies at the
time, paid considerable attention to pollution. Thus, the 1945 proposals for Manchester and district emphasised the problem of smoke
pollution, seeking a solution in smokeless fuels and district heating.[52]
The 1947 advisory plan for a wider area around Manchester sought
the same solution to the problem but also stressed that 'local planning
authorities should be ready to co-operate in any policy which might
further the cause of smoke abatement, and to adopt positive measures to that end in preparing their development plans'.[53] A regional
study of the Birmingham area also looked to district heating as a
method of abatement of smoke pollution. In addition, it suggested a
number of solutions to the derelict land problem in the conurbation.[54]

The consideration of pollution in more recent sub-regional studies
shows a diversity of concern and treatment similar to that in regional
studies. Thus the South Hampshire study briefly discusses the pollution of rivers by sewage effluents and suggests that both effluent and
sewage sludge should be diverted and discharged into the sea.[55][56]
Marine pollution problems from the disposal of sewage are them-

selves briefly discussed in the Tayside report.[57] On the other hand, the Northampton, Bedford and North Bucks study,[58] the Lothians regional survey,[59] the Leicester and Leicestershire study (in either the main report[60] or in the more detailed technical appendices[61]), the North Gloucestershire sub-regional study[62] and the Cambridge sub-region study[63] appear not to mention pollution at all.

Derelict land is briefly mentioned as a constraint on development in the Tyne-Wear plan, but other forms of pollution are not considered.[64] The Severnside study also refers to land pollution as a constraint on major large scale development, together with air pollution, but does not show how these environmental factors were taken into account in deriving a strategy.[65] The Humberside study is also concerned about various types of industrial air pollution (and about noise from this source) and suggests that it may be necessary to zone a cordon of land, one to three miles wide, between the estuarial industrial sites and any major new urban development.[66]

A general evaluation of sub-regional studies[67] quotes the Teesside survey and plan[68] [69] as breaking new ground in the development of this type of planning. One Teesside report contains a chapter on air pollution which lists the various air pollution problems, explains how they can be controlled and describes the local situation in some detail (mentioning the mist as a major element). A section on air pollution trends is followed by one relating the topics of planning and atmospheric pollution together. Air pollution is considered to be a constraint on residential and other development in areas liable to temperature inversion downwind from the main industrial sources of pollution. This factor is marked, with others, on a map of natural constraints on urban development.[69]

The Nottinghamshire and Derbyshire study[70] contains maps showing the derelict land, water and air pollution (smoke and sulphur dioxide) positions. The report recognises the improvement of environmental conditions as a determinant in planning. It recommends that wherever possible residential development should avoid areas particularly liable to static air conditions, such as foggy valleys, and that new industrial buildings in these areas should have chimneys tall enough for the discharged gases to penetrate the lower layers of the air.[70]

The fullest treatment of pollution at the sub-regional level is to be found in the Coventry-Solihull-Warwickshire report, which considers

air, land, water and noise pollution.[71] One of the twenty 'discriminat-
ory' objectives of the study is 'to locate new development in areas
which will not be adversely affected by atmospheric and noise pollution' and it is made clear that the degree to which this objective is
attained will vary between alternative land use proposals. The report
discusses industrial air pollution, grit and dust, smoke and sulphur
dioxide and presents a map of a combination of deposited matter and
the latter two pollutants. Pollution from industrial wastes is discussed
and there is a good review of waste problems and dereliction. Tight
controls over the disposal of solid waste from mineral workings and
the incineration of refuse are recommended. Water pollution problems are described and a planning policy that 'great care should be
taken to ensure that the future growth areas could be drained without
threatening unpolluted rivers' evolved. Noise problems arising from
various sources are discussed and a map of noise from motor vehicles,
aircraft and trains is drawn. Care was taken in the evaluation of
alternative strategies to keep urban growth away from areas polluted
by noise.[71]

The objective relating to pollution was weighted, along with the
other objectives, on the basis of professional and public opinion. It
was given a high priority by both. Four alternative strategies were
then tested for their effectiveness in meeting the weighted objectives
and the preferred strategy chosen. It was, in fact, the third most
effective in fulfilling the pollution objective.[72]

(The construction of an air pollution index and of a noise index on
a 1 km grid square basis is described in a supplementary volume.[73]
These were combined to give an index of 'annoyance' by adding them
together for each grid square. This index was then mapped for 1969
and, using a number of assumptions, for 1991. The factor surface
generated was one of ten used in the generation of alternative
strategies.[74] The water pollution situation is also detailed in a supplementary volume where it is explained that, apart from avoiding
drainage to unpolluted rivers, no simple planning solutions were
found to reduce pollution problems.[75])

It is fair to say, on the basis of this sample of regional and sub-
regional planning studies, that the attention paid to pollution has
been uneven although, in part, this may reflect the variation in the

geographical incidence of the problem. It is clear that, in general, the more recent studies have considered pollution problems to a greater extent than the earlier studies, but many studies still give only cursory acknowledgement to pollution control. Attention has characteristically been confined to locating major new urban developments, whether industrial or residential, away from existing sources and receptors and at sites where dispersion of air pollution is likely to be good. Reclamation of derelict land and restoration of areas after mineral working have also been regarded as planning problems worthy of comment.

With one or two notable exceptions, however, only a limited range of pollutants has been recognised in these studies and the various planning roles, powers and techniques in the control of pollution have been ignored. In the small number of cases where pollution control has been considered important enough to have more than a few sentences devoted to it, objectives have not always been sufficiently precise (or even appropriate) and the range of measures used to gauge the extent to which they are achieved in the proposed plan has been rather narrow.

It is significant that none of the plans explicitly mention the optimal level of pollution control and few mention pollution standards (Chapter 4). Similarly, there is little evidence of an approach to pollution control being agreed with other pollution control authorities. Those reports which do contain more than a 'window dressing' mention of pollution normally prescribe fairly general (and sometimes not even specifically planning) strategic solutions to the problem which take little account of the costs and benefits of control. The subjugation of the pollution control objective to other objectives in these plans is revealing and may, in practice, reflect some balancing of costs and benefits.

REFERENCES

1   Central Statistical Office (1974) *Abstract of regional statistics, 1974* HMSO, London.
2   Ministry of Housing and Local Government (1964) *The South East study* HMSO, London.
3   East Anglia Economic Planning Council (1968) *East Anglia: a study* Department of Economic Affairs, HMSO, London.

4   East Anglia Consultative Committee (1969) *East Anglia: a regional appraisal* EACC, Bury St Edmunds.
5   Department of Economic Affairs (1965) *The North West Study* HMSO, London.
6   Yorkshire and Humberside Economic Planning Council (1966) *A review of Yorkshire and Humberside* Department of Economic Affairs, HMSO, London.
7   Northern Economic Planning Council (1966) *Challenge of the changing North* Department of Economic Affairs, HMSO, London.
8   South West Economic Planning Council (1967) *A region with a future* Department of Economic Affairs, HMSO, London.
9   East Midlands Economic Planning Council (1969) *Opportunity in the East Midlands* Department of Economic Affairs, HMSO, London.
10   Department of Economic Affairs (1965) *The West Midlands* HMSO, London.
11   West Midlands Economic Planning Council (1967) *The West Midlands: patterns of growth* Department of Economic Affairs, HMSO, London.
12   West Midlands Economic Planning Council (1971) *The West Midlands: an economic appraisal* Department of the Environment, HMSO, London.
13   South East Economic Planning Council (1967) *A strategy for the South East* Department of Economic Affairs, HMSO, London.
14   West Midlands Regional Study (1971) *A developing strategy for the West Midlands* WMRS, Birmingham.
15   North West Economic Planning Council (1968) *Strategy II: the North West of the 1970s* Department of Economic Affairs, HMSO, London.
16   Yorkshire and Humberside Economic Planning Council (1970) *Yorkshire and Humberside regional strategy* Ministry of Housing and Local Government, HMSO, London.
17   North West Economic Planning Council (1970) *Smoke control* NWEPC, Manchester.
18   North West Economic Planning Council (1969) *Derelict land in the North West* NWEPC, Manchester.
19   Northern Economic Planning Council (1971) *Report of the working group on environmental pollution* NEPC, Newcastle.
20   Yorkshire and Humberside Economic Planning Council (1973) *Environmental progress report, 1966–73* YHEPC, Leeds.
21   South East Joint Planning Team (1970) *Strategic Plan for the South East* Ministry of Housing and Local Government, HMSO, London.
22   South East Joint Planning Team (1971) *Strategic Plan for the South East. Studies volume 2* Department of the Environment, HMSO, London.
23   Department of the Environment (1974) *Strategic Plan for the North West: 1973 report* HMSO, London. (Abbreviated in subsequent detailed references to *SPNW.*)
24   Strategic Plan for the North West (1971) *Provisional statement of aims and objectives by the North West joint planning team* (NB. This and

other mimeographed technical references marked *SPNWA* are to be published as edited supplementary appendices to SPNW by HMSO, London.)

25   Strategic Plan for the North West (1971) *Issues report* SPNW, Salford.
26   *SPNW* pp. 269–72.
27   Strategic Plan for the North West (1972) *The generation and elaboration of alternative strategies for the location of population and employment at 1981 and 1991* SPNWA.
28   *SPNW* pp. 219–20.
29   Strategic Plan for the North West (1972) *Evaluation of alternative strategies, first cycle* SPNWA.
30   *SPNW* p. 220.
31   *SPNW* p. 273.
32   Strategic Plan for the North West (1972) *The evaluation of alternative strategies—first cycle* SPNWA.
33   *SPNW* p. 230.
34   *SPNW* p. 236.
35   *SPNW* p. 231, para. 10.36.
36   *SPNW* p. 237, para. 10.57.
37   *SPNW* p. 104, para. 6.1.
38   Strategic Plan for the North West *The 1981 situation* SPNWA.
39   *SPNW* p. 47.
40   *SPNW* p. 51 para. 3.30.
41   *SPNW* p. 63.
42   *SPNW* p. 79.
43   *SPNW* p. 120.
44   *SPNW* p. 126, para. 6.74.
45   *SPNW* p. 138.
46   Strategic Plan for the North West (1973) *The urban environment* SPNWA.
47   *SPNW* p. 189.
48   University of Lancaster (1974) *A critique of the 1974 strategic plan for the North West* UL, Lancaster.
49   Melville, B. (1974) Opinion: Strategic Plan for the North West *JRTPI, 60* 770.
50   Wood, C. M., Lee, N., Luker, J. A. and Saunders, P. J. W. (1974) *The geography of pollution: a study of Greater Manchester.* Manchester University Press, Manchester.
51   *SPNW* p. 268, para. 1.
52   Nicolas, R. (1945) *The Manchester and District Regional Planning Committee: regional planning proposals* Jarrold & Sons, London.
53   Nicolas, R., and Hellier, M. J. (1947) *South Lancashire and North Cheshire Advisory Planning Committee: an advisory plan* Bates, Manchester.
54   West Midlands Group (1948) *Conurbation: a planning survey of Birmingham and the Black Country* Architectural Press, London.
55   Ministry of Housing and Local Government (1966) *South Hampshire study: report* HMSO, London.

56 Ministry of Housing and Local Government (1966) *South Hampshire study: supplementary volume 1* HMSO, London.
57 Scottish Development Department (1970) *Tayside: Policies for development* HMSO, Edinburgh.
58 Ministry of Housing and Local Government (1965) *Northampton, Bedford and North Bucks study* HMSO, London.
59 Scottish Development Department (1966) *The Lothians regional survey and plan* (two vols) HMSO, Edinburgh.
60 Leicestershire County Council (1969) *Leicester and Leicestershire sub-regional planning study: report* LCC, Leicester.
61 Leicestershire County Council (1969) *Leicester and Leicestershire sub-regional planning study: technical appendices* LCC, Leicester.
62 Gloucestershire County Council (1970) *North Gloucestershire sub-regional study* GCC, Gloucester.
63 Department of the Environment (1974) *a study of the Cambridge sub-region* (three vols) HMSO, London.
64 Colin Buchanan & Partners (1973) *Tyne Wear Plan: urban strategy* CBP, London.
65 Central Unit for Environmental Planning (1971) *Severnside: a Feasibility study* Department of the Environment, HMSO, London.
66 Department of Economic Affairs (1969) *Humberside: a feasibility study* HMSO, London.
67 Cowling, T. M., and Steeley, G. C. (1973) *Sub-regional planning studies: an evaluation* Pergamon, Oxford.
68 Ministry of Housing and Local Government (1969) *Teesside survey and plan. Volume 1: policies and proposals* HMSO, London.
69 Ministry of Housing and Local Government (1969) *Teesside survey and plan. Volume 2: analysis, part 2* HMSO, London.
70 Nottinghamshire County Council (1969) *Nottinghamshire and Derbyshire sub-regional study* NCC, Nottingham.
71 Warwickshire County Council (1971) *Coventry-Solihull-Warwickshire: a strategy for the sub-region* WCC, Warwick.
72 Warwickshire County Council (1971) *Coventry-Solihull-Warwickshire. Supplementary report 4: evaluation* WCC, Warwick.
73 Warwickshire County Council (1971) *Coventry-Solihull-Warwickshire. Supplementary report 1: data* WCC, Warwick.
74 Warwickshire County Council (1971) *Coventry-Solihull-Warwickshire. Supplementary report 3: alternatives* WCC, Warwick.
75 Warwickshire County Council (1971) *Coventry-Solihull-Warwickshire. Supplementary report 5: countryside* WCC, Warwick.

CHAPTER 7

New town planning proposals

The river Mersey, Warrington, 1964. Not all new towns have been designated in pleasant rural locations, and pollution control is a central planning concern in Warrington New Town.

New town planning proposals are concerned with relatively small areas and therefore tend to be more specific than the larger-scale regional and sub-regional studies described in Chapter 6. Most new towns have been located in areas where there was little previous development; the best possible conditions for effective planning for pollution control. New town studies therefore present the opportunity to consider pollution and other matters as general planning principles (in the same way as regional and sub-regional plans) and then to translate them into physical proposals.

The potential to design a completely new development is denied the planners of the latest sequence of new towns, such as Warrington, which are based on substantial existing settlements. However, the

LIVERPOOL INSTITUTE OF
HIGHER EDUCATION
THE MARKLAND LIBRARY

manifest need to improve pollutant levels in some of these towns must provide an incentive to plan for the control of pollution equivalent to that afforded by greater freedom of design. It is in new town planning, if anywhere, that pollution would be expected to be taken into account and planning control implemented.

RECENT NEW TOWN PROPOSALS

The evolution of new towns may be considered to have progressed in four steps: the pioneering pre-war new towns, like Letchworth; the immediate post-war new towns, like Crawley; the later post-war new towns, like Telford, and the most recent larger new towns, like Warrington.[1] The published proposals for the later new towns make varying reference to pollution. The Runcorn report, for example, appears not to mention the subject at all, although it contains sections on foul sewage and refuse disposal.[2] Nor does that on Telford, although it does refer briefly to the environmental problems associated with refuse tipping.[3]

The study of Hook, Hampshire[4] (which was never designated as a new town), does not mention pollution either, but the need to avoid nuisance from the industries to be located in residential areas is emphasised. This publication contains sections on refuse disposal and sewage treatment (the need for high quality effluent for discharge to the Thames being stated).[4] The Skelmersdale report[5] refers to the advantages of smokeless towns and suggests that measures should be taken to ensure that all development in the new town area incorporates appropriate heating systems. It also indicates that consideration should be given to the possibility of providing district heating to large sections of the town by means of a suitable distribution system. The report contains the usual brief sections on foul drainage and refuse disposal.[5]

The mid-Wales proposals[6] (for another new town which was not designated) mention the necessity to prevent streams from suffering increased pollution as the lower slopes of hills become urbanised. The report does not specify the measures to be adopted and omits further reference to pollution.[6] The Washington report[7] devotes a section to land pollution caused by waste heaps and explains how they can be assimilated into the urban landscape. It states that the tipping of refuse could be carried out without causing great nuisance.[7]

The earliest Irvine report[8] mentions foul sewage and air pollution.

It recommends that 'measures should be taken to ensure that all new development in the area incorporates appropriate heating systems and that industrial processes do not result in the emission of smoke or noxious fumes'[8] but does not elaborate on the nature of the measures. (The study of Redditch repeats these sentiments virtually verbatim.[9]) The later, more detailed, Irvine report[10] expands upon the point, emphasising the need to maintain the air in a clean state, without being more explicit about planning methods of control. This document also explains how water pollution is to be avoided by developing certain areas served by adequate sewage disposal facilities before others which are not[10] but, as with other new town reports, does little more than refer briefly to the pollution problem in passing.

The latest new towns were designated under the New Towns Act, 1965 (which superseded the earlier new town legislation), and have been called 'town expansions' rather than 'new towns' because the additional populations to be accommodated are smaller than those already resident.[1] Of the proposals for these towns, those for Peterborough,[11] Ipswich[12] and Milton Keynes[13] ignore pollution. The report on Central Lancashire also fails to mention the subject but it does state that obnoxious industries should be separated from residential areas.[14] The original Northampton proposals also omit any reference to pollution although concern about sewage effluents is expressed.[15] The master plan, however, contains a very brief statement on the problem and castigates the controlled tipping method of refuse disposal.[16]

In general, the various new town reports reviewed devote at most one or two paragraphs to pollution and tend only to refer to the existence of particular local problems without explaining how they can be overcome by planning methods. It could have been expected, with justification, that air, land, water and noise pollution would each have merited a mention in the new town studies. Further, it would have been reasonable to expect the reports to cover the current pollution situation, to explain how the new development would affect pollution levels and to describe the planning measures to be employed to reduce their effects. The lack of concern about pollution in these reports is the more disappointing because new town planning offers unrivalled opportunities for an effective contribution to pollution control. The Warrington report[17] is more concerned with pollution and its control.

D

WARRINGTON NEW TOWN

Instead of merely presenting a summary of the way in which the pollution problem is dealt with in the Warrington report, it is more instructive to place that document in its context. Accordingly, the development of concern about pollution in the new town is traced from the time its designation was first mooted until 1973. The sequence of events in Warrington falls into three parts; the background to the report, the report, and developments subsequent to the report.

Background

In February 1965 the Minister of Housing and Local Government announced the government's intention to provide for overspill from Manchester in the Risley area, near Warrington. One reason for choosing this location was the presence at Risley of a large and mainly derelict Royal Ordnance Factory. Planning consultants were appointed in October 1965 to recommend an appropriate area for designation under the New Towns Act, 1965, and, later, to propose a master plan for the development of the area. The terms of reference to the consultants included the requirement that: 'the plan should . . . have, as one of its main objects, the provision of a good workable environment in Warrington itself; and the Risley development should be planned to contribute to that'.[18]

The consultants' first report,[18] recommending the designation of some 22,340 acres and setting out a planning strategy, made no reference to pollution, despite the implication in their terms of reference that this was regarded as an important element. (A 'good workable environment' must embrace tolerable pollution levels.) However, the sewerage and sewage disposal situation was briefly touched upon; facilities were heavily overloaded and much of the sewage from the town centre drained untreated into the river Mersey. Dereliction (caused mainly by obsolete buildings) was also mentioned.[18] The Warrington Chamber of Commerce were not particularly worried about pollution either, their main concern being that the proposed new town should be given Development Area status (like adjoining Merseyside) to make it attractive to industrialists.[19]

Following the submission of the consultants' report (in July 1966) a draft Designation Order was made in May 1967, the area of the new town being reduced slightly to 21,500 acres. Air pollution was an important element in the discussion at the public inquiry into the designation held in September of that year.[20] Written objections submitted to the Minister had criticised the proposed designation on the ground that an area subject to as much air pollution as Warrington was unsuitable for a new town. After argument about smoke and sulphur dioxide statistics the inspector found that 'there is undoubtedly a very high level of pollution at Warrington, though it is being reduced as a result of a programme of smoke control orders'.[20]

The inspector concluded: 'if a town is not established, I have no doubt that the population of the Warrington area as a whole will continue to increase by voluntary migration. If the level of pollution is not a bar to such a voluntary immigration, there is no reason why it should be regarded as a factor inhibiting the establishment of a new town.'[20] The Minister agreed with this assessment, stating that he concurred with the inspector's finding that the air pollution objection, and others, were not sufficiently material to raise doubts about the suitability of the location, and in April 1968, he made an order designating a reduced area of about 18,650 acres as a new town.[21] A development corporation was set up, under the New Towns Act, 1965, with responsibility for planning and developing the new town in close association with the Warrington County Borough Council. Its members were appointed in spring 1969 and staff appointments commenced shortly afterwards.[22]

There is no doubt that the air pollution situation was brought to the attention of the consultants by a series of complaints about emission from the power station, due to be closed in the near future, and about a number of industrial sources.[23] [24] The county borough public health inspector prepared detailed statistical records of deposited matter, smoke and sulphur dioxide readings in the town[25] and these were analysed in relation to wind speed and direction.[26]

Shortly before the publication of their second, and main, Warrington New Town report the consultants published proposals for the re-development of an inner housing area in the town.[27] Derelict land, noise from industry and road traffic, air pollution and water pollution are included in an appraisal of the environment of the redevelopment area. Maps showing the incidence of these problems are presented (the air pollution map showing the areas affected by 50 per cent of the maximum ground level concentration and by the maximum concentration of sulphur dioxide from tall chimneys). The report states that houses which are affected by adverse pollution and noise conditions, which are unlikely to be eliminated in the foreseeable future, were not considered for long term improvement.[27]

Warrington New Town report

The consultants' main report, setting out detailed planning proposals, was presented in October 1969.[17] Possibly reflecting the concern about the environment expressed at the public inquiry, this report considers pollution problems more closely than that for any other new town. In an early section on the regional and sub-regional context it is stated that one of the largest single tasks facing the area is environmental rehabilitation: tidying up its derelict land and cleaning its polluted rivers and dirty atmosphere.[28]

Environmental matters are considered important in the siting of those industries which would be appropriately accommodated in areas which were currently derelict or had been left undeveloped by virtue of neighbouring land uses (for example, motorway buffer zones).[29] The report suggests that 'firms emitting pollutants should be located wherever possible in the lee of prevailing winds' and mentions that shelter belts might be necessary. It states that 10 per cent of new employment might be suitable for location in proximity to residential areas on the grounds of 'its performance with respect to noise, smell, smoke, fumes, pollution, traffic generation and generation of waste'. The report refers to the existing problem of non-conforming industries in Warrington, which should, it says, provide a reminder of the danger of ignoring environmental objectives (including pollution) in industrial location.[29]

The section on sewerage and sewage disposal emphasises the need for full treatment of sewage and the restriction of storm overflows to curb pollution. It states that 'full treatment will be required at all sewage works to alleviate the present problems of river pollution'.[30] The section on refuse disposal mentions the problem of odours from controlled tipping and reviews the advantages of the various disposal methods. It concludes that more positive and creative uses of tipping are needed, even if incineration is used and quotes the development of noise barriers by such methods.[31]

The consultants canvassed the views of older school-children about their town in order to provide a realistic context for their proposals. Many were scathing about the domestic and industrial air pollution, about river pollution and about land pollution from waste tipping.

The schoolchildren put forward a number of solutions to deal with what they regarded as a serious problem affecting Warrington.[32]

The objectives quoted in the report as underlying the consultants' proposals did not specifically refer to pollution other than by specifying the need to minimise aural intrusion from roads.[33] The development proposals earmarked most of the derelict sites for building and other positive purposes.[34] The report mentions that air pollution had been an issue at the public inquiry and states that this problem is more likely to constitute a phasing constraint on redevelopment, than an absolute one. It presents a review of smoke, sulphur dioxide and industrial air pollutants together with a map showing the areas affected by maximum concentrations of pollutants emitted from the main industrial sources[35] (similar to that in the redevelopment report).[27] Individual redevelopment recommendations, the report suggests, 'must be reviewed in terms of their compatibility with the level of pollution throughout the implementation of the plan.[35] The proposals for renewal of older housing areas mention the need for traffic management in order to, among other things, minimise noise intrusion.[36] The report states that dereliction and non-conforming uses will need to be eliminated from such areas. It stresses that any potentially serious industrial pollution sources 'should be sited up to a mile from any residential development, depending on the height of specific emissions. The use of tree shelter belts will help to reduce pollution'.[37]

Subsequent events

On receiving the consultants' report the Development Corporation proceeded to study the proposals in detail, since they were intended to form the basis for the preparation of a draft outline plan for the new town. New sewers were laid to improve the water pollution situation. Meanwhile the rationale for the new town's existence began to change from providing accommodation for an overspill population to providing for voluntary migration.[38] Despite the absence of development Area status the town's new role emerged in sharper definition during 1971–72: it had become that of a natural growth point, with excellent communications attracting voluntary in-migration.[39] Local public inquiries had to be held into the designations of a residential area and of an industrial area in advance of the publication of the outline plan for the New Town. From the evidence of the annual New Town Report on Warrington, the problems of environmental pollution continued to exercise the corporation.[39]

The corporation arranged the setting up of an anti-pollution working party of the various authorities responsible for pollution control in 1971. This must have been one of the first occasions on which planners, water authority and environmental health officers, engineers and others had been assembled to consider the types of pollution to which an area was subject, the means of controlling it and the responsibility for the enforcement of that control. Matters considered included the provision of refuse dumps in Warrington, pesticides, motor vehicle emissions and other topics. Plans of noise levels and derelict sites in the designated area were prepared.[40] This working party was no doubt responsible for recommending that the corporation, with other neighbouring authorities, commission an industrial waste study of the sub-region. The ensuing report sets the new town's tips in their context and emphasises the need to improve the methods employed in disposing of solid wastes—of toxic wastes in particular.[41]

It appears, however, that the number of members of the working party made proceedings cumbersome and that there was difficulty in getting the representatives of the various local authorities to recognise the 'whole town' concept. After a few meetings, the size of the working party was reduced and the Development Corporation's planning representation was withdrawn.[23] This action marked the end of the working party as a forum for broad interdisciplinary concern about, and action on, pollution problems in Warrington and terminated a very interesting exercise in co-operation. The departure of the Development Corporation planner from the working party was particularly disappointing in that it rendered it more difficult to make an effective planning contribution to pollution control.

The outline plan[42] for the development of the new town was published in April 1972. One of its objectives is 'to make Warrington a good place in which to live and grow up' and the plan recognises the derelict land, air pollution and water pollution problems facing the town. Apart from its sections on sewage and refuse disposal, the plan quotes the need to reduce traffic noise and fumes. It states that 'any applications from industries where there is any chance of adding to the problem (of industrial emissions) must be examined with care'. Again: 'parts of the area are marred by non-conforming and incompatible land uses. The Corporation will assist the County Borough

Council and the other Authorities in the relocation of these uses'.[42] The plan is essentially similar to the earlier Warrington New Town report,[17] although there are a number of relatively minor amendments to the proposals.

The air pollution question was no longer an important issue at the public inquiry into the outline plan held in September 1972.[43] In its place objections were raised about the environmental effects of new roads. The visual intrusion, noise and atmospheric pollution likely to result from the new road system was debated at length at the inquiry, particular emphasis being placed upon the effects of a new high-level crossing of the Manchester Ship Canal. Estimates of the numbers of properties affected by different noise levels were put forward and dust, dirt and fumes were also discussed. The inspector did not find that these objections to the new road system could be sustained and recommended that the outline plan be accepted with only minimal modifications.[43] These environmental issues were not considered sufficiently important to warrant mention in the Secretary of State's decision letter of June 1973.[44] It did state, however, that the Secretary of State would, in due course, wish to examine detailed road proposals with particular reference to the extent to which they have been designed to limit environmental intrusion. The voluntary, as opposed to planned overspill, growth of Warrington was now fully recognised.[44]

The latest New Town Report[45] to be published (as at 1975) states that the Warrington New Town Development Corporation 'has become increasingly sensitive of its responsibility for the improvement of the environment'. It also expresses the hope that better working relationships can be established with the new local authorities (Cheshire County and Warrington District) than were achieved with the old.[45] It appears from this that there may have been a number of conflicts between the Development Corporation and the various local authorities concerned (Lancashire and Cheshire Counties, Warrington County Borough, Warrington Rural District and Runcorn Rural District). These may have had unfortunate effects upon pollution control, since public health is not a new town development corporation function—responsibilities lie with the local authorities, as do most planning powers. It is known, for example, that in one case the Development Corporation recommended that planning permission be refused for the development of a chemical works likely to emit sulphurous fumes and to pollute its environment but that the local authority granted permission.[23]

The Development Corporation published a district plan during 1973 which makes some reference to pollution and is concerned with building on the large area of derelict land at Risley[46] (the original reason for the designation of Warrington). It states that a noise attenuation zone (perhaps incorporating barriers and mounds) has been adopted to reduce the effects of major roads upon residential areas. Protection zones around a small nuclear reactor in the area and provision of sewage treatment are also referred to.[46]

Commentary
The treatment of pollution in the Warrington New Town report is better than in any of the other new town studies reviewed in this chapter. The report shows a real awareness of environmental pollution problems in Warrington and makes a number of proposals to improve conditions. However, pollution control is not mentioned among the objectives forming the basis for the planning proposals. This is particularly disappointing because the need to control pollution was implicit in the original terms of reference to the consultants and was an important issue in discussions and at public inquiries at various stages in the development of the New Town planning proposals.

The main report does not demonstrate how concern about pollution was translated into physical planning proposals. The physical planning measures suggested are generally rather naive: industrial development to be sited to the leeward of housing, no improvement of housing areas close to major roads, etc. There is no explanation of the basis for adopting these measures, either by reference to the costs and benefits of control, to standards, or to alternative planning techniques for achieving the same effects. Indeed, no appreciation of the range of physical planning techniques available, or of the desirability of attacking the problem on a town-wide basis is displayed. (However, the recommendation relating to industrial shelter belts does demonstrate recognition that trees absorb air pollutants—their use for this purpose being a relatively sophisticated planning measure.)

In view of the importance of air pollution at the inquiry into the designation of the new town, the treatment of this subject in the report is inadequate. More could easily have been made of the various types of air pollution in Warrington and their potential control by planning and other methods. More crucially, the effects of the development proposals in reducing pollution could have been explained. Overall, despite the fact that its general coverage of pollution marks it out from other new town studies, the treatment of pollution in this large report still leaves something to be desired and the discussion of control of pollution by planning methods leaves considerably more, there being inadequate recognition that many planning decisions will inevitably affect pollution levels, whether intentionally or not.

Despite increasing mention in the annual reports pollution may perhaps have become a slightly less important issue in Warrington New Town since the consultants' report was published. The setting up of the anti-pollution working party probably marked the height of concern about pollution. This was a novel and potentially very useful innovation, which could have provided the basis for effective, concerted action to control all types of pollution. The short-lived nature of the Development Corporation's planning representation was perhaps an indication of lessening interest in the problem. There is some mention of pollution in the outline plan (a much shorter document than the consultants') but it was not a critical issue at the inquiry into objections to it.

It is interesting that the emphasis changed between the inquiries from concern about air pollution (mainly smoke) to road traffic pollution (mainly noise). This is quite possibly a fair reflection of the change in the relative impact of pollution problems in Warrington in the five year intervening period though industrial air pollution and noise, land pollution and water pollution still adversely affect the town. The only mention of pollution in the local plan published recently relates to noise from roads. It would be a great mistake if Warrington were to lose the impetus generated by the consultants' report: there is still considerable scope for the control of pollution by the exercise of planning powers in the New Town.

Even the discussion of pollution in the Warrington New Town report does not compare with the best treatment in regional and sub-regional studies. There may be a number of reasons why new town planning proposals have paid scant regard to the issue. It may be that pollution is not a problem at most new town locations chosen although Peterlee and Runcorn, for example, immediately spring to mind as having pollution problems. Even if it is generally true, the planning proposals ought to be concerned with maintaining unpolluted conditions. New town reports tend to be less recent than regional and sub-regional studies, but there are a sufficient number of older sub-regional studies dealing with pollution and sufficient recent new town studies not mentioning the problem to indicate that the relatively recent increase in public concern about pollution cannot be a universal reason for the discrepancy.

It is possible that planners recognise pollution only as a large-scale problem, and believe it to be unimportant at the level at which detailed planning exercises have to be carried out. If this is the case, there are sufficient local pollution problems in most areas to render the position untenable. Indeed, it can be argued that pollution is essentially a local concern. It is also possible that new town planning proposals do, in fact, pay considerable regard to pollution control but that this is an implicit design constraint which is little emphasised in the reports. It is certainly true that new town reports tend not to explain their methodology as clearly as the larger-scale planning studies but this explanation still seems somewhat unlikely.

On the whole the conclusion that pollution has been largely ignored in new town planning proposals is inescapable. In the circumstances, discussion of the way in which the planning measures do or do not accord with the principles of control and of the reconciliation of pollution control objectives with other planning objectives (Chapter 4) is irrelevant. It appears that the framing of pollution control objectives, recognition of the role of planning and the use of planning techniques in the control of pollution are all largely missing from new town planning, where there is most scope for the control of pollution. There is not even any indication that the position is improving: the control of pollution is no better handled in the most recent new town proposals than in the older ones.

REFERENCES

1   Osborn, F. J., and Whittick, A. (1969) *The new towns* Leonard Hill, London.
2   Ling, A. (1967) *Runcorn New Town* Runcorn Development Corporation, Runcorn.
3   John Madin Design Group (1969) *Telford development proposals* (two vols) JMDG, Birmingham.

4   Greater London Council (1965) *The planning of a new town* GLC, London.
5   Wilson, L. H. (1964) *Skelmersdale New Town planning proposals. Volume 1* Skelmersdale Development Corporation, Skelmersdale.
6   Welsh Office (1966) *A new town in Mid-Wales* HMSO, London.
7   Llewelyn-Davies, Weeks & Partners (1966) *Washington New Town: master plan and report* Washington Development Corporation, Washington.
8   Scottish Development Department (1966) *Irvine New Town* HMSO, Edinburgh.
9   Wilson and Womersley (1966) *Redditch New Town* Redditch Development Corporation, Redditch.
10 Irvine Development Corporation (1971) *Irvine New Town plan* IDC, Irvine.
11 Peterborough Development Corporation (1970) *Greater Peterborough master plan* PDC, Peterborough.
12 Ministry of Housing and Local Government (1968) *Ipswich draft basic plan* HMSO, London.
13 Llewelyn-Davies, Weeks, Forestier-Walker & Bor (1970) *The plan for Milton Keynes* (two vols) Milton Keynes Development Corporation, Bletchley.
14 Ministry of Housing and Local Government (1967) *Central Lancashire: study for a city* HMSO, London.
15 Ministry of Housing and Local Government (1966) *Expansion at Northampton* HMSO, London.
16 Wilson & Womersley (1969) *Northampton master plan* Northampton Development Corporation, Northampton.
17 Austin-Smith/Lord Partnership (1969) *Warrington New Town* Warrington New Town Development Corporation, Warrington. (Referred to as *WNT* in subsequent detailed references.)
18 Ministry of Housing and Local Government (1966) *Expansion of Warrington* HMSO, London.
19 Warrington Chamber of Commerce (1966) *Planning Warrington's future* WCC, Warrington.
20 Ministry of Housing and Local Government (1967) *Report of the inquiry: the draft Warrington New Town (Designation) Order 196* MHLG, London.
21 Ministry of Housing and Local Government (1968) *Decision letter: Warrington New Town designation* quoted in *WNT* p. 465.
22 Ministry of Housing and Local Government (1970) *Reports of the Development Corporations, 31 March 1970* Warrington, 543–58, HMSO, London.
23 Warrington New Town Development Corporation (1973) Personal communication.
24 Ward, E. W. (1971) Air pollution and planning *Proc. Symp. on Env. Poll. Lancaster* North West Association of Public Health Inspectors, Wigan.

25 Warrington County Borough (1967) *Measurement of atmospheric pollution in Warrington: statistical studies* mimeo, WCB, Warrington.
26 Austin-Smith/Lord Partnership (1967) *Measurement of atmospheric pollution in Warrington* mimeo, A-SLP, Warrington.
27 Austin-Smith/Lord Partnership (1969) *Urban renewal proposals: Whitecross, Warrington* A-SLP, Warrington.
28 *WNT* p. 52, para. 5.
29 *WNT* p. 115, paras. 2–5.
30 *WNT* p. 205, para. 8.
31 *WNT* p. 215.
32 *WNT* p. 228, paras. 1 and 2.
33 *WNT* p. 318, paras. 7–10.
34 *WNT* p. 241, para. 2.
35 *WNT* p. 242.
36 *WNT* p. 448.
37 *WNT* p. 267, para. 3.
38 Department of the Environment (1971) *Reports of the Development Corporations, 31 March 1971* Warrington, 569–95, HMSO, London.
39 Department of the Environment (1972) *Reports of the Development Corporations, 31 March 1972* Warrington, 591–618, HMSO, London.
40 Warrington New Town Development Corporation (1971) *Minutes of meetings: Anti-pollution Working Party* mimeo, WNTDC, Warrington.
41 Harwell Hazardous Wastes Service (1973) *The disposal of industrial waste in the upper Mersey valley* HHWS, Harwell.
42 Warrington New Town Development Corporation (1972) *Warrington New Town outline plan* WNTDC, Warrington.
43 Department of the Environment (1973) *Report of the inquiry: Warrington New Town outline plan* DoE, London.
44 Department of the Environment (1973) *Decision letter: Warrington New Town outline plan* DoE, London.
45 Department of the Environment (1973) *Reports of the Development Corporations, 31 March 1973* Warrington, 589–623, HMSO, London.
46 Warrington New Town Development Corporation (1973) *Birchwood district plan area* WNTDC, Warrington.

CHAPTER 8

Structure plan formulation

Structure plans represent the most recent form of development plan presentation and the focus of a great deal of planning activity. It could therefore be expected that of all the different types of plans prepared, structure plans would provide the greatest evidence of planning control of pollution. It is useful to set the scene for the discussions of structure plans by first briefly reviewing pollution considerations in a number of 'old-style' development plans.

'OLD-STYLE' DEVELOPMENT PLANS

Certain pre-1947 plans laid considerable emphasis on pollution. That for Manchester in 1945[1] highlighted water pollution and especially smoke pollution problems. River pollution was to be mitigated by reducing the density of development, and hence storm overflows, and by building new relief sewers. A long treatment of air pollution ended by recommending district heating as a method of planning control.[1] The 1946 Middlesbrough survey and plan[2] contained a lengthy and virtually unique section on air pollution, describing a special survey of the problem, its influence on planning, and pollution control methods. It recommended that no housing should remain in the areas most affected by pollution, that hospitals and other sensitive land uses should be relocated in cleaner parts of the town and it expressed confidence that the reduction in housing density engendered by redevelopment would improve the situation.[2]

The Westminster plan (1946) mentions the authority's pioneering district heating scheme and its advantage of preventing atmospheric pollution.[3] The early plans for Kingston upon Hull,[4] Swindon[5] and Worcester,[6] on the other hand, made no mention of pollution, and Abercrombie's famous Greater London plan refers to pollution only in relation to smoke from electricity generating stations.[7] (Although his earlier plan for the county had discussed the smoke problem in London and suggested that the use of cleaner fuels than coal, more efficient fuel utilisation, district heating and a reduction in the number of dwellings would considerably alleviate the situation.[8])

The 1947 Town and Country Planning Act [9] imposed on every

Many structure plans contain sections devoted to the control of pollution. Domestic waste dumped at Warley shows that the policies they contain must gain general acceptance if they are to prove effective.

local planning authority the obligation to carry out a survey and to prepare a development plan for their area. The survey involved a physical, economic and sociological analysis of the potentialities and future requirements of the area dealing, for example, with natural resources, distribution of industry, communications, housing requirements and the community structure. A circular elaborating on the survey requirements[10] made no mention of pollution—public utilities (water supply and sewerage, electricity supply, gas supply and land drainage) perhaps being the most closely related topic. An official document which sought to explain development plans likewise contained no hint of concern about pollution.[11]

With so little official encouragement it is hardly surprising that many plans failed to mention pollution. West Suffolk[12] and Cambridgeshire,[13] both admittedly fairly unpolluted parts of the country, were two such. The plan for West Hartlepool, a rather more polluted place, also omitted any reference to pollution.[14] The preliminary plan for Lancashire made a fleeting reference to derelict land and its reuse,[15] while the analysis of survey for the first Devonshire review considered derelict land and mentioned the intention to control discharges of sewage direct to streams.[16]

The Newcastle development plan review[17] discussed river pollution—stressing the need for better treatment and for separate sewers—and, briefly, smoke control. However, the smoke abatement programme is the only approach to control described, as is the case in the Coventry review.[18]

In view of the attitude prevalent in both central government and in other local authorities, it is notable that Glasgow corporation dealt with air pollution, river and canal pollution and the reclamation of derelict land in the first review of its plan.[19] Pollution problems from motor vehicles and oil burning were envisaged and a planning measure, redevelopment, was seen as one of the methods of controlling smoke pollution. The opening up of waterways, their cleansing and continued co-operation with the water pollution control authorities were proposed as control measures.[19] Despite the considerable attention paid to smoke in the earlier Manchester plan, the official development plan for Manchester completely failed to mention pollution.[20] The County of London plan (1962) omitted to refer to the problem,[21] although the analysis section of the earlier, 1951, plan emphasised air pollution, referring to smoke abatement, gas washing

and cleaning, district heating, the siting of industrial uses to the leeward of residential areas and the use of buffer zones as control measures.[22]

There were several local authority plans for the area which was
later to constitute Teesside County Borough. Of these, Stockton on
Tees, in the written analysis—a non-statutory document also referred
to by different authorities as the report of survey or analysis of survey—mentioned the question of treating sewage (then discharged
crude to the Tees). It also dealt with derelict land and its reclamation.[23] As might have been anticipated from the earlier plans, the
Middlesbrough report of survey referred to air pollution from industry, the clearance of old housing close to industry and the question of
river pollution from sewage effluents, stating that 'strong economic
arguments will be required to justify the expense that would be
involved' in treating sewage.[24] Neither approved written statements—the statutory documents—touched upon pollution, however.[25] [26] The Billingham written analysis referred to derelict land
and the surface deposit of waste as problems,[27] but the written statement did not.[28]

The authorities which once constituted Warley made even less play
of pollution matters. The Smethwick[29] and Staffordshire[30] reports of
survey mentioned dereliction but neither written statement did.[31] [32]
The Oldbury report of survey[33] and written statement[34] both completely neglected pollution.

The various reports of survey submitted for the South Hampshire
area[35-40] and the written statements forming part of the approved
town maps[41-45] and of the submitted county plan[46] conspicuously fail
to mention pollution at any point, despite the fact that an earlier plan
for the whole of this area had referred to severe sewage disposal
problems and the consequential difficulty of accommodating overspill
from Portsmouth.[47]

STRUCTURE PLANS GENERALLY

It is logical to commence an analysis of the treatment of pollution
control measures in structure plans by questioning whether this
figures as an important element in the official guidance on the preparation of plans. Next the results of a 1972 survey into structure plan
preparation are compared with the evidence obtained from a brief
review of the consideration of pollution in a sample of published

structure plans.

Guidance on preparation
The structure plan is intended to perform seven closely related functions:[48]

1   Interpreting national and regional policies, in terms appropriate to the area in question.
2   Establishing aims, policies and general proposals designed to achieve the aims.
3   Providing a framework for local plans.
4   Indicating 'action areas', being areas where intensive change is expected.
5   Providing guidance for development control.
6   Providing a base for co-ordinating decisions.
7   Bringing the main planning issues and decisions before the Secretary of State for the Environment and the public.

The Department of the Environment's guide to structure plan preparation, published in 1970, stated that the plan should show how individual aspects of planning are dealt with.[48] It suggested that policies, general proposals and related information be set out in the structure plan 'written statement' whereas supporting information be presented in a 'report of survey' and be summarised in the written statement. The twelve individual subject headings mentioned in the guide do not include 'pollution', but it is recognised that there will be occasions when a particular aspect of one of these main subjects is of such importance, and the development of policies and proposals is likely to be so complex, that separate treatment is justified. An example quoted is the restoration of derelict land.[48] Pollution could clearly be considered under the miscellaneous heading 'other subjects'.

   However, the guide mentions the restoration of derelict land under 'housing', noise and fumes under 'industry and commerce', impact on the environment under 'transportation', absence of noise under 'education', noise in relation to 'recreation and leisure', derelict land and smokeless zones under 'conservation', 'townscape and landscape' and the reduction of the adverse impact of 'utility services'.[48] Although these topics embrace some consideration of pollution, it is frequently in connection with local planning and development control. No

requirement to examine pollution problems over the area as a whole
or as a part of the preparation of the structure plan itself is set out at
any stage. There is no reference to pollution in the accompanying
circular.[49]

Less than a year after the publication of the guide a memorandum
on the interpretation of the 1968 Town and Country Planning Act
(see Chapter 3) stressed that proposals in a structure or local plan
should be related to the need to combat and prevent pollution, even
though responsibility and specific action in this field would often be
for bodies other than the local planning authority.[50] This very specific
advice is in marked contrast to the piecemeal references to pollution
matters in the guide and probably reflects the growing concern about
pollution at the time. It remains to examine how far local planning
authorities heeded the advice.

Survey and review

A survey of local planning authorities was conducted in 1972 to
discover what progress was being made in the preparation of structure plans.[51] The survey revealed a widespread use of a subject classification based on topics such as housing, transport, etc. An analysis
of the replies[52] to a question requesting information about the topics
to be discussed in structure plans has been made to examine whether
pollution was being considered in plan preparation.

Questionnaires were returned by seventy-four local planning
authorities, of which fifty-two answered the relevant question. Only
one of these authorities did not refer to environmental matters.
Unfortunately, the questionnaire did not mention pollution by name,
the most closely related topics specified in the appropriate question
being 'conservation, townscape and landscape', 'public utilities' and
'other matters'. However, eleven local planning authorities mentioned pollution related subjects under this last category.

Of these authorities four were in south-east England, four in
northern England, two in Wales and one in Scotland. Three
authorities were dealing with 'environmental pollution' (including
Teesside), one 'pollution and derelict land', three 'derelict land' one
'reclamation and environmental improvement', one 'the environmental context', one 'aircraft and traffic noise' and the last 'public protection'. South Hampshire and Warley were not amongst those return-
ing questionnaires.[52]

Although it is quite possible that authorities regarded pollution as falling within one of the categories listed in the questionnaire, it is notable that only eleven authorities felt the subject to be important enough to mention separately, particularly in view of environmental conditions in some of the areas concerned. Some discrepancies between the results of this survey and the treatment of pollution in completed structure plans are apparent.

The Ipswich sub-region plan mentions dereliction in the report of survey[53] but not, seemingly, in the strategy report.[54] The North Riding of Yorkshire also appears to pay little attention to the problem.[55] Solihull's report on the environment barely mentions pollution,[56] but the Herefordshire[57-60] and Worcester[61] [62] structure plans do refer to the problem. The West Midlands planning authorities have clearly worked closely together, since West Bromwich,[63] Wolverhampton[64] and Walsall,[65] like Warley (see below), have prepared reports on the environment in which pollution is given some prominence. It also figures in the corresponding written statements.[66-68]

Pollution is considered important by Dudley[69] and Coventry,[70] and is referred to frequently by Birmingham.[71] [72] Worcestershire includes a section on pollution under public utilities[73] and Stoke on Trent is also concerned about the problem.[74] [75] Staffordshire deals with dereliction and waste disposal in its report of survey[76] and these topics together with water pollution in its written statement.[77] The Leicester and Leicestershire structure plan contains numerous references to pollution,[78] [79] and, finally, Brighton gives pollution a separate section in its report on the physical environment.[80] A structure plan for Manchester has not yet been completed (1975), but it appears that pollution will be an important element.[81] Other local planning authorities are known to be giving pollution considerable weight in the preparation of structure plans. For example, Cumberland County Council and the Peak Park Planning Board included all types of pollution in surveying their areas, and appear to have attempted to formulate a consistent policy for locating various activities with respect to waste disposal and pollution control. Glamorgan County Council have also given pollution problems some prominence and have made a waste and pollution survey of the county.

It is of interest to note that the planning authority in this sample of published structure plans which stated that it was examining pollution in McLoughlin's survey[52] gave a rather below-average account of the subject, whereas four authorities which did not mention pollution in the survey did, in fact, give it considerable emphasis in their structure plans.

In practice most local planning authorities in this sample have considered pollution to be a relevant structure planning issue, whereas the survey tended to indicate that the opposite was the case. At least a year elapsed between the survey and the submission of most of the plans and it may be that a change in planners' attitudes to pollution was reflected in the plans. However, it seems likely that the indications provided by the survey may be somewhat unreliable in this instance because pollution was not specifically referred to in the relevant question.

It is quite clear, nevertheless, that there has been a very significant improvement in the consideration of pollution in the years between the preparation of the old-style development plans and preparation of the structure plans. Not only is pollution generally regarded as a relevant issue in structure plans but the level of treatment tends to be of a completely different order from that in old development plans and demonstrates a detailed appreciation of both problems and planning solutions to them.

GREATER LONDON DEVELOPMENT PLAN

The Greater London development plan, published in 1969, was not originally intended to be a structure plan but it does incorporate many of the features of such plans, predating subsequent plans by several years. Because there has been an exhaustive inquiry into the plan, guidance on the relevance and importance of pollution as a structure planning issue is available, although it has to be borne in mind that the Greater London Council is a quite exceptional metropolitan county rather than a county or district planning authority. The Greater London development plan is consequently probably more akin to a regional strategic plan than a normal structure plan.

Like the old-style development plans, the plan is divided into two parts, the report of survey and the written statement, as advised in the guide to structure plan preparation[48] circulated a year later. The survey report[82] contains impressive sections on pollution. Smoke, sulphur dioxide, industrial air pollutants and motor vehicle pollutants are all reviewed, the results of a number of analyses of traffic pollutants being given. There is also a clear, full and factual statement on road traffic and aircraft noise, noise levels for the main central London roads and for the area around Heathrow airport being quoted. Vehicle vibration and visual impact are also discussed. River pollution is briefly mentioned and there are sections on foul sewage and refuse disposal.[82]

The written statement[83] contains a number of provisions relating to pollution control. It mentions the need to reclaim derelict land: to be carried out within the context of local development plans. Although the statement contains a section on rivers and canals it does not mention water pollution; nor does it refer to pollution in discussing sewerage and sewage disposal or refuse disposal. However, there are two paragraphs on the problem of air pollution, one explaining progress in smoke control and the other providing a general description of air pollution problems generally. Recognising the pollution attributable to power stations and motor vehicles, the statement 'trusts that the various Ministries and local authorities concerned will press forward with all practicable means of improvement.'[83]

The paragraph on traffic noise is more specific, recommending the London boroughs to accept the Wilson standards[84] and stating that the council's own developments will protect building interiors from traffic noise by careful siting and layout and by appropriate design and construction. The three paragraphs on aircraft noise state the position regarding possible development control policies within certain noise contours and that regarding soundproofing.[83]

The inquiry into the plan was a prodigious affair and generated vast quantities of evidence. Among the papers, however, were a number of documents dealing with pollution from motor vehicles which were of considerable planning relevance. One paper discussed the detailed noise and air pollution effects of traffic on local and secondary roads in an area of inner London.[85] Another dealt with pollution from proposed secondary roads[86] and another with that from primary roads.[87] A study of the environmental effects of the construction of Westway is contained in another paper.[88] These papers and the Greater London Council's proof of evidence on transport[89] show that they do not consider air pollution to be a significant problem but that they are well aware of the range of planning techniques for controlling noise (and of the financial difficulties of implementing them). The evidence states that 'it is not expected that traffic noise alone will frequently be sufficient reason for removing properties indirectly affected by a major road scheme'.[89] The council undoubtedly has more experience than any other British planning authority of planning to control the environmental effects of roads. The Layfield inquiry tested that experience.

The panel of inquiry heard a great deal of evidence about pollution and considered it sufficiently important to devote a chapter of their report to it.[90] They made a number of recommendations about the provisions of the written statement on the basis of evidence presented both by the Greater London Council and by objectors to the development plan. On noise, they recommended that environmental effects be taken fully into account in considering facilities for vertical and short take-off aircraft. The Greater London Council agreed to modify the relevant section of the statement.[91] The panel drew attention to the inadequacies of the Wilson standards and recommended the deletion of the three paragraphs on aircraft noise, as the members did not think 'the statements made in them are of strategic significance or contain sufficiently firm policies to warrant inclusion in a strategic plan'.[90]

The panel, noting the absence of mention of water pollution, recommended the inclusion of a statement on this topic. The GLC agreed to insert 'the council also proposes to continue its policy, in conjunction with other appropriate authorities, to reduce the level of pollution as part of a comprehensive programme for improving the cleanliness of the Thames, its tributaries and the canals'.[91] The panel did not feel that the two paragraphs on air pollution were worth retaining (indeed, they thought it inappropriate that a statutory document should include views about what the GLC wished the government to do) and recommended their deletion.[90]

The Layfield panel dealt with air pollution and noise from roads separately. The members recommended that all new roads should be tested against explicit, easily understood and unambiguous environmental criteria (including noise and air pollution levels) and that the Department of the Environment should develop these. They stated that new roads could be designed to minimise environmental impact by such methods as depression, screening and landscaping and they advocated the use of protective devices for affected buildings. They did not specifically recommend the deletion of the paragraph on traffic noise, but it is not to be found in their suggested statement.[91] The panel also suggests amendments which effectively delete the paragraph on derelict land and the sections on sewage and refuse disposal.

It would appear, then, that the panel of inquiry, while being perfectly clear about the significance of the pollution problem and equally clear that the GLC should show its awareness of environmental issues, did not feel that the paragraphs on pollution in the submitted written statement were generally appropriate as strategic policies. The panel's own recommended statement, a substantial revision of the GLC version, showed that the members felt pollution to be an important strategic issue, to be considered in making policy decisions.

However, despite this clear concern, the absence of policies relating specifically to air pollution, noise and land pollution is disappointing. Although most of the policies concerned with the planning control of pollution are undoubtedly administered at London borough level, they could be best operated in the context of an overall GLC planning strategy. In fairness, however, it has to be said that the GLC's original statements, with the exception of that relating to traffic noise, were rather imprecise and that the panel was probably correct in deleting them. It was obviously not crucial that the panel replaced them with more appropriate statements, since their opinions were recorded as recommendations in their report.[90] If the GLC had formulated their policies more precisely, the panel's view about inclusion of the relevant sections might well have been different. The government's formal opinion is still awaited (in 1975).

TEESSIDE

Teesside lies on the industrial north-east coast of England and is probably one of the more polluted urban areas in the UK. Apart from fairly high smoke, sulphur dioxide and grit and dust levels, the town also experiences significant concentrations of other air pollutants from industrial sources. The situation has been exacerbated by the recurrent meteorological conditions, which caused sea mist, polluted by ammonia and sulphur dioxide, to be transformed into 'Teesside mist'.[92] A 1965 study of the effects of air pollution on a housing estate in Teesside described it as very probably the most heavily polluted settlement in the country and stated a strong case for its demolition.[93] This area clearly represented an extreme case but the air pollution situation in Teesside and indeed pollution levels generally leave scope for improvement. It must be stated, however, that pollution concentrations (and particularly air pollution levels) have shown significant decreases over the last decade.

Teesside was formed in 1968 by combining Middlesbrough County Borough, Stockton on Tees Municipal Borough, Thornaby on Tees Municipal Borough, Redcar Municipal Borough, most of Billingham Urban District and Eston Urban District with parts of other authorities. Since April 1974 it has formed part of the county of Cleveland, being re-divided to form (with other local authorities), the districts of Stockton on Tees, Middlesbrough and Langbaurgh. Teesside County Borough, the single local authority responsible for preparing the structure plan, was able to draw heavily upon the conclusions of a previous comprehensive sub-regional study[94] and to maintain close co-operation with neighbouring authorities. The area is continuing to attract heavy industry on a considerable scale and both parts of the Teesside structure plan lay great emphasis on the need to remedy the polluted conditions in the town.

Report of survey

The Teesside report of survey[95] devotes considerable attention to pollution. Air pollution is regarded as an important factor in making decisions about development and the section devoted to this latter topic[96] states that the location and expansion of industries requiring special pollution controls in Teesside should be carefully considered for their effect on neighbouring areas. It recommends that residential development should not be permitted north-east of the major industrial complexes or along the banks of the Tees and that where housing exists in polluted areas consideration should be given to its eventual removal.[97] (This policy reflects earlier statements to the same effect,[2 24] which have culminated in the demolition of the housing estate mentioned previously.)

Derelict land is discussed in another section.[98] Much of this land is polluted by industrial and local authority tips, slag and chemical waste. A programme for the reclamation of derelict land, one of the main purposes of which is the improvement of amenity by the removal of eyesores, has been adopted.

Environmental pollution is given a complete section,[99] subdivided into air pollution, water pollution and noise. Motor traffic impact (which includes noise and air pollution) and visual blight (which includes derelict land) are also discussed within the section. Relying partly upon a previously published document[100] the air pollution review describes the sources of pollution, the main pollutants involved, the meteorological conditions prevailing on Teesside, the areas worst affected by pollution, the responsibilities of the air pollution control authorities and the improvements made.[99]

It is recognised that industrial air pollution is unlikely ever to be completely eliminated and it is stated that all new industrial development is vetted to minimise prospective additions to the current pollution levels and that the local authority will have to maintain positive control over new development. The report expresses the conviction that the effects of traffic pollution would be considerably ameliorated by the construction of an efficient vehicular circulation system on which traffic can flow freely, and by the implementation of schemes allowing the separation of pedestrians and vehicles at congested locations.[99]

The discussion of water pollution covers the condition in the tidal river Tees and the Tees Bay area, which appear to be poor enough to dampen any incentive to exploit the river frontage or to use the water for recreation. The difficulties of controlling estuarial discharges are described and the main domestic and industrial effluent problems are reviewed.[99]

Noise problems arising from road traffic and industry are discussed. The report states that a major highway system proposed for Teesside would eliminate the through-route commercial vehicles from central areas and would have the effect of much reducing the problem of increasing traffic noise in areas of intensive human activity. The Teesside housing clearance programme is expected to remove most of the dwellings affected by industrial noise and the report states that detailed recommendations can be made for isolating or insulating major noise generators at the local planning level. The report expresses the hope that Teesside noise standards based upon the Wilson recommendations will be set up which could be used for planning control purposes in the future.[99]

A section of the report[101] deals with sewerage and sewage disposal. The poor condition of the river and sea is stressed and a very large programme now under way to reduce the pollution caused by effluents from sewage works is described. In the absence of legislation, the value of liaison with industrial concerns as a method of controlling pollution from large manufacturing plants is stressed.[101]

The refuse disposal section does not mention pollution,[102] but this topic is a feature in the discussion of district planning.[103]

Written statement

As would be expected from the report of survey, pollution is discussed in some detail in the Teesside written statement.[104] The chapter summarising the report of survey also contains a section on amenity in which the problems of pollution, urban decay and dereliction are stressed and their alleviation urged.[105]

Much of the written statement is devoted to aims and objectives which are generally derived from sub-regional objectives. Teesside County Borough and the other two planning authorities involved in the Teesside Survey and Plan (which covered the whole sub-region) broadly accepted the consultants' report[94] and agreed three sub-regional aims based upon it. One of these is: 'living conditions: the provision of satisfactory conditions for work, residence and leisure'. Fourteen sub-regional objectives were developed to pursue these aims, of which two of the 'living condition' objectives relate to pollution. They are: 'to improve and renew areas of dereliction and urban decay' and 'to minimise the effect of all forms of environmental pollution and hazards, including atmospheric and river pollution, traffic noises and danger'.[106] The document states that balancing the needs of the environment against the needs of the economy is a key issue. Environmental considerations are said to be among the reasons supporting proposals to develop new housing areas away from the concentration of new capital-intensive industry.[106] Similarly, environmental needs were considered in formulating the transport, leisure and housing proposals as well as in determining activities to be implemented as part of the amenity and public health and protection programmes.[106]

The nine Teesside County Borough primary objectives, which were evolved from the sub-regional aims and objectives and from the report of survey, include provisions relating to pollution control. Although atmospheric pollution is recognised as contributing to the objective of protection from personal harm and damage to property, the main primary objective relating to pollution is: 'to encourage the development of an attractive environment'.[106] The clearance of dereliction and the suitable treatment of pollution are regarded as important factors in the improvement of Teesside's environment which, it is stated, should be a constant consideration.[107]

The primary objectives are used to identify sub-objectives in the main section of the report entitled 'environmental strategies'. This section is divided into a number of sub-sections in which policies and proposals designed to meet the relevant objectives and sub-objectives are advanced. Pollution is considered in a large number of policies and proposals for the different subject areas. Thus housing is to be cleared from the areas most grossly affected by atmospheric pollution,[108] the environmental impact of pollution from any new steelworks or other large industrial developments must be weighed against their benefits,[109] and reclaimed derelict land will be re-used by industry wherever possible.[110]

It is stated that amenity constraints (which include pollution) are to influence decisions on the selection of routes for new highway schemes.[111] The recreational and amenity potential of the river Tees and the coast is to be developed wherever possible, necessitating the control of river pollution.[112] [113] All domestic sewage is to be suitably treated before being discharged to the river or estuary,[114] The risk of contamination of water or the atmosphere as a result of a major accident is recognised in one of the public protection policies[115] and, finally, the possibility of the purity of the water supply being endangered by pollution is recognised and regular tests are to be made.[116]

It is apparent that environmental needs have indeed been considered in formulating proposals in nearly all subject areas. However, one of the sub-sections (amenity) brings all the pollution policies and proposals together.[117] The primary Teesside County Borough environmental objective is subdivided into four amenity sub-objectives, of which one is: 'to minimise all forms of environmental pollution and dereliction'. In all, seventeen policies are relevant to pollution control and the alleviation of damage and these, together with the proposals to implement them, are reproduced in Appendix 2. A diagram showing the amenity proposals does not, however, refer to pollution.[117]

The implementation of the numerous plan proposals is clearly a complex matter. Five implementation objectives were established to enable the proposals to be carried out efficiently and with the minimum amount of disruption to the social and economic life of the community.[118] To ensure a proper phasing of the developments proposed over the next ten to twenty years four key policies were identified, of which one is the construction of the Teesside sewerage and sewage disposal scheme.[119] Delay in implementation of the scheme would both postpone improvements in river pollution levels and seriously affect the proposed housing programme by putting back necessary residential developments. The expenditure involved in the scheme is the largest item in the proposed amenity strategy and is equivalent to spending on the primary road network over the period concerned.[119]

Commentary

The report of survey presents a full review of pollution problems in Teesside. If criticism had to be made, it could be pointed out that discussion of a number of important pollution topics, especially land pollution, is omitted. The additional subjects which might have been considered in more detail include pollution from refuse, industrial wastes, sewage sludge and litter, pollution of tributary streams and aircraft and neighbourhood noise. It could also be said that there is a lack of statistical data in the report, although it seems that many of the proposals were based on available information (for example, that on sulphur dioxide and other air pollutant levels and that on biochemical oxygen demand for water courses). When the treatment of pollution in the report is compared with that in most regional, sub-regional and new town studies, however, these criticisms are reduced to their proper perspective, since it is markedly more comprehensive.

The written statement recognises both the need for a wide variety of actions to control pollution and the distinctive role of planning in pollution control. (It also recognises, implicitly, the co-ordinating function of the planning authority.) Thus, the location of new polluting industries is to be strictly controlled, land affected by air pollution will not be allocated for residential uses and houses will be cleared from areas suffering serious atmospheric pollution. (However, the provision prohibiting housing development north-east of the major industrial complexes betrays a somewhat simplistic approach, since winds other than the prevailing south-westerlies are frequently associated with the highest pollution levels.) In addition, noisy industry will be located away from housing areas and vice versa, the types of industry to be located close to residential areas will be controlled to ensure that noise and vibration are not caused, and new roads will be located and designed to minimise noise levels in adjacent residential properties. It is clear from this catalogue that the Teesside planning authority not only recognised its role in controlling pollution but intended to discharge many of its powers and responsibilities in the control of the problem. (One omission from the proposals reproduced in Appendix 2 is a policy relating to the planning authority's control over new sources of river pollution, although an awareness of their powers in this regard is inherent in the council's proposals.) Teesside County Borough also appeared to be preparing to use a considerable number of the techniques available to them (one notable omission, however, being the use of planting to reduce air pollution). The pollution control policies adopted seem unlikely to conflict with the activities of other pollution control authorities.

Turning to the principles governing the use of these techniques and powers, it is apparent that the policies adopted express the desirability of a very high degree of control, probably well above the optimum level discussed in Chapter 4 (for example, 'minimise the noise level', 'housing will be cleared from areas suffering serious atmospheric pollution', and 'residential development will not be allowed close to likely noise sources'). Pollution standards are not mentioned and the basic problem in providing positive guidance for planning control of pollution on Teesside, as elsewhere, is the lack of operational target pollution levels to which land use controls can be directed.

On the other hand, policies listed in Appendix 2 are only a few of the large number formulated in the plan as a whole, some of which conflict with pollution control; for example, 'every effort to attract new job opportunities to Teesside' will be made, and, 'action where necessary on proposals which can in any way change Teesside's communications' will be taken. Policies are not weighted and there is no formal reconciliation of those which may conflict. However, many are phrased to take account of such difficulties, phrases like 'provision will be made for', and 'where possible' being employed, and the implementation and programming policies tend to partially reconcile some conflicts. It is apparent that proposals intuitively take account of conflicting objectives and that pollution policies which imply high levels of control may, in practice, be reflected in proposals which not only do not attain these levels but may promote a degree of damage well above the optimum. In brief, there is no consideration of the optimal level of pollution control and too little account is taken of the costs of control, of the effects of pollution, or of realistic pollution standards. Having said that, the structure plan suggests an extremely impressive planning contribution to the control of pollution in Teesside.

WARLEY

Warley lies to the west of Birmingham, in the south-eastern corner of the Black Country, and forms part of the West Midland conurbation. Reflecting the title 'black', the air pollution situation in the area is poor, the streams and canals are polluted and there exist large areas of dereliction. The Warley structure plan recognises that pollution conditions leave much to be desired and makes a number of proposals to alleviate them. Although a number of regional plans for the West Midlands have been published, none have made specific proposals for the Warley area. The structure plan, which was prepared by a single county borough, therefore had little precedent from which to draw. Created by amalgamating Smethwick County Borough, Rowley Regis Municipal Borough and Oldbury Municipal Borough in 1966, Warley was itself amalgamated with West Bromwich County Borough to become part of Sandwell Metropolitan District in April 1974. The population of the area covered by the county borough has been declining for some years.

Report of survey

Pollution is a relevant matter in several volumes of the report of survey. Air pollution and noise are mentioned in the housing report,[120] dereliction under land resources[121] and noise, fumes and dust under transport.[122] However, the salient points from these reports, together with other material relating to pollution, are presented in the report of survey on the environment.[123] The chapter on the 'social environment' in this report contains sections on atmospheric pollution, water pollution, dereliction, non-conforming land uses, noise, vibration and smell.

   This chapter regards pollution arising from industrial firms registered under the Alkali Act in Warley as generally less significant than that from domestic smoke.[124] The report presents results obtained from smoke and sulphur dioxide gauges and relates the substantial improvements in concentrations to the introduction of smoke control areas in the borough.[125] Other air pollutants—grit and dust and carbon monoxide (as a motor vehicle pollutant)—are described, but prevailing levels and problems in Warley are not discussed.[125]

The section of the chapter on water pollution contains a general description of biochemical oxygen demand and dissolved oxygen measurements, together with the standards set by the Severn–Trent Regional Water Authority. The results of measurements of canal water quality throughout the structure plan area are described (pollution levels being generally high) and the visual quality of discharges into the canal system is also mentioned.[126] Since the borough straddles a major watershed, the report states that analyses of the quality of the small streams in the area are seldom made.[126] It also mentions that some firms in Warley have been fined for disposing of unsuitable waste into canals and streams.[126]

Dereliction is a major problem in Warley and the report describes the reclamation which has been carried out and proposals for the future. The depressing effect of derelict land on neighbouring areas of land is stressed.[127] Detailed statistics relating to dereliction are presented in the land resources volume of the report of survey.[121]

The section of the chapter dealing with 'non-conforming' uses contains a number of planning proposals to alleviate pollution. A survey and analysis of non-conforming industrial land uses in residential areas is described, noise and smell being among the criteria considered. Concerns registered under the Alkali Act are stated to be totally unacceptable in such areas.[128] The report relates how a number of firms were selected as being the most noxious and in need of priority treatment[128] (the nature of which is not specified). Non-conforming residential uses suffering from noise, vibration, smell and air pollution have also been identified, the ultimate removal of 1,500 dwellings on environmental quality grounds being stated to be a possibility.[129] In addition, detailed studies of certain mixed use areas are recommended, and, here too, the need for demolition of older non-conforming dwellings is recognised.[129]

Noise is discussed in some detail in the report. Measurements, sources and the concept of noise abatement zones are described in general terms[130] before Warley's specific problems are dealt with. The industrial processes giving rise to noise in Warley are listed and analyses of traffic noise levels within the borough are then presented, those areas suffering excessive noise levels being detailed.[130] Road traffic noise levels for 1981 are forecast and it is made clear that the

borough has a substantial noise problem, one example being the
effect of the M5 motorway (which dissects the structure plan area) on
a nearby housing estate.[131] The impact of railway noise on Warley
and the need for sound insulation of certain buildings are mentioned.[131]

The problems of vibration from railways, roads and industry are
discussed; first generally, and then specifically in relation to Warley.
An indication of the roadside locations likely to suffer most is
given.[132] The chapter contains some discussion of the variation in
intensity of smells. It then mentions the odours caused by polluted
waters and chemical wastes tipped on land, but describes the problem
of smells from industrial processes and sewage works in Warley as
limited.

Written statement
The almost universally high pollution levels in Warley were an important element in framing the environmental policies laid down in the
written statement. It was felt that the problems facing Warley both at
the time of preparing the structure plan and in the future could be
solved in several alternative ways and the policies, proposals and
choices open to the council were published in a 'report on the
options'.[133] After assessment, the publication of a draft[134] and public
participation, the preferred policies and proposals were finalised in a
written statement.[135]

The overall goal of the structure plan, in common with the other
West Midland conurbation authorities, is to 'provide the maximum
opportunity for individuals and the community to choose their own
concept of a "better life" '.[136] One of the six main aims of the plan is:
'environment—to maintain and improve the quality of the physical
environment in Warley'.[136] To go some way toward achieving these
aims, fifty-five objectives were laid down. Those relating to or imp-
inging upon pollution control are shown in Appendix 2.[137]

The written statement declares that the standard of the environment in the borough is generally below that in the neighbouring
authorities and that the residents of Warley feel that the improvement of the environment is very important.[138] This deficiency,
together with certain others, formed the basis for improvement proposals put forward in the written statement as a fundamental theme of
the structure plan.[39] The importance of environmental improvement

was recognised in the adoption of a vital policy: 'The Council in considering solutions to problems in other fields has favoured policies which will help to secure improvements to the environment'.[140]

A separate section of the written statement is devoted to policies and proposals relating to the environment. In treating traffic problems a policy of 'segregation of pedestrians from large volumes of traffic . . . on environmental grounds in addition to safety grounds' has been adopted.[141] It is explained that the environmental grounds include noise and fumes. Another environmental policy relating to roads was also formulated; 'in so far as it is possible, the Council will take action to reduce the detrimental effect of traffic using inappropriate routes,'[142]

Other pollution problems in Warley are stressed, attention being drawn to the problems associated with the important metal industries, particularly air pollution from smelting. The document states that the council intends to continue to apply such pressures as are available to achieve as much as possible in controlling emissions from polluting firms.[143] Another policy relates to the declaration of further smoke control areas, the intention being that the whole of Warley should eventually be smoke controlled.[142]

An important general policy regarding various forms of pollution was formulated: 'The Council will take all actions available to it, to prevent the incidence of new sources of pollution. Where sources of pollution already exist the Council will continue the present policy of making routine inspections and will take such action as it reasonably can to reduce or remove that pollution.[144] Were this policy to be rigorously interpreted, it must result in a substantial decline in the levels of all types of pollution in Warley.

The written statement enunciates the council's policy to reclaim the total acreage of derelict land except that expected to remain in private ownership. In addition, 'where unsightly land . . . exists, the Council will use what powers are available to obtain an improvement in appearance'.[145] The control of water pollution also merited the declaration of a policy: 'the Council will actively support the appropriate authorities in their fight against water pollution'.[146] On the subject of poisonous wastes and tipping the document claims that 'land reclamation' is extremely beneficial but recognises that adverse environmental consequences can accrue by adopting the following policy: 'the Council will exercise the powers available to it to prevent pollution of the land while reclaiming suitable sites'.[147]

The written statement makes little mention of noise. However, the report on the options (which was prepared as a precursor to the written statement) explains that 'the Council intend to pursue a policy of creating noise abatement zones. . . . Control will be exercised through conditions attached to planning approvals.'[133] That report also discusses traffic noise and the possibilities of screening with earth banks and barriers, channelling traffic into selected routes and sound insulation.[133] The problems of neighbourhood and traffic noise, while not mentioned specifically in the written statement, and hence not adopted as council policy, could certainly be included within the general policy previously quoted.[144]

The written statement does not include a section on implementation. However, the document consists mainly of specific proposals which, after extensive public participation, were accepted as council policies and as such should be implemented. The response of the public to the proposals relating to the environment was positive, both when a carefully selected sample was interviewed and when a self-selected sample returned questionnaires. The great majority of those expressing an opinion wished for a better environment, favouring the rapid improvement of the situation in regard to derelict land and canals. Smell, noise and danger from traffic were also felt to be significant environmental problems by the inhabitants of the borough.[148] The proposals and policies relating to the alleviation of pollution are thus believed to reflect the general desire of the people of Warley.[138] The written statement finds that, from an examination of the financial implications of all council programmes, effort will have to be concentrated on particular environmental problems, rather than spread over a range.[149] As consolation, however, 'actions taken to remedy other deficiencies will, by themselves, significantly improve the environment'.[149]

Commentary

The report of survey volume on the environment gives a good coverage of pollution problems in general terms. However, the incidence of these problems in Warley is not always specifically recognised, although relevant statistics are presented where they are available. The volume mentions neighbourhood noise but makes no specific suggestions about reducing levels. It does not deal with litter (except very incidentally), mineral working wastes, industrial waste tipping, sludge tipping or the pollution associated with refuse tipping. (Refuse disposal is mentioned separately in the report on public utilities.[150]) Some mistakes of fact, of a relatively minor nature, are made in the treatment of general water pollution issues.

The report of survey recognises that planning action may be necessary to relocate a number of non-conforming uses and hence to reduce the effects of pollution. However, there is no explicit recognition that planning could contribute to the control of other types of pollution. Thus there is no mention of such methods as reducing density, or the use of screens, planting and traffic management in the sections dealing with air pollution, water pollution, dereliction, noise, vibration and odours.

The written statement devotes adequate coverage to pollution and its control. However, it is difficult to say whether the potential planning contribution to pollution control is adequately recognised. There is no clear reference to the use of the various planning powers or indeed to the discharge of the planning authority's roles in the control of pollution. The co-ordinating role of the local planning authority in pollution control may be implicit in the general policy statement but the text provides little evidence of awareness of the numerous planning techniques of pollution control. However, it is quite clear that the need to alter the location of certain non-conforming uses is recognised as a priority and it is only fair to point out that, since there is very little additional building land available in Warley, the authority's scope for directing the location of new development is limited.

The rather general policies relating to pollution control are never illustrated by more specific planning proposals. It is, therefore, not very clear by what means the policies are to be implemented. Only in relation to noise control is it explained how a policy is to be carried out and that explanation appears in the report on the options, not in the written statement. It is unfortunate that the planning contribution to the achievement of the general policies is not brought out. (These policies are, incidentally, unlikely to conflict with those of other pollution control authorities.)

It seems that the various policies could conflict with each other even though they are often phrased so that incompatibilities are notionally obviated. For example, 'in the circumstances', 'will be kept under review' are used in policy statements. The objectives cannot strictly be reconciled. 'To facilitate the growth and increased production of industry within the overall national and regional policies' could easily conflict with several other objectives (for example, 'to ensure that the detrimental environmental effects of mineral extraction are kept to a minimum', since extended quarrying is certain to lead to further pollution). How objectives are to be mutually implemented is not explained. However, objectives of this type are rarely complementary and planning authorities tend to use them to provide some direction for policy implementations, rather than to expect them to be achieved.

The principle of the optimum level of pollution control is not followed since each objective is phrased so as to imply the minimisation of pollution. Limitations to this possibility are recognised, for example in the form of the statement 'as much as possible' in the first tier environmental objective quoted in Appendix 2. Such limitations apparently relate more to problems of fit with other conflicting objectives than to the concept of optimal control.

The concern of the structure plan about pollution and the determination to improve conditions are quite apparent: the environmental objective is ranked fourth of fifteen. However, there is a notable absence of express awareness of the contribution of planning powers, roles and techniques in the implementation of the policies on control of air, land, water and noise pollution in the plan. There must be a question of balance here, since it would be unreasonable to expect a structure plan to proceed beyond a reasonable level of generality as the detailed application of general policies would be more appropriately dealt with at local plan level.

SOUTH HAMPSHIRE

South Hampshire, bounded by the sea, the South Downs chalk ridge, Southampton and Portsmouth, is one of the fastest growing areas in the UK. The South East study identified it as a major growth area capable of accepting considerable overspill population in addition to its own natural growth.[151] A detailed study by consultants confirmed the feasibility and indeed the inevitability of growth[152] and the three local planning authorities (Hampshire, Southampton and Portsmouth), formed a centralised Technical Unit to prepare a master plan for the area under the guidance of an advisory committee. The various reports of the Technical Unit formed the basis of the South

Hampshire structure plan, which was published jointly by the three authorities at an early date (1972). As an excellent background description of planning policies in South Hampshire points out, the question of overspill had by now been forgotten.[153]

In contrast to Teesside and Warley, South Hampshire is a predominantly rural area, rich in recreational resources and consequently has few environmental quality problems, the most serious undoubtedly being water pollution. Rivers, tidal inshore waters and the sea are all polluted by sewage effluents as a result of years of infra-structure underprovision, and concern about this problem is reflected in the structure plan.*

Report of survey

No section of the report of survey[154] is devoted specifically to pollution. However, the problem is raised at a number of points in the report, for example in the chapters on minerals,[155] refuse disposal,[156] transport[157] and airports.[158] The most detailed discussion of pollution is to be found in the chapter on foul and surface water drainage,[159] where it is stated that although the provision and maintenance of a foul and surface water drainage system is not the responsibility of the local planning authority, the disposal of effluent must be considered in the interests of combating and preventing pollution.

The chapter presents the main conclusions of a detailed Technical Unit report on drainage,[160] a consulting engineer's report on the feasibility of foul and surface drainage, a water pollution control consultant's report on marine disposal of sewage and a consulting engineer's report on the location of a large sewage outlet.[161] It explains that there has been a general underprovision of both foul sewerage and sewage disposal facilities in South Hampshire for many years (as previously mentioned[47]), and recognises the problem of local harmful pollution, the need to alleviate it and the need to ensure that additional pollution is not caused by future drainage works. Only parts of the larger rivers were regarded as being capable of accepting further sewage effluent and then only if volumes were limited. Improving the quality of other effluents would not provide a solution, according to the report, since 'the quantities involved would probably

*South Hampshire was divided into six districts of the county of Hampshire under local government reorganisation in 1974: Southampton, Eastleigh, Fareham, Gosport, Portsmouth and Havant.

drastically alter the character of the chalk rivers by promoting dense
plant growth, which could affect land drainage, possibly kill game
fish, and render the water unsuitable for domestic use'. A new drainage system using sea outfalls was therefore recommended.[159]

The report relates that it was established that it would be physically
feasible to drain the structure plan area for foul and surface water
purposes and at the same time to avoid harmful pollution of rivers,
estuaries, harbours and sea by installing trunk sewers and a treatment
works and by discharging the effluent to sea. A suitable disposal point
was located and, although partial treatment was felt to be satisfactory, the possibility of further treatment should not be ruled out,
according to the report.[159]

The chapter emphasises that 'it is essential that the local planning
authorities should work in close co-operation with the drainage
authorities, including the South Hampshire Main Drainage Board [a
joint local authority board] and the River Authorities, to ensure that
development is co-ordinated with additional drainage capacity, to
control the development of piecemeal drainage systems and to maintain the standards of receiving waters'.[159]

The establishment of aims, objectives and criteria was central to
the process of plan preparation and much of the detailed material
relating to aims establishment, the generation of alternative strategies
and the preparation of the preferred strategy is to be found in the
report of survey rather than in the written statement. Nine broad
strategic aims were set to point the general direction in which planning action was needed.[162] Objectives were then derived from the
aims and from the identified problems facing the area. Planning
criteria were in turn derived from objectives and represented detailed
evaluation yardsticks to measure the achievement of objectives. The
preferred planned growth strategy evolved from the following processes:[162]

1   The postulation of thirty-one alternatives as sketch strategies and
    their reduction to four best representatives.
2   The development of the best representatives as 'four possibilities'
    and their subsequent evaluation in terms of more detailed
    criteria. Thirteen prime objectives emerged at this stage, which
    were then employed to generate the preferred strategy.
3   On the basis of the evaluation of the 'four possibilities', and
    through the consideration of further options, the preparation of

the preferred strategy to form the basis of the structure plan. The successive refinement of this strategy was based upon evaluation against criteria relating to all the objectives of the plan, a cyclical incremental planning approach thus being employed.[162]

The two broad strategic aims most relevant to pollution and its control are 'environment: to create high-quality surroundings for living, working, shopping and recreation' and 'conservation: to conserve the important natural resources and man-made features of the area, with the least disturbance to the existing urban and rural areas'.[162]

A number of objectives under these heads embrace pollution, without specifically mentioning it, for example: 'To ensure the maintenance and improvement of the quality of the environment in the existing built-up areas'. Other objectives more clearly include pollution among other considerations. These are: 'To ensure that the traffic and associated environmental effects of mineral extraction are kept within acceptable levels'; 'To ensure that the methods of refuse disposal adopted do not harm the important natural resources of the area and cause the least possible disturbance to the existing rural and urban areas'; 'To ensure the minimisation of environmental damage caused by the provision and management of transportation facilities, and *inter alia*, the reduction of pedestrian/vehicle conflicts'; and 'To ensure that airport use and development does not cause harmful disturbance by noise'.

Pollution is, in fact, specifically mentioned in one of the eighty-two objectives. Not surprisingly, in view of the history of concern about drainage, it is: 'To ensure that no harmful pollution is carried to the land, rivers, water-courses, estuaries, harbours or sea by domestic, industrial or agricultural discharges'.[163] It should be noted that this is not a prime objective. Although atmospheric emissions are clearly included in 'discharges', the effects of atmospheric pollution and noise could, arguably, fall outside the scope of the objective, which appears to relate mainly to water pollution.

Written statement

The written statement[164] consists largely of policies and general proposals for particular subject areas and geographical areas. These crucial policies and proposals are intended to meet the objectives, which themselves were framed against the problems and opportunities revealed by the detailed studies upon which the report of survey was based.

Appendix 2 gives examples of many of the policies which relate to pollution and the criteria which are to be used in putting them into effect.[165] These criteria are thus of considerable importance as a link between the policies of the structure plan and the objectives and proposals put forward.[165] They are derived from the objectives and other matters considered in the course of preparing the structure plan, and they are intended to supplement and strengthen the standards and requirements currently used by local planning authorities.[165] In considering a planning application all the policies and criteria relevant to the proposal would be weighed.[165]

As in the report of survey, pollution is included in environmental considerations at a number of points. Thus in the chapter on refuse disposal it is stated that the 'efficient removal and inoffensive disposal of refuse is an important factor in maintaining the quality of the environment' and a policy is adopted which related specifically to pollution control[166] (see Appendix 2). The chapter on foul and surface water drainage contains the most forceful account of the structure plan's pollution control proposals and enunciates three policies relating to the active participation of the planning authorities in the control of pollution.[167] These are set out in detail in Appendix 2.

Apart from the proposals, policies and criteria the written statement contains several chapters concerned with implementation. One of these details the various roles of the local planning authority.[168] It is stated that the three local planning authorities would use the strategic policies of the structure plan, supported by criteria, to govern development both by means of development control and by preparing local plans.[168] The planning policies and criteria relating to pollution control are thus intended to be implemented by both these methods. In a wider context the county planning officer of Hampshire has said that 'the authorities are only just beginning to grasp the scale of the implementation task and its involvement of many departments and committees. By contrast, the work on the structure plan itself may later seem to have been relatively straightforward, complex though it was'.[169]

Commentary
The report of survey neglects to consider a large number of aspects of

pollution, despite its concentration on the problem of water pollution. Even here it is possible to make some criticisms as, for example, of the rather simplistic view that the sea is the only logical location for sewage effluents. Air and land pollution are hardly mentioned and noise is not given any prominence. This may only reflect a view of the currently good environmental situation, however, since the written statement certainly lays emphasis on the control of pollution liable to arise from new development. Unlike Teesside and Warley, the South Hampshire concern is principally to prevent future pollution rather than to improve an already poor environment.

Although not reviewed in the main body of the report of survey, pollution problems are dealt with in the policy sections of the volume. The policies and criteria spell out in some detail the measures to be adopted in the control of pollution. There is considerable recognition of the planning authority's powers to control pollution in the statement. For example 'the local planning authorities will seek to remove or discourage through traffic from residential areas where the environment is being degraded by noise' (Appendix 2). Despite the range of policies adopted, the true degree of appreciation of the planning authorities' own roles, as opposed to those in co-operation with other bodies, may not perhaps be as substantial as it first appears. Thus the role of detailed design in minimizing air and noise pollution is not referred to. The central co-ordinating role of the planning authority is implicitly recognised in several policies, for example those relating to drainage. The policies and criteria in Appendix 2 reveal the planning authorities' awareness of numerous planning techniques for pollution control but not all are mentioned specifically, however. (Thus many criteria are unaccompanied by discussion of techniques: for example, that on minerals stating that the authorities will 'take account of the provision for avoiding . . . pollution', not that they will impose conditions on relevant planning permissions.)

The South Hampshire structure plan goes rather further than the other two examined in generating aims, objectives, policies and criteria. Although the policy is often expressed in forceful terms: 'to ensure that no harmful pollution is carried to the land, rivers, watercourses, estuaries, harbours or sea by domestic, industrial or agricultural discharges', the criteria generally reflect appreciation of conflicting factors; 'the local planning authority will have particular regard to the generation of noise, fumes, etc', or 'where practicable and finance is available, uses which pollute will be abated or extinguished'. However, some criteria are expressed very uncompromisingly: 'in preparing local plans, design briefs or considering other proposals for change, the local planning authorities will secure the relocation or removal of uses which are noisy, noxious or otherwise objectionable, particularly in residential areas'.

On the whole, policies and criteria have been phrased to avoid conflict with each other, although this is not universally the case. The use of the term 'harmful' pollution is noteworthy in that it implies an appreciation of the costs and benefits of control. If, in fact, the optimum level of pollution were achieved, it would be a happy accident resulting from the reconciliation of pollution control objectives with other objectives rather than from a deliberate intention. None of the policies or criteria seems likely to conflict with the activities of other pollution control authorities.

The South Hampshire structure plan, then, reveals a very real concern to prevent a currently good environment from deteriorating. Planning powers and techniques are expected to play a very considerable part in the implementation of policies designed to control pollution.

There can be no question that structure plans do indeed provide the best reflection to date of the planning control of pollution at the plan-making stage. In comparison with regional, sub-regional and new town studies and with the old-style development plans which preceded them, structure plans demonstrate:

1 A much greater grasp of air, land, water and noise pollution problems.
2 A much greater recognition of planning powers in the control of pollution.
3 A much greater appreciation of the roles of planning in pollution control.
4 A much greater awareness of planning techniques for controlling pollution.

They do not, however, show an approach more clearly geared towards achieving the optimum level of pollution control.

The Layfield panel struck out a number of sections of the Greater

London development plan written statement which referred to pollution because the members believed that they were inappropriate to the statutory document prepared by an 'upper tier' planning authority. However, the panel expressed no doubts about the relevance of pollution control measures in a structure-type plan, even in one prepared by an authority largely concerned with strategy. All the structure plans examined above were prepared by authorities responsible for implementing the policies formulated (although this situation has changed since 1 April 1974). The strictures of the panel of inquiry would probably not, therefore, be universally appropriate but the place of general statements about pollution, rather than specific policies, in the written statement (as opposed to the report of survey) could still be questioned.

There are a number of probable reasons for the improved treatment of pollution in structure plans. The plans are all very recent and therefore better able to reflect a growing public awareness about the environment. They are more concerned with the use of planning powers than regional and sub-regional studies, appertain more to policy matters than new town plans, and are thus more likely to be involved with pollution control. Perhaps more important, structure planning authorities have received positive encouragement from central government (most notably in the 1971 memorandum[50]) to frame proposals relating to pollution control. Of similar significance is the role of public participation, which must have brought home to planning authorities the increasingly general desire for an unpolluted environment.

The test of the structure plan, of course, lies in the implementation of the policies it contains. It is appropriate to examine the practical application of the very specific drainage policies and criteria contained in the South Hampshire structure plan. Chapter 9 is devoted to a discussion of this question.

REFERENCES

1   Manchester Corporation (1945) *City Manchester plan* MC, Manchester.
2   Middlesbrough County Borough (1946) *Survey and plan* MCB, Middlesbrough.
3   Westminster City Council (1946) *City of Westminster plan* WCC, London.
4   Lutyens, E., and Abercrombie, P. (1945) *A plan for Kingston upon*

Hull Kingston County Borough, Kingston upon Hull.

5   Swindon Borough Council (1945) *Planning for Swindon* SBC, Swindon.

6   Worcester County Borough (1946) *Outline development plan* WCB, Worcester.

7   Abercrombie, P. (1945) *Greater London plan, 1944* HMSO, London.

8   Forshaw, J. H., and Abercrombie, P. (1943) *County of London plan* London County Council, London.

9   *Town and Country Planning Act, 1947* s. 5(2).

10 Ministry of Town and Country Planning (1948) *Survey for development plans* Circular 40, HMSO, London.

11 Collins, B. J. (1951) *Development plans explained* Ministry of Housing and Local Government, HMSO, London.

12 West Suffolk County Council (1951) *County plan: the analysis of the survey* WSCC, Bury St Edmunds.

13 Cambridgeshire and Isle of Ely County Council (1968) *Development plan review: report of survey* CIECC, Cambridge.

14 West Hartlepool Corporation (1948) *The Hartlepools: a survey and plan* WHC, West Hartlepool.

15 Lancashire County Council (1951) *A preliminary plan for Lancashire* LCC, Preston.

16 Devonshire County Council (1964) *Development plan: analysis of survey* DCC, Exeter.

17 Newcastle City Council (1963) *Development plan review* NCC, Newcastle.

18 Coventry County Borough (1966) *Review plan* CCB, Coventry.

19 Glasgow Corporation (1960) *Survey report: first quinquennial review* GC, Glasgow.

20 Manchester Corporation (1951) *Development plan: written analysis* MC, Manchester.

21 London County Council (1962) *Development plan: statement* LCC, London.

22 London County Council (1951) *Development plan: analysis* LCC, London.

23 Durham County Council (1957) *Stockton on Tees: written analysis* DCC, Durham.

24 Middlesbrough County Borough (1952) *Middlesbrough development plan: report on the survey* MCB, Middlesbrough.

25 Durham County Council (1961) *Stockton on Tees town map* DCC, Durham.

26 Middlesbrough County Borough (1953) *Middlesbrough development plan: written statement* MCB, Middlesbrough.

27 Durham County Council (1965) *Billingham written analysis* DCC, Durham.

28 Durham County Council (1965) *Billingham written statement* DCC, Durham.

29 Smethwick County Borough (1960) *Smethwick development plan: report of survey and analysis* SCB, Smethwick.
30 Staffordshire County Council (1952) *Development plan: survey report and analysis* SCC, Stafford.
31 Smethwick County Borough (1960) *Smethwick development plan: written statement* SCB, Smethwick.
32 Staffordshire County Council (1958) *Development plan: written statement of proposals* SCC, Stafford.
33 Worcestershire County Council (1952) *County development plan: report of survey* WCC, Worcester.
34 Worcestershire County Council (1957) *County development plan: written statement* WCC, Worcester.
35 Hampshire County Council (1961) *Hampshire development plan: first review: report of survey* HCC, Winchester.
36 Hampshire County Council (1962) *Eastleigh: report of survey* HCC, Winchester.
37 Hampshire County Council (1961) *Southern parishes of Winchester Rural District: report of survey* HCC, Winchester.
38 Hampshire County Council (1961) *Gosport: report of survey* HCC, Winchester.
39 Hampshire County Council (1961) *Fareham: report of survey* HCC, Winchester.
40 Hampshire County Council (1957) *Havant and Waterlooville: analysis of survey* HCC, Winchester.
41 Hampshire County Council (1967) *Eastleigh: town map* HCC, Winchester.
42 Hampshire County Council (1966) *Southern Parishes of Winchester Rural District: town map* HCC, Winchester.
43 Hampshire County Council (1968) *Gosport: town map* HCC, Winchester.
44 Hampshire County Council (1968) *Fareham: town map* HCC, Winchester.
45 Hampshire County Council (1961) *Havant and Waterlooville: town map* HCC, Winchester.
46 Hampshire County Council (1961) *Hampshire development plan: county map: amendment map* HCC, Winchester.
47 Lock, M. (1949) *Outline plan for the Portsmouth district* Portsmouth County Borough, Portsmouth.
48 Ministry of Housing and Local Government (1970) *Development plans: a manual on form and content* HMSO, London.
49 Ministry of Housing and Local Government (1970) *Development plans* Circular 82/70, HMSO, London.
50 Department of the Environment (1971) *Memorandum on Part 1 of the Town and Country Planning Act, 1968* Circular 44/71, HMSO, London.
51 McLoughlin, J. B. (1973) Structure planning in Britain *JRTPI, 50* 115–21.

52 McLoughlin, J. B. (1973) Personal communication of questionnaire returns.
53 Ipswich County Borough Council and East Suffolk County Council (1972) *Structure plan for the Ipswich sub-region: report of the survey: conservation, townscape and landscape* ICBC and ESCC, Ipswich.
54 Ipswich County Borough Council and East Suffolk County Council (1973) *Structure plan for the Ipswich sub-region: the strategy report* ICBC and ESCC, Ipswich.
55 North Riding County Council (1973) *Structure plan: report of survey for public participation* NRCC, Northallerton.
56 Solihull County Borough (1972) *Structure plan: report of survey: environment* SCB, Solihull.
57 Herefordshire County Council (1973) *Urban structure plan: report of survey* HCC, Hereford.
58 Herefordshire County Council (1973) *County structure plan: report of survey* HCC, Hereford.
59 Herefordshire County Council (1973) *Urban structure plan: written statement* HCC, Hereford.
60 Herefordshire County Council (1973) *County structure plan: written statement* HCC, Hereford.
61 Worcester County Borough (1973) *Structure plan: report of survey 7: social and public services* WCB, Worcester.
62 Worcester County Borough (1973) *Structure plan: report of survey 8: public utilities* WCB, Worcester.
63 West Bromwich County Borough (1973) *Structure plan: report of survey: environment* WBCB, West Bromwich.
64 Wolverhampton County Borough (1973) *Structure plan: report of survey 9: environment* WCB, Wolverhampton.
65 Walsall County Borough (1972) *Structure plan: report of survey: environment* WCB, Walsall.
66 West Bromwich County Borough (1974) *Structure plan: written statement* WBCB, West Bromwich.
67 Wolverhampton County Borough (1973) *Structure plan: written statement* WCB, Wolverhampton.
68 Walsall County Borough (1973) *Structure plan: draft written statement* WCB, Walsall.
69 Dudley County Borough (1973) *Structure plan: report of survey* DCB, Dudley.
70 Coventry County Borough (1972) *Corporate planning survey report 8: the provision of a satisfactory physical environment* CCB, Coventry.
71 Birmingham County Borough (1973) *Structure plan: report of survey: recreation and leisure, environment, public utilities* BCB, Birmingham.
72 Birmingham County Borough (1973) *Structure plan: written statement* BCB, Birmingham.
73 Worcestershire County Council (1973) *Structure plan: report of survey: general* WCC, Worcester.

74 Stoke on Trent County Borough (1972) *Structure plan: report of survey* SCB, Stoke.

75 Stoke on Trent County Borough (1973) *Structure plan: written statement of policies and proposals* SCB, Stoke.

76 Staffordshire County Council (1973) *Structure plan: report of survey* SCC, Stafford.

77 Staffordshire County Council (1970) *Structure plan: policies and proposals* SCC, Stafford.

78 Leicester County Borough and Leicestershire County Council (1973) *Structure plan: report of survey* LCB and LCC, Leicester.

79 Leicester County Borough and Leicestershire County Council (1973) *Structure plan: written statement* LCB and LCC, Leicester.

80 West Sussex County Council, Brighton County Borough Council and East Sussex County Council (1970) *Brighton urban structure plan: physical environment* WSCC, BCBC and ESCC, Brighton.

81 Joint Working Group on Structure Plans (1972) *Greater Manchester: first review of the study* Manchester County Borough, Manchester.

82 Greater London Council (1969) *Development plan: report of studies* GLC, London.

83 Greater London Council (1969) Development plan: statement GLC, London.

84 Committee on the Problem of Noise (Wilson Committee) (1963) *Final report* Cmnd. 2056, HMSO, London.

85 Greater London Council (1970) *Road traffic and urban environment in inner London* GLDP inquiry background paper 486, GLC, London.

86 Greater London Council (1971) *Proposals for secondary roads–illustrative examples* GLDP inquiry background paper 443, GLC, London.

87 Greater London Council (1970) *Environmental effects of the construction of primary roads–illustrative examples* GLDP inquiry background paper 383, GLC, London.

88 Greater London Council (1971) *Westway: an environmental and traffic appraisal* GLDP inquiry background paper 494, GLC, London.

89 Greater London Council (1970) *GLDP inquiry proof E 12/1: transport* GLC, London.

90 Department of the Environment (1973) *GLDP: report of the panel of inquiry 1: report* HMSO, London.

91 Department of the Environment (1973) *GLDP: report of the panel of inquiry 2: appendices* HMSO, London.

92 Eggleton, A. E. J., and Atkins, D. H. (1972) *Results of the Teesside investigation* United Kingdom Atomic Energy Authority Research Group Report, AERE R 6983, HMSO, London.

93 Gregory, P. (1965) *Polluted homes* Occasional Papers on Social Administration, No. 15, Bell & Sons, London.

94 Ministry of Housing and Local Government (1969) *Teesside survey and plan 1; policies and proposals* HMSO, London.

95 Teesside County Borough (1973) *Teesside structure plan: report of survey, 1972* TCB, Middlesbrough. (Referred to in subsequent

detailed references as *TRS.)*
96   *TRS* p. 59, para. 8.7.
97   *TRS* p. 59, para. 8.8.
98   *TRS* p. 62.
99   *TRS* pp. 67-71.
100 Teesside Health Department (1970) *Clean air for Teesside* THD, Teesside County Borough, Middlesbrough.
101 *TRS* p. 209.
102 *TRS* p. 261.
103 For example, *TRS* p. 266, para. 38.21.
104 Teesside County Borough (1973) *Teesside structure plan : draft written statement* TCB, Middlesbrough. (Referred to subsequently as *TWS.)*
105 *TWS* p. 25.
106 *TWS* p. 56.
107 *TWS* p. 62.
108 *TWS* p. 78.
109 *TWS* p. 86.
110 *TWS* p. 92.
111 *TWS* p. 116.
112 *TWS* p. 152.
113 *TWS* p. 182.
114 *TWS* p. 194.
115 *TWS* p. 197.
116 *TWS* p. 199.
117 *TWS* pp. 169–86.
118 *TWS* p. 203.
119 *TWS* p. 205.
120 Warley County Borough (1973) *Structure plan report of survey: housing* WCB, Smethwick.
121 Warley County Borough (1973) *Structure plan report of survey: land resources* WCB, Smethwick.
122 Warley County Borough (1973) *Structure plan report of survey: transportation* WCB, Smethwick.
123 Warley County Borough (1973) *Structure plan report of survey: environment* Smethwick. (Referred to in subsequent detailed references as *WRS.)*
124 *WRS* p. 27, para. 9.74.
125 *WRS* p. 28.
126 *WRS* pp. 29–30.
127 *WRS* p. 30.
128 *WRS* p. 32.
129 *WRS* p. 33.
130 *WRS* pp. 33–5.
131 *WRS* p. 36.
132 *WRS* p. 40.
133 Warley County Borough (1973) *Structure plan: report on the options* WCB, Smethwick.

134 Warley County Borough (1973) *Structure plan:draft written statement* WCB, Smethwick.
135 Warley County Borough (1974) *Structure plan: written statement* WCB, Smethwick. (Subsequently referred to as *WWS.*)
136 *WWS* p. 8.
137 *WWS* pp. 6–10.
138 *WWS* p. 13, para. 2.26.
139 *WWS* p. 15.
140 *WWS* p. 16.
141 *WWS* para. 4.10.20.
142 *WWS* para. 4.10.21.
143 *WWS* para. 4.10.23.
144 *WWS* para. 4.10.24.
145 *WWS* para. 4.10.25.
146 *WWS* para. 4.10.26.
147 *WWS* para. 4.10.27.
148 *WWS* pp. dxiii–dxv.
149 *WWS* para. 4.10.31.
150 Warley County Borough (1972) *Structure plan report of survey: public utilities* WCB, Smethwick.
151 Ministry of Housing and Local Government (1964) *The South-East study* HMSO , London.
152 Ministry of Housing and Local Government (1966) *South Hampshire study* (three vols) HMSO, London.
153 Hall, P. (1973) South Hampshire. In Hall, P., Gracey, H., Drewitt, R., and Thomas, R. *The containment of urban England I* 484–503, Allen & Unwin, London.
154 South Hampshire Plan Advisory Committee (1972) *South Hampshire structure plan: report of survey* Hampshire County Council, Winchester (*HRS*).
155 *HRS* p. 137.
156 *HRS* p. 149.
157 *HRS* p. 187.
158 *HRS* p. 215.
159 *HRS* pp. 141–44.
160 South Hampshire Plan Advisory Committee (1968) *Drainage* Study report, Group B, 2, South Hampshire Plan Technical Unit, Winchester.
161 Watson, J. D. and J. D. (1972) *Marine disposal of sewage and sewage sludge* South Hampshire Plan Advisory Committee, Winchester.
162 *HRS* p. 228.
163 *HRS* p. 237, No. 35.
164 South Hampshire Plan Advisory Committee (1973) *South Hampshire structure plan* Hampshire County Council, Winchester. (*HWS*).
165 *HWS* pp. 4a–60a.
166 *HWS* p. 69, para. 10.3.
167 *HWS* p. 121.

168   *HWS* p. 326.
169   Smart, A. D. G. (1973) Comments on structure planning in Britain *JRTPI, 59,* 123.

CHAPTER 9

Structure plan implementation

This chapter is devoted to a single case study of the implementation of structure plan pollution control policies as exemplified by the proposal to build a large new sewage work at Peel Common, Fareham, Hampshire. The South Hampshire structure plan contains three policies relating to foul and surface water drainage (Appendix 2):

1 Development requiring foul or surface water drainage facilities will be permitted only where such facilities can be made available.
2 No development will be permitted which would hinder the efforts of the drainage authorities to avoid harmful pollution of the rivers, watercourses, estuaries, harbours and sea of the plan area.
3 Planning powers will be used to assist the drainage authorities in exercising their functions, including, where necessary, the provision of water pollution control works on suitable sites, the safeguarding of foul and surface water drainage sewers and channels and other appropriate matters.

The chief planning officer of Hampshire has said that the implementation of structure plan policies seemed likely to be more difficult than their formulation (Chapter 8). The Peel Common case lends support to that view and provides an illuminating insight into some of the planning problems encountered in pursuing pollution control objectives.

SOUTH HAMPSHIRE'S WATER POLLUTION AND DRAINAGE PROBLEMS

As mentioned in Chapter 8, the growth of South Hampshire has been accepted for some time. The position was confirmed in 1970 in the Strategic Plan for the South East,[1] which emphasised the need for heavy investment on foul drainage so that growth would not be inhibited. The South Hampshire structure plan, published in draft form in September 1972,[2] made a number of projections of likely growth which confirmed the need for an adequate system of main drainage.

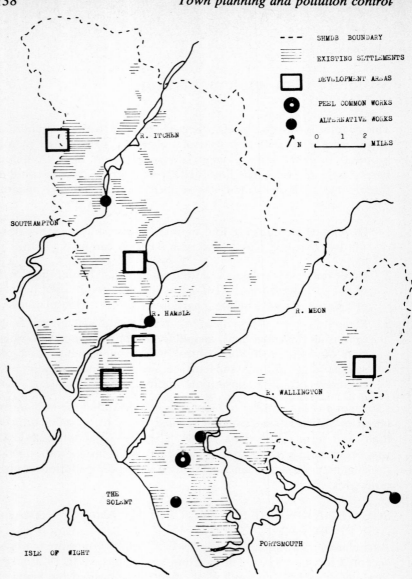

The South Hampshire Main Drainage Board area. Although a structure plan objective
to provide sewerage and sewage treatment facilities to serve existing and planned
development without causing harmful pollution was accepted by all, the method chosen to implement it proved to be controversial.

The area between Southampton and Portsmouth has a complex set-tlement pattern provided in parts with sewers which lead to a number of existing water pollution control works discharging effluents of varying standards. Hampshire County Council, the planning authority, were therefore faced with a real problem of inadequate foul drainage and sewage disposal and had to decide whether the planned development should use and extend the existing infrastructure or whether the design of a new trunk sewer and effluent and sludge disposal system was required.[3]

A working party was set up by the planning authority to study drainage and sewage disposal in the structure plan area in 1968. It reported in June 1969 that the eighteen sewage disposal works and six sea outfalls in the area were generally causing water pollution and were incapable of coping with further population growth.[4] One of the members (representing the river authority) submitted a report to the working party stating that 'it is considered that the streams in the study area cannot be used for disposal of large volumes of trade and sewage effluents, that it would be unwise to provide for the volume of the effluents at present discharged to the estuaries and harbours to be increased significantly and that it would be desirable for some of the existing discharges to be diverted to new outlets'.[5] This report was clearly extremely important in deciding the working party to recommend the abandonment of existing works in favour of a system of major new trunk sewers and marine disposal of effluent.[4]

In making this recommendation the working party assumed that:

1   The water of streams and rivers should be sufficiently pure to ensure their retention for salmon and trout fishing and for water supply.
2   Existing potentially harmful pollution should not be aggravated and should, in time, be eliminated.[4]

The members rejected the alternative of improving the existing system and discharging effluents to rivers, estuaries and harbours because:

1   The character of the rivers would be altered.
2   A dense growth of weeds, including unsightly algae, would occur which would adversely affect land drainage and possibly kill fish.
3   The water could be made unsuitable for public supply.
4   It could make it impossible to store the water in reservoirs.[4]

A number of further, more detailed, studies were undertaken following the working party's report. Consulting engineers were asked to investigate possible schemes of main drainage for the area. They reported that a trunk sewerage system was perfectly feasible and suggested two potential coastal locations for partial treatment works. They were then asked to report on the suitability of a works at Peel Common, apparently because of powerful opposition to the coastal sites from the local authority concerned. They reported on Peel Common's practicability in May 1970.[6] Studies of the effects of sewage outfalls on the Solent were made using a tidal model and a biological assessment of these effects was carried out.[7] No investigations relating to improving the existing system were, however, commissioned.[8]

In the meantime the foul drainage system deteriorated and an embargo had to be placed on new planning permissions in Fareham from February 1971 as a result of overloading at the local sewage works. A similar situation applied in other parts of South Hampshire, and, in dismissing appeals against refusal of development, the Secretary of State for the Environment stressed the need to make additional sewage disposal facilities available. The local planning authority was instrumental in setting up, in September 1971, the South Hampshire Main Drainage Board as a joint local authority board charged with implementing improvements to the foul drainage situation.[3] The chairman was a councillor of the coastal local authority mentioned previously.

Shortly after the inauguration of the board, the planning authority undertook a study to select a site for a works to receive sewage from the net trunk sewerage system, to partially treat it and to discharge it to sea.[3] This study identified five sites employing engineering criteria and evaluated these using planning criteria consisting of conservation and implementation objectives and two environmental objectives, of which one was 'to avoid nuisance through noise, smell or traffic'.[9] Reporting in November 1971 the study found that, in relation to the preferred site—Peel Common—'the amount of residential property immediately adjacent is small'.

In March 1972 the Main Drainage Board decided to give full treatment to sewage before discharging it to the sea. This decision was partly the result of growing public concern about marine pollution[3] and partly the result of a report from the Southern Sea Fisheries Committee. This report had reviewed the pollution situation in the Solent and concluded that any sewage discharges should be fully treated and that the resulting sludge should not be dumped there.[10] As a result of this change in treatment strategy the question of using several existing works, as opposed to a single new one, was reopened and four sites were evaluated,[11] presumably against the same planning criteria as used previously;[9] it being assumed that the smell could be controlled at a cost and that it would not be significant beyond 400 yards.[12]

The evaluation, dated November 1972, concluded that:

> None of the four sites studied is without objection as a sewage disposal works. However, if the effects of possible harm to water quality are ignored and if there were no reasonable alternative it is unlikely that there would be sufficiently strong land use planning reasons to object to the sites. Even so in view of possible River Authority objection and environmental deterioration due to water pollution it is likely that the Local Planning Authority would need to be satisfied that no economically feasible alternatives exist before granting permission.[11]

The local planning authority accordingly recommended the single works at Peel Common because, among other reasons, 'the concentration of environmental harm in one site constitutes an overall gain in this respect'.[11]

SEWAGE DISPOSAL WORKS PLANNING APPLICATION

The South Hampshire Main Drainage Board made a compulsory purchase order for 32·5 hectares of farm land at Peel Common in November 1972. In the accompanying statement the board explained that 'the location of the site selected for the sewage disposal works has been determined in the first instance by the need to use a sea outfall instead of a river outfall owing to the limited capacity of the rivers in the Board's district to accept additional sewage effluent even if fully treated'.[13] In December the board applied for planning permission to construct the works.

Following statutory advertisement, a number of objections were made to both the planning application and the purchase order. The local authority concerned, Fareham Urban District Council, objected on the following grounds:

1   The proposed sewage disposal works will have a serious detrimental effect on the amenities of the area and the proposed sewage works are sited too near to residential properties.
2   The site of the proposed sewage works has been adopted without adequate investigation of possible alternatives.

3   The proposed scheme will be extremely expensive, and there have been insufficient detailed cost investigations into possible more economic alternatives.
4   The sewage disposal scheme proposed is inflexible in that it involves a commitment to a high initial cost before the required capacity will be ascertained.
5   The present proposals do not show how the Drainage Board propose to dispose of sludge. Incineration of the sludge would cause major air pollution in the surrounding residential districts and disposal by road would have a serious effect on the road system on the area.
6   The concentration of all the sewage effluent in the South Hampshire area into one outfall direct into the Solent will reduce the flow in the main rivers of the area and there are no proposals by the Drainage Board to compensate for this.
7   The site is affected by by-pass proposals.'[13]

On receiving the application the planning authority undertook a number of consultations. One response, that of the Hampshire River Authority, considered 'that the only satisfactory method of preventing pollution of the rivers and tidal waters in the area of the South Hampshire Main Drainage Board was by discharging effluent direct to the Solent'.[13] The Secretary of State called in the application in March 1973 prior to holding a local inquiry into both the planning application and the compulsory purchase order. The following were stated to be relevant to the Secretary of State's consideration of the application:

1   the need for a sewage disposal works of the proposed size and nature in southern Hampshire;
2   the suitability of the site for such a development;
3   the effect the nature of the proposed development is likely to have on neighbouring land.[14]

Later in March the planning authority resolved to inform the Secretary of State that they would have been prepared to grant outline permission subject to appropriate conditions.[3] The Main Drainage Board, in making its statutory statement under the Public Health Act in September 1973, relied largely on the statement which had accompanied the compulsory purchase order but inserted an additional paragraph to the effect that any alternative scheme based on the expansion of existing treatment works and supplementing these with new works as and when required would be unsatisfactory because of:

1   limitations on the discharge of effluents to rivers;
2   the greater flexibility of an integrated system to meet changes in pro-
    jected development and long-term needs;
3   the physical constraints of existing sites and the adverse effect on
    environmental amenities of expanding existing works and creating new
    ones;
4   the financial disadvantages of such a scheme.[15]

The reason for this belated insertion presumably lay in Fareham
Urban District Council's objections, just as the planning authority's
investigation of this alternative strategy[11] had probably arisen from
similar objections raised by Fareham's representatives on the South
Hampshire Main Drainage Board.[16] The objectors to the Peel Common proposal never doubted the need to increase the capacity of the
foul drainage system or to implement the South Hampshire structure
plan objective of reducing water pollution. They did, however, dispute that the means of improving the existing situation adopted were
appropriate. They were not convinced of the advantages of a single
works discharging treated effluent to sea (served by a system of trunk
sewers) compared with those of a number of works discharging
treated effluent to rivers or estuaries.

It is quite clear that the actions of the planning authority were
directly concerned with implementing their three drainage policies,
since they had limited development where adequate sewage disposal
facilities were not available and had rendered great assistance to the
drainage authorities in providing a sewage works. Indeed, their role
in promoting the improvement of drainage facilities appears to have
been central throughout. Whether or not their actions were directed
towards implementing the structure plan pollution control objectives
in the most apposite manner was a central point at the public inquiry.

THE PUBLIC INQUIRY

The public inquiry into the application for planning permission and
the compulsory purchase order was a lengthy affair, commencing in
October 1973 and lasting a total of twenty-three days. Numerous
documents were submitted, together with over a hundred plans. Several of the many witnesses were called more than once, either to give
further evidence or to be re-examined a second or third time. The
complexity of the proceedings arose from Fareham Urban District
Council's presentation of an alternative proposal for draining and
treating South Hampshire's sewage, together with supporting techni-

cal evidence. Apart from debate about the degree of pollution damage, population and cost projections, the flexibility of alternative schemes and the time needed to commission improvements were the chief issues argued at the inquiry. The planning inspector sat with an engineering assessor to advise him on technical points.

Following a preliminary statement by counsel, the first witness to be called was the chief planning officer of Hampshire, appearing in support of the Main Drainage Board, who elaborated upon the county's Rule 6 statement.[3] He said that the possible need for a sewage disposal works at Peel Common had been mentioned in the draft structure plan[2] and that representations against this provision had been received. Overall the planning authority made a full and clear answer[17] to the three points raised by the Secretary of State in his call-in letter.[14]

The next witness to appear was the engineer to the South Hampshire Main Drainage Board. He stated the board's statutory duties and described the reappraisal of the drainage situation which they had undertaken following formation.[18] He made it clear that the river authority's advice had been crucial in causing the board to decide upon marine discharge of effluents. He went on to describe the proposed works and the various alternatives which the board had evaluated.[18] The engineering assessor asked a considerable number of technical questions.

Other witnesses were called to attest the minimal environmental impact to be expected from the proposed works at Peel Common. A landscape architect described how the works would be made attractive,[19] an agricultural consultant demonstrated that the surrounding farmland could still be properly managed[20] and a traffic engineer detailed how Fareham's by-pass objection could be overcome and stated that there was no highway authority objection to the proposal on traffic grounds.[21] A noise consultant produced a noise contour plan and concluded that 'the proposed plant at Peel Common will not be a source of significant noise in the residential areas surrounding the site.'[22] A consultant on air pollution emphasised that incineration of sewage sludge would produce no odour and minimal sulphur dioxide concentrations.[23] A consultant on public health engineering dismissed odour problems: 'with efficient maintenance of the sewers and operation of the treatment works, in my view it should be possible for the surrounding area to be completely free from odour nuisance'.[24]

The consultant who had previously assessed the effect of marine discharge of partially treated sewage[7] stated that the proposed disposal of treated sewage to the sea would not cause any significant detriment to the amenity and fisheries of the Solent.[25] Finally the board called their consulting engineer to discuss cost and basic engineering.[26] There can be no question that this collection of eminent witnesses presented an excellent defence of the impact of the Peel Common works on its immediate surroundings.

Following the address of a second counsel, the technical director of the Hampshire River Authority gave evidence concerning the authority's powers and described the use of water, the rivers and sewage discharges in the area they administered.[27] He stated that the authority considered four factors in determining effluent discharges:

1 The location of the proposed discharge points.
2 The quantity of effluent to be discharged.
3 The nature and composition of the effluent.
4 Its anticipated effects on the receiving water.

He also declared that the authority would not give consent for additional discharges to be made in the vicinity of several sites, whereas disposal from a single new works would be approved.[27] [28]

The principal water quality officer of the river authority then related the conditions prevailing in the various rivers concerned and the reasons for preferring the Main Drainage Board's scheme.[29] The three main advantages were: 'it . . . permit[s] the elimination of existing pollution and also the preservation of the purity of the "inland" waters, many of which are used, or will be used, intensively for recreational purposes. It would also make it possible to eliminate the potential threat to the safety of an important public water supply.'[29] The question of treatment to a high standard was discussed in a supplementary proof, where it was dismissed as expensive and likely to malfunction, thus putting rivers at risk.[30]

Two other witnesses appeared to represent the river authority, the engineer to a water company (who argued strongly against increasing the volume of effluent, of whatever quality, discharged to a river above a water abstraction point on the grounds that the public water supply might be endangered)[31] and an officer of the Nature Conservancy (who considered that further increases in effluent discharges to a harbour could ultimately be biologically disastrous).[32] Two local authorities also presented a case in support of the proposal[33-36] but their evidence did not add significant weight to that already heard.

By this stage in the inquiry it was quite clear that the excellent case prepared by the planning authority and those prepared by the Main Drainage Board and the river authority in support of the Peel Common works had not taken sufficient account of the alternative of utilising the existing system to produce effluents of very high quality. The proposers had received copies of Fareham's proofs of evidence in advance of their being read and were therefore able to make some belated rebuttal of this alternative. The central role of the water quality officer of the river authority had also emerged. It was he who, acting as the representative of the river authority, advised the original working party not to consider discharges to rivers and harbours,[5] it was he who advised the Main Drainage Board in a similar manner and it was presumably he who advised the planning authority likewise. (It was becoming clear that the planning authority had never adequately considered an alternative drainage strategy because they were not sufficiently aware that another was environmentally or economically feasible.) Throughout, the river authority's water quality officer appears to have been the only person offering technical information about the effect of effluents on inland waters.

The objectors were led by Fareham Urban District Council, who also retained counsel to present their case. Rather than suggesting an alternative site for the works, Fareham suggested an alternative approach, as their grounds for objection foretold. Their first witness was a consulting engineer, who demonstrated that four existing works and one new works could be employed to satisfy anticipated drainage needs.[37] (These were not precisely the same works as those evaluated by the planning authority.[11]) He concluded that this alternative:

1   Was cheaper, both in capital cost and in rate of expenditure.
2   Was more flexible, since each works could be expanded to serve the population in its own catchment area.
3   Involved only limited trunk sewer construction.
4   Enabled sources of atmospheric and water pollution to be dispersed and therefore to have less effect.
5   Improved environmental pollution problems more quickly.[37]

The engineering assessor did not question the strategy put forward.
An ecologist was then called to discuss the biological effects of this

alternative strategy.[38] He concluded that the use of five sites was
preferable on water conservation and ecological grounds (with the
possible exception of one of the works, which might eventually cause
deoxygenation of the adjacent tidal water), provided that high quality
effluents were discharged from three of the five. He was able to state
that he had carried out some of the research on which the river
authority had based much of their case and to assert that in four of
the five situations the level of pollution would be reduced, not merely
remain constant, if the proposed treatment were carried out.[38]

Finally, a planning consultant gave evidence on the land use planning implications of the alternative strategy. He showed that the five
sites were quite acceptable on land use planning grounds and he completed his proof by stating that, apart from the advantages referred to
in other evidence, the Fareham alternative would, in comparison with
the Peel Common proposal:

1   Require less additional land, much of that required being
    under-used.
2   Require far less agricultural land of good quality.
3   Have less serious visual impact on the localities of the sites.
4   Be preferable on Green Belt grounds and avoid diversion of
    footpaths.
5   Not affect areas of valuable landscape by constructing trunk sew-
    ers.

He also suggested that the Main Drainage Board had 'failed to
demonstrate a proper relevance for their drainage strategy to either
the objectives or evaluation procedures of the South Hampshire draft
structure plan'.[39]

Other objections were made by the Ministry of Defence (who are
responsible for two establishments close to Peel Common), by the
landowners and by individual residents. The landowners presented a
strong case for locating a centralised works closer to the sea.[40] Following this a great deal of additional material was submitted by both
proposers and opposers and a number of supplementary proofs of
evidence were presented. These included evidence by the engineer to
the Main Drainage Board[41] (endeavouring to refute Fareham's
engineer) and by the objectors' planning consultant[42] (presenting new
evidence on population forecasts and on the damage caused by the
board's trunk sewers and refuting the earlier ecological evidence[32] on

the effect of additional discharges to the harbour). As previously mentioned, considerable debate about forecasts and costs took place and the engineering assessor became more and more closely involved. Because certain figures which he requested were not forthcoming from the board, the inquiry was adjourned to recommence some weeks later for a single day. Four days were devoted to visiting the various sites in question.

Counsel for both the opposers and the proposers cross-examined witnesses with vigour. The degree to which the planning authority had provided additional justification of the Peel Common decision after it had been reached was revealed during the first period of questioning. (Hampshire County Council had, of course, been party to the evaluation of alternatives throughout.) The engineer to the Main Drainage Board admitted that the treatment of sewage effluents to higher than normal standards and their discharge to rivers had never been seriously considered. (On the other hand, the evidence of the various witnesses to the effects of Peel Common remained unshaken after cross-examination.) The officers of the river authority conceded that high-quality effluent discharge had not been fully considered or evaluated in reaching their decisions and in giving evidence, and some of the Nature Conservancy officer's statements were refuted during questioning. Although the evidence of the opposition witnesses was also subjected to rigorous cross-examination, no very significant points were conceded. Some doubt about minor elements of their statements was sown, however.

At the end of the inquiry the viability of the alternative schemes had been established and an impressive array of statistics had been employed to demonstrate or dispute its advantages. It had become quite clear that, in implementing the drainage policies in the structure plan, the planning authority had become embroiled in a difficult, complex and highly technical sphere of activity. The opposers of Peel Common could also argue that, in following the policies, the authority had run into conflict with other structure plan objectives, notably those relating to conservation and economy.

INSPECTOR'S REPORT
As might be anticipated, the inspector's report is a lengthy document, running to some 200 pages.[43] The early sections of the report are devoted to preliminary legal points and to descriptions of Peel Com-

mon and its surroundings and of the sites of Fareham's alternative works. Peel Common is described as 'a large featureless area which at present is used for extensive pig rearing and for the production of winter wheat and potatoes'.[44] Favourable comments are made about the environs of four of the five works suggested by Fareham. In the fifth case, where expansion under the alternative strategy would take place entirely within the perimeter fence of an existing works, the inspector states that in spite of the very pleasant landscape seen from a local viewpoint the area around the sewage works 'does present a rather mixed character'.[45] These opinions must anticipate future proposals for the areas concerned, since few would declare that they are particularly attractive at present (with one notable exception).

The report then devotes just under a hundred pages to summarising the case for the South Hampshire Main Drainage Board, the Hampshire County Council, the Hampshire River Authority and the other supporters of the proposal. A few of the points made in cross-examination appear in this section, but substantial errors which were pointed out at the inquiry remain uncorrected. The evidence for the objectors is then presented, each submission being followed by a rebuttal by the Main Drainage Board. Thirty-five pages are devoted to Fareham's case and the board's reply is given six pages. The cases for the other objectors, together with replies by the board to each objector or grouped objection, take up around forty pages, of which at least a third are devoted to the proposer's comments. The general reply by the board to all the objections is then presented. This is not the way in which matters proceeded at the inquiry and, while this method of organising the report is perfectly reasonable, both the detailed arrangement of evidence and the space devoted to the respective cases are, perhaps, open to question.

The inspector's findings of fact are not always easily distinguishable from his conclusions, which they precede. He finds that 'it is agreed that there are no unsurmountable technical problems to Fareham Urban District Council's preferred scheme'.[46] He also finds that the Fareham scheme would be cheaper.[47] However, he finds that a footpath diversion would be necessary at one works,[48] that another is located within an area of high landscape value,[49] that a third would impinge on an existing public open space[50] and that a fourth represents a potential recreational area.[51] He makes a number of findings relating to the opposition of the river authority and other bodies to

L. I. H. E.
THE MARKLAND LIBRARY
STAND PARK RD. LIVERPOOL L16 9JD

further discharges but he does not include any relating to the actual polluting effect of discharges. The number of findings of fact relating to the proposal and the alternative are in a similar ratio to the number of pages devoted to each in the main body of the report.

The conclusions section is fairly extensive and presents a summary of much of the earlier part of the report. One conclusion is that 'although the Peel Common site is good Grade II agricultural land within the draft Green Belt it is at the same time entirely featureless compared with, say, any part of an alternative site'.[52] Another states that 'an accurate evaluation of the extra cost of a works at Peel Common cannot be calculated on the basis of the evidence submitted at the inquiry although it does appear that Fareham's scheme would be cheaper over a forty-year period by perhaps 10 per cent of the total cost of £130 million'.[53] The inspector's conclusions concede the technical feasibility, flexibility and, indeed, relative economy of the Fareham scheme but, like the findings of fact, they do not deal with the relative merits of marine or river disposal of sewage effluent.

The inspector suggests, in dealing with the other environmental effects of the Peel Common proposal, that in relation to incineration 'the Secretary of State might also wish to consider whether there is a need to impose a limitation on the sulphur dioxide emission in the event of planning permission being granted'.[54] While conceding the cost advantages of the Fareham scheme, the inspector states that 'against that, however, must be weighed the long-term environmental benefits of the Board's scheme over those of Fareham'.[55] Mentioning the inevitable delay if any other course of action were taken, the inspector then states:

The evidence has shown that the technical problems of various alternative schemes can be overcome so a choice of schemes does in the last resort appear to depend very largely upon environmental factors. Having considered all these matters and the various objections, I am persuaded that from a planning point of view the Peel Common site appears to have least disadvantages and that the Board's scheme should be supported.[56]

I prefer the Board's scheme because it ensures that essential sewage and sewerage facilities will be available to serve the forecast population requirements of the structure plan, whilst at the same time it will bring about a substantial improvement in the elimination of pollution of the rivers, estuaries and harbours, which can be expected to react favourably upon the ecology of these areas, and render them more attractive for the enjoyment of future generations.[57]

Since it was demonstrated at the inquiry that the Fareham scheme could achieve an earlier improvement in the level of pollution and since this represents the inspector's first and only assessment of the relative merits of the two schemes on pollution grounds, it would seem that the decision must have been made 'from a planning point of view'. The engineering assessor is stated to agree 'with the technical aspects of this report' (not 'with this report') and it is clear from the technical engineering sections of the document that the assessor inclined favourably to the Fareham scheme, certainly on cost grounds. However, despite (or possibly because of) all the complex technical argument about population forecasts, costs, efficiency and pollution, the inspector appears to have made the decision on his assessment of the merits of the various sites concerned. Pollution seems not to have been a factor in this decision, but to have been an element quoted in its support. No attempt was made to evaluate the advantages of the alternative schemes in controlling pollution and any endeavour to weigh this and other relative merits against monetary costs (£13 million–10 per cent of £130 million—was in question) is missing from the inspector's report.

DECISION LETTERS

Two decision letters were released in September 1974. The first[58] deals with the compulsory purchase order and summarises the two paragraphs of the inspector's report quoted above. It mentions the economy inherent in Fareham's scheme but states that:

Nevertheless, the Secretary of State has come to the conclusion that the Board's scheme is to be preferred. He shares the inspector's general conclusion that it would ensure that essential sewerage and sewage disposal facilities will be available to serve the forecast population and requirements of the area; that it is necessary to implement a satisfactory long term sewage disposal scheme as quickly as possible, otherwise the housing programmes will suffer; and that in this connection the Board's proposals have the advantage over Fareham's preferred scheme in that the assembly of land required at several of the sites proposed would inevitably take time. He also agrees that the Board's scheme would substantially reduce pollution of the rivers, estuaries and harbours of South Hampshire with resultant beneficial effects on the quality of the river water abstracted for public supply purposes, on the conservation and ecology of the areas concerned and on recreational facilities. He does not consider that the financial advantages of the alternative scheme are sufficient to over-ride the advantages as a whole of the Board's proposals.[58]

F

The second letter[59] relates to the planning application. It quotes several paragraphs from the inspector's report, including those referred to in the first letter. In discussing growth in South Hampshire it states that in the Secretary of State's opinion:

> The precise rate of growth is not critical in the present context and he therefore accepts the need for the proposals. He notes that the proposed scheme could be implemented relatively quickly which will benefit housing programmes, and at the same time improve the quality of the area's rivers, estuaries and harbours. The Secretary of State agrees with the inspector's conclusions and accepts his recommendations.[59]

(It should be mentioned that the inspector's conclusion relating to sulphur dioxide control was ignored.)

From these letters it would appear that the Secretary of State viewed time as the critical element. The improvement of the foul drainage system is quite clearly of paramount importance to the continuing growth of South Hampshire, and the difficulties of securing additional land at five different locations to serve the eventual population may well have been the decisive issue. The advantages of reducing pollution are mentioned in both decision letters but these seem ancillary to the time element as do 'planning grounds' and cost advantages. Even here no attempt is made to weigh the relative advantages of the alternative proposals in reducing pollution or even to systematically compare benefits with £13 million. If Fareham's scheme was capable of rapid implementation, as its proponents claimed, this fact was obviously not spelt out in sufficient detail to convince either the inspector or the Secretary of State.

The intervention of the planning authority in the inquiry was probably crucial, since their evidence clearly swayed the inspector and lent considerable weight to the evidence of the Main Drainage Board. The implementation of the first two structure plan drainage policies by controlling development had led to serious conflict with numerous other structure plan objectives and was definitely hindering the growth of South Hampshire. The planning authority therefore attached considerable importance to implementing their third policy: to secure a site for a water pollution control works. In so doing they met three of the four criteria for putting the policy into practice (Appendix 2), since the scheme adopted should cope with future extensions of growth, should be well landscaped and should not give rise to significant smell or other nuisance. The fourth criterion was 'minimising the costs of development commensurate with environmental considerations'. This is well qualified and the planning authority could argue that the inspector decided that the Peel Common scheme met the criterion.

There is evidence, however, that the planning authority was not fully aware that a more economical alternative scheme might exist. They were advised throughout by the Drainage Board and the river authority. The former body had submitted that the alternative to their proposal suffered from physical constraints, offered less flexibility than the Peel Common system and had financial disadvantages in comparison with it. That these claims had never been fully tested was proved by the inspector's conclusions. The planning authority were clearly not to blame in accepting the best advice available. They are open to criticism, on the other hand, on the grounds that they could be said to have employed the objectives of the structure plan ostensibly to evaluate alternative sites but in reality (as the dates of the relevant documents testify) to support a decision which had already been taken. (The provision regarding Peel Common in the structure plan is phrased to escape this charge.) The planning authority's priorities may well have been correct at the time, but such a procedure can only call structure plan policies and criteria into some question (as some of the evaluation statements quoted earlier suggest).

There is a more fundamental issue concerned with the planning control of pollution. The role of a river authority officer, acting on behalf of his authority, in influencing sewage disposal policy in South Hampshire has become apparent. It appears that alternative policies were, in fact, feasible on ecological grounds and the question therefore arises: should the planning authority have taken independent advice on pollution and its effects? There can be no clear answer but it would appear that in this case such advice might have been taken when opposition to the centralised scheme first became vocal. The planning authority would then have been confident that they were achieving their objective of reducing harmful water pollution in the most appropriate way. As it is, they might be thought to have considered waste (effluent) to be the same as pollution (the effluent diluted) in the receiving waters, a frequent and dangerous assumption. They might also have avoided conflict with structure plan objectives relating to landscape and water conservation and economy by adopting, or at least fully evaluating, an alternative approach.

The complexity of implementing what appear to be relatively straightforward planning objectives and policies relating to pollution control are clear from this case study. While the planning authority were able to further the achievement of certain policies, it seems likely that they were unaware of the technical and ecological feasibility of an alternative means of doing so which, had it been pursued from the first, might have been quicker, more flexible, cheaper and brought faster control of existing pollution, and hence met the structure plan's fourth criterion more completely.

REFERENCES

1   Ministry of Housing and Local Government (1970) *Strategic plan for the South East* HMSO, London.
2   South Hampshire Plan Advisory Committee (1973) *South Hampshire structure plan* Hampshire County Council, Winchester.
3   Hampshire County Council (1973) *Statement of case of the local planning authority* (Rule 6 statement), HCC, Winchester.
4   South Hampshire Plan Advisory Committee (1968) *Drainage* Study Report, Group B, 2, South Hampshire Plan Technical Unit, Winchester.
5   Wright, S. L. (1969) *Report on river pollution by sewage effluents* Hampshire River Authority, Eastleigh.
6   John Taylor & Sons (1970) *South Hampshire plan main drainage and sewage disposal* JTS, London.
7   Southgate, B. A. (1970) *Report on proposals for sewage disposal* Hampshire County Council, Winchester.
8   Smyth, A. H. M. (1970) *South Hampshire plan main drainage* (letter of 13th May and appendices) Hampshire County Council, Winchester.
9   South Hampshire Plan Technical Unit (1971) *Study of sites for a water pollution control works* DTE 195, Hampshire County Council, Winchester.
10 James, G.V. (1972) *Report on proposals for South Hampshire plan sewage disposal* Southern Sea Fisheries District Committee, Bournemouth.
11 South Hampshire Plan Technical Unit (1972) *Alternative sewage disposal works sites—planning appraisals* DTE 224, Hampshire County Council, Winchester.
12 South Hampshire Plan Technical Unit (1972) *Salterns Lane sewage disposal works—a planning appraisal* DTE 213, Hampshire County Council, Winchester.
13 South Hampshire Main Drainage Board (1972) *Preliminary statement of reasons* SHMDB, Eastleigh.
14 Call-in letter reproduced as appendix A of reference 3.

15 South Hampshire Main Drainage Board (1973) *Statement of reasons* (Rule 4 statement), SHMDB, Eastleigh.
16 South Hampshire Main Drainage Board (1972) *Minutes of Board meetings* SHMDB, Eastleigh.
17 Smart, A. D. G. (1973) *Peel Common inquiry: proof of evidence* Hampshire County Council, Winchester.
18 Kirkaldy, I. D. (1973) *Peel Common inquiry: proof of evidence* South Hampshire Main Drainage Board, Eastleigh.
19 Graham, M. (1973) *Peel Common inquiry: proof of evidence* South Hampshire Main Drainage Board, Eastleigh.
20 Maclay, M. P. (1973) *Peel Common inquiry: proof of evidence* South Hampshire Main Drainage Board, Eastleigh.
21 Fairless, G. D. (1973) *Peel Common inquiry: proof of evidence* South Hampshire Main Drainage Board, Eastleigh.
22 Gordon C.G. (1973) *Peel Common inquiry: proof of evidence* South Hampshire Main Drainage Board, Eastleigh.
23 Craxford, S. R. (1973) *Peel Common enquiry: proof of evidence* South Hampshire Main Drainage Board, Eastleigh.
24 Stanbridge, H. H. (1973) *Peel Common inquiry: proof of evidence* South Hampshire Main Drainage Board, Eastleigh.
25 Southgate, B. A. (1973) *Peel Common inquiry: proof of evidence* South Hampshire Main Drainage Board, Eastleigh.
26 Taylor, O. M. (1973) *Peel Common inquiry: proof of evidence* South Hampshire Main Drainage Board, Eastleigh.
27 Speight, H. (1973) *Peel Common inquiry: proof of evidence* South Hampshire Main Drainage Board, Eastleigh.
28 Speight, H. (1973) *Peel Common inquiry: supplementary proof of evidence* Hampshire River Authority, Eastleigh.
29 Wright, S. L. (1973) *Peel Common inquiry: proof of evidence* South Hampshire Main Drainage Board, Eastleigh.
30 Wright, S. L. (1973) *Peel Common inquiry: supplementary proof of evidence* Hampshire River Authority, Eastleigh.
31 Simpson, L. J. (1973) *Peel Common inquiry: proof of evidence* Hampshire River Authority, Eastleigh.
32 Tubbs, C. P. (1973) *Peel Common inquiry: proof of evidence* Hampshire River Authority, Eastleigh.
33 Ling, L. P. (1973) *Peel Common inquiry: proof of evidence* Portsmouth City Council, Portsmouth.
34 King, E. E. J. (1973) *Peel Common inquiry: proof of evidence* Portsmouth City Council, Portsmouth.
35 Bennett, G. (1973) *Peel Common inquiry: proof of evidence* Gosport Borough Council, Gosport.
36 Jones, J. H. (1973) *Peel Common inquiry: proof of evidence* Gosport Borough Council, Gosport.
37 Martin, C. (1973) *Peel Common inquiry: proof of evidence* Fareham Urban District Council, Fareham.

38   Hawkes, H. A. (1973) *Peel Common inquiry: proof of evidence* Fareham Urban District Council, Fareham.
39   Herbert, J. R. (1973) *Peel Common inquiry: proof of evidence* Fareham Urban District Council, Fareham.
40   Mann, G. E. (1973) *Peel Common inquiry: proof of evidence* Richard Austin & Wyatt, Fareham.
41   Kirkaldy, I. D. (1973) *Peel Common inquiry: supplementary proof of evidence* South Hampshire Main Drainage Board,
42   Herbert, J. R. (1973) *Peel Common inquiry: supplementary proof of evidence* Fareham Urban District Council, Fareham.
43   Department of the Environment (1973) *Peel Common inquiry: inspector's report* DoE, London. (Subsequently referred to as *IR*.)
44   *IR* p. 6, para. 1.31.
45   *IR* p. 15, para. 1.87.
46   *IR* p. 181, para. 8.
47   *IR* p. 182, para. 15.
48   *IR* p. 183, para. 35.
49   *IR* p. 183, para. 36.
50   *IR* p. 183, para. 37.
51   *IR* p. 184, para. 38.
52   *IR* p. 187, para. 34.21.
53   *IR* p. 192, para. 34.35.
54   *IR* p. 187, para. 34.17.
55   *IR* p. 193, para. 34.65.
56   *IR* p. 193, para. 34.67.
57   *IR* p. 194, para. 34.68.
58   Department of the Environment (1974) *Peel Common inquiry: compulsory purchase decision letter* DoE, London.
59   Department of the Environment (1974) *Peel Common inquiry: planning application decision letter* DoE, London.

CHAPTER 10

Development control

Fertiliser plant at Ince, Cheshire, 1975. The location of new residential development too close to large industrial complexes can lead to serious pollution problems, since significant damage may result.

It has been shown that provision for pollution control in the preparation of plans has been somewhat uneven. Structure plans demonstrate the most constructive approach to the pollution problem and the policies incorporated in some of the plans should make a significant contribution to control. The previous chapter showed how the implementation of pollution control policies in one structure plan involved development control issues of strategic importance. Not all such issues are decided by local planning authorities in the light of published pollution control policies, however.

Most development control still involves reference to an 'old style' development plan since few structure plans have been approved by the Secretary of State for the Environment. These older plans seldom refer to pollution. Since planning authorities do not generally formulate separate positive pollution control policies, it is necessary to examine not just how the control of pollution is considered at the development control stage of the planning process but whether it is considered and what criteria are employed. Some local planning authorities, however, have prepared development control policies relating to pollution abatement, at least in the case of noise.

POLICIES FOR POLLUTION CONTROL
Cheshire County Council has published noise standards for new development which relate to noise generated within the site concerned, to sound levels within buildings in noisy areas and to noise levels in open spaces.[1] Noise levels at the boundary of a site where new industrial or entertainment development is to take place will not be permitted to exceed 45 dB(A) on the L_{10} (eighteen hour) scale in rural areas, 50 dB(A) in residential areas and 55 dB(A) in busy urban areas. (Noise units are referred to in Appendix 1.) There will be a strong presumption against new residential development in areas where ambient noise is likely to exceed 70 dB(A). Where such development is permitted in noisy areas, internal noise levels will not exceed 40, 45 and 50 dB(A) in the corresponding types of area. Other standards relating to churches, hospitals, shops, offices and schools have also been laid down. New external sources generating noise are not to cause levels in private, communal and other recreational open space in residential areas to exceed 45, 55 and 60 dB(A) respectively, for more than 10 per cent of the time between 08.00 hrs and 20.00 hrs.[1] These development control standards appear to be among the first sets of reasonably comprehensive noise criteria to be laid down, and they rely heavily on the Wilson Committee's recommendations.[2]

Surrey and West Sussex County Councils adopted the following development control policy in relation to noise from Gatwick airport in 1968:[3]

Zone 1: In the noisiest zone bounded by the 60 NNI day and 45 NNI night contour where noise is 'very annoying or worse', most development to be refused, i.e. other than factories, warehouses and hotels with sound insulation.
Zone 2: In the next noisy zone bounded by the 50 NNI day and 35 NNI night contour where noise is 'annoying', no major development, but infilling dwellings permitted with sound insulation.

Zone 3: In the outer zone bounded by the 40 NNI contour where noise is 'intrusive' no major development but infilling dwellings permitted without sound insulation.

An environmental study of the airport later recommended that the 35 NNI contour should be accepted as the limit within which major urbanisation should not take place.[3] Surrey County Council were a pioneer planning authority in this sphere of pollution control when they first adopted a zoned development control policy for noise abatement.

Manchester corporation have adopted a similar policy in relation to noise arising from Manchester airport.[4] They used the same noise contours, refusing virtually all development within the 60 NNI contour and imposing a standard soundproofing condition on any development within the 40 NNI contour which was permitted: 'the proposed development shall be subject to the submission of detailed drawings indicating the soundproofing measures necessary to secure a noise reduction of . . . .'[4] Cheshire County Council accepted a virtually identical policy for the large area affected by aircraft noise that fell within their jurisdiction.[5,6] The standard condition employed in this case was:

'All bedrooms and at least one other habitable room shall be insulated to meet the local authority's specification for noise reduction and details of the works involved shall be submitted to and approved by the local planning authority before the development is commenced.'

The Department of the Environment indicated their acceptance of the policy when consulted.[5]

In 1966 the Greater London Council adopted the Wilson standards[2] for traffic noise, resolving that all major road and redevelopment schemes should pay full regard to the problems of traffic noise and that L_{10} (eighteen hour) noise levels of 45 dB(A) by day and 35 dB(A) by night be applied to new residential development in suburban areas away from main traffic routes and 50 dB(A) (35 dB(A) by night) be applied in busy urban areas.[7] The council noted that it might not always be possible to implement such standards because of high ambient noise levels, especially in the case of existing dwellings. They were, nevertheless, to be used as strongly desirable design aims.[8]

Telford New Town, acting in the clear belief that environmental conditions in new towns should be above average, has decided to employ outdoor noise standards in residential areas, both because of the attenuation afforded by the shell of a building and because of the importance of quiet private open space.[9] The corporation here stated that an L_{10} (eighteen hour) level of 55 dB(A) should not be exceeded in residential parts of suburban areas away from main traffic routes, and that the equivalent standard for busy urban areas is to be 60 dB(A). They extended these standards to existing (as opposed to planned) development, and resolved that 'a standard of 60 dB(A) should apply for all residential property adjoining existing or proposed major roads'.[9]

Manchester Corporation similarly has adopted traffic noise standards in relation to their new development.[10] Measured on the L_{10} (eighteen hour) scale:

External noise level within the residential development	65 dB(A)
Internal noise level (where external level unattainable)	50 dB(A)
Internal noise level where there is substantial traffic during late evening	40 dB(A)

Such standards would also be employed in evaluating the effect of new roads.[10]

DEVELOPMENT CONTROL GENERALLY

The use of such standards must enable a local planning authority to make better development control decisions where pollution is an issue than would otherwise be the case. Examples of poor decisions abound and inadequate consultation on pollution issues in some areas has led to situations comparable with those pertaining before planning legislation was first introduced. For example, the construction of a group of twelve storey blocks of flats overlooking a gasworks led to many complaints about odours in one town.[11] In another town a block of flats was erected within a few hundred yards of the cupolas and steel converters of an iron and steel works. The inevitable air pollution problem was resolved to the satisfaction of residents only when the firm concerned transferred steel converting operations to another part of the country.[12]

A proposal to extend a hospital on land opposite an iron foundry was made in another area. Despite the Alkali Inspectorate's opposition, planning permission was granted and informal representations had to be made to the Department of Health and Social Security to prevent the development. Elsewhere a proposal was allowed which involved building a twenty-six storey block of offices and multi-storey blocks of flats adjacent to a chemical works stack emitting ammonia. Again, extensions to a lead works in the heart of an inner urban area led to fears of poisoning of local residents. On Canvey Island the hemming in of urban development by a series of polluting oil refineries has aroused strong indignation. It would appear that the liaison between planners, health officers and other pollution control authorities has by no means been all that it might have been throughout the country.[13]

It is clearly difficult to determine the precise extent to which the control of pollution or its effects is taken into account at the development control stage. A survey of development control procedure in seventeen local planning authorities revealed that, although nuisance aspects—noise, fumes, smoke, etc—often formed part of the content of standard conditions attached to permission by planning authorities, consultations on these issues were infrequent.[14] Noise and undesirable neighbouring uses were among topics frequently discussed with the public, however. The survey found that acts of parliament, statutory instruments, circulars and government bulletins were the documents most frequently referred to by development control officers, but it did not, unfortunately, classify the material consulted by topic.[14]

A more limited investigation revealed that pollution was fairly widely considered in making certain development control decisions.[15] The factor most taken into account was generally noise from the proposed development, but air pollution from fuel burning was also important. The public health department was frequently involved, because of its role in the grant of Building Regulations approvals, and its opinion about the appropriate height of a new chimney generally prevailed. Water pollution and land pollution seemed to be less frequently considered, although the water authority was normally consulted on riverside development. It was clear that consultation on pollution control normally occurred only if the potential problem was readily apparent.[15] Both this and the previous survey were carried out before public concern about pollution and its control reached its highest level.

The same is true of two further surveys relating to the planning control of pollution. Replies to a questionnaire to river authorities showed that the degree of consultation by local planning authorities varied.[16] Formal procedures for referring developments with water pollution implications existed in most of the 20 former river authority areas for which information was obtained. Where this did not apply, informal consultations were often felt to be satisfactory. Nevertheless, it appeared that consultations on applications by some planning authorities left much to be desired. On the other hand, the nine sea fisheries committees replying to a questionnaire survey were mostly satisfied with the level of consultation by coastal planning authorities.[17] It would appear from these investigations that some authorities take much more account of pollution problems than others in making development control decisions, and that consultation could be improved in several areas. Nevertheless, there is evidence that control of pollution at the development control stage of the planning process is now much more important than used to be the case.

Many planning decisions are clearly affected by pollution control implications and local planning authorities sometimes cite pollution as the reason for refusing permission or attaching conditions. Thus reasons for refusal of quarrying development have included the effects of dust and noise on local communities, the introduction of noise to an unspoilt area and the damage to amenity caused by solid waste pollution. Permission to tip domestic and industrial refuse has been refused because the water authority considered 'that the nature of the wastes to be tipped would be likely to give rise to contamination of underground water'.[18] Conditions attached to permissions for industrial or mineral working development have included the following:

The best practical means shall be adopted to control the emission of dust from the proposed buildings to the reasonable satisfaction of the planning authority.

The proposed dust arresting equipment shall at all times be maintained in good working order.

All practicable means shall be employed by the applicants for preventing or minimising the emission of dust or the creation of noise of more than 55 dB(A) measured at any point outside the site during operations authorised or required under this permission.

Any waste resulting from the proposed workings shall be disposed of either underground or within the excavated area of the adjoining limestone quarry.

Adequate precautions shall be taken in running the washing plant to ensure that solid material in suspension does not enter the adjacent stream.[19]

There have been a number of public inquiries where pollution and its control have been important issues; some being concerned with appeals specifically relating to the refusal of planning permission on pollution generation or damage grounds or to the attachment of planning conditions to approvals intended to control pollution.

PUBLIC INQUIRIES
Decisions published in the literature
The consideration of pollution control in early post-war public inquiries tended to concentrate on 'injury to the amenities of an area' caused by industrial development of one type or another. Thus, in relation to smoke and fumes from a proposed pottery in an area provisionally zoned residential, the Minister allowed an appeal subject to the boilerhouse and chimney being located away from houses.[20] In another case complaints about nuisance from fumes and smell led to a refusal of planning permission which the Minister had to quash because development was not involved.[21] Again, the Minister decided that soundproofing arrangements in premises proposed for light engineering use were adequate to prevent noise annoyance and allowed an appeal.[22] Similarly, where it was proposed to rebuild a brewery which had given rise to complaints about noise and smells in a residential area, the Minister dismissed the appeal because 'the development, if permitted, would have a severely adverse effect on the amenities of the neighbourhood'.[22] Where it was proposed to manufacture potato crisps the Minister refused to accept an appeal, as he considered that the premises would cause 'serious injury to the neighbourhood by reason of smell, fumes and noise'.[22]

An application for planning permission to erect piggeries (submitted after the applicant had received complaints about effluent from the local council's sanitary inspector) was refused partly because 'it would be likely to cause injury to public health through contamination of the subsoil and pollution of water supplies over a wide area'. The Minister allowed the appeal and 'considered that any control necessary to protect water supplies from the risk of pollution should be exercised by the appropriate bodies under any statutory powers available to these bodies'.[22]

In another case the council considered that the use of noisy processes meant that an industry no longer fell within the classification 'light industry'. The Minister allowed the appeal, since he 'considered that if alterations and improvements designed to minimise noise were carried out as proposed' no change of use was involved.[23]

In an inquiry concerned with the installation of a crushing plant in a quarry in a national park the local authority argued that the noise and dust inseparable from such a plant would injure the amenities of the area. The Minister allowed the appeal, subject to conditions governing the siting of the plant, requiring the use of soundproof materials and dust extractors and limiting the times of operation.[24] There are a number of other examples of early inquiries into appeals against planning permission where pollution was a prominent, if not central, issue.[25] Other factors were generally involved also.

Pollution has, if anything, become more important in recent years. Certainly the language employed at the inquiry has changed from 'injury to amenity' to more specific reference to the pollution problem arising. Thus smell was an important issue at an inquiry into tipping industrial wastes where a technical assessor sat with the inspector. The appeal was allowed by the Minister subject to conditions relating to the types of waste tipped, the method of tipping, screening and covering with earth.[26] Noise was a factor at an inquiry involving the extension of a non-conforming use, and was one reason for the Minister dismissing the appeal.[27]

Noise, air and water pollution were all considered at an inquiry into an oil refinery at Milford Haven. Although construction noise would result, the inspector concluded that there would be no significant increase in pollution of the atmosphere of the Haven. He recommended that conditions relating to smell be attached to the planning permission. The Secretary of State gave planning permission, but deleted the 'smell condition' on the grounds that the matter was more appropriately dealt with under the Alkali Act. This is in keeping with other central government decisions designed to prevent the duplication of specific pollution control authority responsibilities by planning conditions. However, he insisted that detailed designs to reduce environmental pollution be submitted to the planning authority, that sound insulation and siting of noisy plant be agreed with them, and that no construction work took place at night.[28]

The legitimacy of refusing planning permission because of water pollution from a sewage works (Chapter 3) was confirmed by the rejection of an appeal to build a single house that would drain to a seriously overloaded works.[29] After the inspector's report of another inquiry had been received, the Department of the Environment asked the Water Directorate to examine the pollution situation. Because the directorate felt that some spare capacity at the sewage treatment works existed, the Secretary of State ruled that additional development could be allowed, but made provisions for the inquiry to be reopened to challenge the new evidence if required.[30]

The measurement of noise was the central feature of a rare inquiry into a discontinuance order. The defendants engaged a consultant on noise to measure levels and he and the council public health inspector gave conflicting evidence. The inspector concluded that 'the scientific measurement of noise by meter and more sophisticated equipment and the use of criteria has become a highly technical matter, but even if there had not been such an obvious difference of opinion in this case, one should not, I consider, be exclusively dependent for degree and duration of noise on purely objective measurements.' The Secretary of State agreed and confirmed the order.[31]

The conflict between amenity and pollution control considerations was symbolised by the inquiry into the erection of a 175 ft chimney, at the natural gas terminal at Bacton, Norfolk. The chimney, required to achieve effective dispersion of pollutants, was approved and built.[32] Pollution was a central consideration in the inquiry into the development of Holme Pierrepoint power station, close to Nottingham. The objectors stated that the power station, would 'increase the atmospheric pollution in the built-up area and further endanger the health of the large population nearby'. The technical assessor (sitting as chief engineering inspector) concluded that 'there would be very little risk that the proposed station would seriously pollute the atmosphere' but that it would be better sited away from residential areas. The planning inspector felt noise would not be a problem but still recommended that permission should not be granted. The Minister agreed and refused planning permission.[32],[33] (Air pollution is frequently an issue at power station inquiries.)

The first refinery at Milford Haven was permitted despite considerable objection on air pollution and, especially, water pollution grounds. The Minister, who called in the application, included an amenity clause with his permission to develop. This was related mainly to appearance, but pollution control was also considered in reaching his decision.[33]

Other decisions

Accounts of inquiries where pollution has been an important factor are often chosen for publication for reasons other than their significance to the planning control of pollution. It is therefore instructive to examine also a number of public inquiries where pollution issues figure large but which have not been reported in the literature.

The effect of sewage effluent on drinking water was an important consideration at a public inquiry into a proposal to abstract water from a chalk river a mile or so downstream of the discharge point. A great deal of evidence about the water treatment necessary and about the impact of storm overflows was heard before the inspector recommended that the scheme be accepted, subject to the provision of holding capacity for raw water in case the river temporarily became too polluted for abstraction to proceed, and certain other conditions.[34] The Minister concurred.

There have been a number of inquiries concerned with the refusal of planning permission on the grounds that the sewage works concerned was overloaded, and was already causing pollution. Thus in an appeal settled by a decision based on written representations 'the overriding disadvantage of the appeal development is, however, thought to lie in the inadequate local sewage disposal arrangements'. Development as a caravan site would 'add unacceptably to the current substantial overload at the existing treatment works'.[35] In a similar case concerning thirty-eight houses the local authority were restricting development pending the completion of a new sewage disposal works and the Secretary of State felt that 'on drainage grounds alone, and if there were no other planning objections, the proposed development would . . . be regarded as premature'.[36]

In another appeal concerning sewage treatment the inspector found that the sewage works had no spare capacity but that an extension, to be completed in four years' time, would be able to treat sewage from the appeal site. He therefore found that 'no acceptable reasons had been advanced why development should be permitted before the provision of the necessary treatment and disposal capacities'.[37] The Secretary of State agreed and dismissed the appeal.[38] In a second appeal relating to the same sewage works another inspector also found that they were at present overloaded and concluded, 'as far as foul drainage is concerned, I feel the proposal must be considered as premature until such time as the disposal works have been extended. To allow the development under present conditions, and thereby overburden an already overloaded disposal works could well endanger public health'.[39] The Secretary of State accepted the inspector's recommendations and dismissed the appeal.[40]

Perhaps the fullest account of such matters was presented at another inquiry where the planning authority had refused planning permission on the sole grounds that 'it is considered that, as this area is drained into the . . . sewage disposal system, which is at present seriously overtaxed by existing development, and will be further overloaded by development already approved, any development on this site is premature pending the improvement on the present sewage disposal system'. The inspector, an engineering rather than a planning official, heard evidence by the water authority that the estuary into which the works discharged had a very low dissolved oxygen content, well below the level at which fish would survive and within the range where the water might begin to smell, as it already did in the vicinity of the works. He inspected the works and observed the very poor quality of the effluent. He concluded that 'the present overloading of the sewage works and the resulting heavy pollution of the estuary are such that further development within areas draining to the works is likely to increase to an unacceptable extent the risk of smell nuisance affecting a wide area and that the planning authority were justified in refusing planning permission'.[41] After some discussion about the interpretation of 'sewerage services' in the Town and Country Act, 1971, the Secretary of State decided that the adequacy of the sewage works was relevant and dismissed the appeal.[42]

Proposals to deal with serious river pollution led to a public inquiry into an application for planning permission to build a large sewage works on Tyneside. As confirmation of the multi-medium nature of the pollution problem, the possibility that air pollution in the form of hydrogen sulphide from sewage might discolour the products of an adjoining lead manufacturer formed the principal ground for objection. Both parties accepted that the condition of the Tyne needed urgent improvement and the water authority submitted that the discharge of untreated sewage to a river 'was a revolting practice that should not be resorted to in any civilised community'. Apart from evidence about river quality and the benefits of river and sea outfalls, much of the inquiry was taken up with technical information relating to the threshold level for discolouration of various lead compounds by hydrogen sulphide and the ambient level of the gas in the air. No firm conclusions were reached, just as the two parties had been unable to agree on a basis for compensation, the concentration in question (of the order of a few parts per thousand million) being well below the limit of detection by smell and the sensitivity of many analytical methods.

The engineering inspector, who sat with a chemical assessor, accepted the need to improve the condition of the Tyne, but was not satisfied that discharge to sea should not be practised. He therefore concluded that sewer construction should be commenced but that 'on the evidence submitted, it is impossible to be certain that the products manufactured at the lead works would not be affected by gases generated in the proposed sewers or at the proposed sewage works. I therefore conclude that it would be wrong to permit construction of a central sewage works'.[43] While pressing for urgent implementation of a sea outfall scheme, the Secretary of State refused planning permission for the works, since 'the objections to the proposals outweigh the need to provide works on land at Tynemouth'.[44]

The effect of noise on dwellings has been important in some inquiries. After hearing an appeal concerning refusal of planning permission to construct twelve houses within the second noise zone (40–50 NNI) around Gatwick airport, the inspector had to decide whether the development, which was to have incorporated sound-proofing, constituted infilling or not. There were other factors to be considered, and he concluded that 'where other planning factors are favourable a case could possibly be established for permitting a small development of twelve houses in an area where the policy is to restrict development because it is affected by aircraft noise'. Here, however, they were not favourable and he recommended that the appeal be dismissed.[45] The Secretary of State concurred.[46]

Noise levels of a different order were involved at an inquiry relating to an area 400 m from Heathrow airport. Here permission to build one hundred dwellings had been refused because 'the site is immediately adjacent to the air safeguarding zone associated with runway No. 5 of London (Heathrow) Airport, and is subject to very considerable nuisance from aircraft noise. The local planning authority considered that such noise would detract considerably from the amenities of the environment associated with residential development of this land'. The site fell within the 60+ NNI contour and the planning authority submitted that although sound-proofing would reduce noise considerably the occupants would have to live in 'virtually a sealed box without opening windows', and that soundproofing did not reduce the level of noise in the garden.

The inspector concluded that the only material question in the case was whether houses should be erected in such a noisy area. He found the noise level at the site to be extremely high but stated that, since houses in the area were freely bought and sold, 'it would seem to be an incorrect application of planning principles to refuse consent on the grounds that this was an area in which, because of noise, it is undesirable to live'.[47] He recommended that the appeal should be allowed subject to soundproofing conditions. The Minister agreed that noise was the central issue, the essential question being 'whether the proposed dwellings and their gardens would afford sufficient residential amenity'. He decided that 'people living on the site would be exposed to very serious disturbance, especially out of doors. In the absence of an overriding need for the provision of housing in this particular situation, he is not satisfied that it would be right to give permission for the erection of dwellings which would lack amenity in this important respect' and dismissed the appeal.[48]

Noise generation from activities for which planning permission was sought has also been very important in several inquiries. In an appeal against a condition attached to the planning permission to land and park a helicopter which imposed a time limit to the consent, the Secretary of State concluded that the planning authority were right to employ the condition. He felt that although the noise levels recorded during test flights were useful, there was no substitute for a trial period of operation to establish how the proposal would affect the noise climate of the locality.[49]

On a larger scale there have been two recent public inquiries into expansion at Luton airport, originally a small municipal airstrip and now an extremely important operating base for several charter companies. The end of the runway is within two miles of the centre of Luton, and a large number of people are affected by the noise generated. The reports of the inquiries contain a wealth of technical detail on the effects of noise and its measurement. In both cases the inspector sat with assessors expert in noise problems.

The first inquiry, in 1970, was into the provision of additional hard standing for planes, additional car parking and other works. The inspector did not believe that refusal of planning permission would curtail aircraft movements over the next two years and hence reduce either the daytime or night noise exposures. While recognising the widespread concern about noise, therefore, he recommended that planning permission be granted in the belief that the third London airport would ease the problem in the near future.[50] The Minister agreed, although he wished 'to record clearly that any further proposals for development of the airport will be subjected to a rigorous scrutiny'.[51]

Despite the choice of Foulness and the confidence that the previous planning permission would have little effect on aircraft movements, the number of passengers using Luton almost doubled in the years before the second inquiry, in 1972. This related to further extensions of a similar nature to those already permitted, strengthening the runway and increasing the capacity of the terminal buildings. The central issue was again whether or not the development would, of itself, increase the degree of noise nuisance. The inspector had to consider the type and mix of movements, including those of wide-bodied aircraft. He concluded that 'the development would add to, rather than reduce, the injurious impact which flights to and from the airport had on amenities, 'and that activities at Luton should be kept within bounds. He therefore recommended that planning permission be refused.[52]

The Secretary of State did subject the proposal to rigorous scrutiny and was obviously impressed by the strength of public opposition to the proposals. He agreed that 'the proposed development would be directly associated with a rapid and progressive build-up of activity at Luton Airport which would inevitably be accompanied by a substantial increase in aircraft noise', and refused planning permission.[53] It is hard to understand why this view was not taken on the earlier application, and it can only be concluded that current government airport policy determined the issue in both cases. It would be interesting to know how the application would have been treated after the cancellation of Foulness.

Finally, in this coverage of unpublished inquiries, it is instructive to look at an application to tip solid waste which would cause damage to amenity. A lengthy inquiry into the working of china clay and the disposal of the waste sand on the edge of Dartmoor resulted from a planning application to extend extraction being called in. A great deal

of evidence about tipping methods, which have changed since Aber-
fan from the methods which created the familiar conical white land-
marks, landscaping and visual intrusion was heard at the inquiry, the
central issue of which was land pollution from the disposal of the
waste.

The inspector felt that it would be wrong to restrict the continued
growth of the china clay industry by planning measures, stating that
his main concern would be to minimise its impact on the environment. It was accepted that the working out and back-filling of tips was
not generally possible and that transport of waste sand to distant mar-
kets was uneconomic. He recommended that permission be granted
for most of the proposals, but because waste heaps would look out of
place in certain locations in the beautiful countryside on the edge of
the national park he found that permission to tip waste at these
particular sites should be refused.[54]

The Secretary of State broadly agreed with this recommendation
and gave permission for about twenty years' tipping space, subject to
numerous conditions relating to design, height and precise siting of
heaps, landscaping, the erection of plant and its removal after completion of working.[55] This and the previous decisions indicate the
fairly enlightened way in which pollution and its control have been
approached in central government development control decisions.
The role of the local planning authority in some of these examples has
been inferred, but it is now necessary to look in slightly more detail at
the attitude of planning authorities to pollution problems in the
administration of development control.

EXAMPLES OF DEVELOPMENT CONTROL PROBLEMS

Carrington

There has been petrochemical-related development at Carrington,
situated on the Mersey south-west of Manchester, since the war and
the site has been expanded and redeveloped to become a large complex producing a variety of chemicals derived from naphtha. The
nearest residential areas are more than a mile away, and the works
are located close to other large industrial land users. A planning
application was made to Cheshire County Council in 1958 for permission to build a 300 ft chimney and boiler house to serve the
extensions envisaged (routine plant building was covered by existing

permissions). This was called in and an inquiry into both the application and the refusal by Bucklow Rural District Council to approve the chimney under the Clean Air Act was held in November 1958. The county council, after taking advice from the Medical Officer of Health and the county analyst, argued that planning permission should be refused on air pollution grounds. They held that the use of planning powers to protect the atmospheric environment was quite analogous to refusing planning permission for development creating water pollution because of inadequate sewage treatment facilities and that they were bound to consider all the effects of the development. The inspector and the Minister disagreed and, after considering but rejecting the use of planning conditions relating to the sulphur content of fuel, granted permission provided that the chimney was increased in height to 375 ft.

During the next ten years a number of planning applications for residential development close to the works were rejected, partly on the grounds that they would be adversely affected by them. As the works grew, further expansion became necessary and in May 1967 Shell Chemicals (UK) Ltd submitted an application to construct a new boiler house and a triple-flue 400 ft chimney to provide additional capacity. The letter accompanying the planning application pointed out that the chimney would not discharge any process gases, only the products of combustion, and would emit above inversion level. Cheshire County Council carried out consultations with all the local authorities concerned, with the local hospital board, with various national bodies and took expert opinion. At this time the company were experiencing real problems commissioning a new chemical process and were having to flare volumes of waste gas, generating noise and smoke and creating nocturnal visual intrusion. As a result the public became alarmed and indignant. The local press also grew very concerned and the local authorities most closely affected reacted to local feeling by writing to the Minister of Housing and Local Government, who called in the application. Cheshire County Council, aware that the proposed development was unrelated to the source of justified complaints, nevertheless decided that they would wish to see a number of conditions relating to the sulphur content of fuel attached to any planning consent.[56]

The inquiry, held in spring 1968, was concerned only with air pollution issues, and the planning inspector sat with a technical assessor from the Central Electricity Generating Board. A great deal of detailed evidence about emissions of sulphur dioxide and about the effects of the various ground level concentrations of gas likely to arise was presented. Shell called an impressive array of expert witnesses marshalled by a queen's counsel and a junior barrister. Cheshire, on the other hand, merely read a prepared statement (perhaps indicating that they might have been satisfied with a very tall chimney as the sole control device) and left the other local authorities affected to contest the issue with counsel and witnesses. The District Alkali Inspector was called as a neutral witness to describe how control under the Alkali Act was administered. Mentioning the need to render sulphur dioxide harmless, he explained that the chimney height of 400 ft had been suggested by the inspectorate and indicated that he was content with the proposals.

The inspector felt that the main issue was the emission of sulphur dioxide from the the proposed chimney and dismissed pollution from chemical processes as immaterial (despite the fact that further process expansion was dependent upon construction of the boiler house and chimney). He noted the local planning authority's concern about total emissions, but believed that the ground level concentration of sulphur dioxide was the most important factor. The increase in the level of this pollutant as a result of the development, he was advised, would be very small. Despite admitting the need to reduce sulphur dioxide emissions as a whole, he felt that the imposition of conditions relating to the sulphur content of fuel would be unfair, unpractical and administratively difficult, giving rise to conflict with the existing control by the Alkali Inspectorate. He therefore recommended that planning permission should be granted unconditionally.[57] The Minister agreed, feeling that the proposed planning conditions would give rise to practical and administrative difficulties (namely that control under the Alkali, etc, Works Regulation Act, 1906, should not be duplicated by planning conditions) and he granted permission without conditions.[58]

There can be no doubt that Shell handled this application with very considerable skill. The company engaged the support of eminent experts in the air pollution field and gained the agreement of the Alkali Inspectorate to the proposals in advance. Shell also carried out detailed negotiations with the planning authority (who had learned from the previous inquiry that co-operation was probably the most effective method of achieving planning objectives in a case of this type), and were completely vindicated at the inquiry. The fact that the technical assessor was a Central Electricity Generating Board man must have helped considerably because that body's 'hot and high' policy of pollutant dispersal was now being followed by Shell. What is more, Shell's evidence relating to likely increases in sulphur dioxide concentrations has been more than justified by subsequent minimal recordings. Continuing complaints about process pollution do, however, arise but it is hard to see how the planning authority could have improved this situation. Planning permission was won in the face of great local hostility and Shell or the planning authority might, with hindsight, have appreciated the need to inform local residents and authorities of the proposals and to explain them, once the application had been called in.

Copeley Hill
Copeley Hill was a residential road of mature houses, but dwellings on one side of it have now been demolished to allow construction of the junction of the Aston Expressway and the M6 at Gravelly Hill, Birmingham. The local planning authority, Birmingham Corporation, were asked to grant permission for the development of sixteen maisonettes on a 1·1 acre site previously occupied by a single house and garden, in August 1967. The planning authority consulted the Ministry of Transport, because of the proximity of the site to the motorway junction (only 60 ft at the nearest point), observing that the site formed part of a larger area bounded by the proposed motorway junction and a railway and that the whole area should be redeveloped in a comprehensive manner. After considerable delay they were advised, in January 1968, that the Ministry did not wish to restrict grant of permission. (In a letter accompanying the official notice the Ministry said that if permission were given they did not, however, wish drivers on the interchange to be distracted.) Planning permission was nevertheless refused in February 1968 on the grounds that 'redevelopment of this individual site at this time would be premature and may prejudice the future comprehensive development and layout of the area as a whole'.

In 1971 the house which formed the subject of the 1967 application became dilapidated, and the Chief Public Health Inspector served a notice requiring the house to be secured or demolished. In

February 1972 a property company submitted a proposal for the redevelopment of this site together with the land occupied by six adjoining houses, in two phases. The first phase was to consist of the original site together with another derelict house site and the second was to consist of land occupied by three existing houses, one of which was currently derelict, and two cleared sites. Phase 1 would consist of twenty-four flats, twenty-four garages and twelve parking spaces. This application took no account of the encroachment of the motor-way link roads and a revised layout was requested of the applicants. The planning authority noted that Copeley Hill itself ran in a dip but that the proposed development site was on a similar level to the motorway, which is elevated at this point. They felt that two-storey development might be better than three-storey on noise grounds, that the blocks needed to be as far from the motorway as possible, and that the living rooms ought to be protected from noise. The Ministry of Transport were consulted again.

The applicants submitted a revised plan in late May in which the whole layout was altered, garages being placed in front of the flats as partial screens. The blocks (still three-storey) were mostly end-on to the motorway to protect the living rooms. The Ministry of Transport again had no comment, provided an access strip was provided adjacent to the interchange embankment. Outline planning permission was therefore granted in June 1972 for the erection of sixty one-bedroom and two-bedroom flats, in three-storey blocks, and sixty garages. Phase 2 would be implemented as and when control of neighbouring properties was obtained. Two of the conditions attached were that no room should be less than 100 ft from the motorway and that windows in two elevations should be double-glazed and unopenable. The applicants were asked to discuss the question of motorway noise with the Medical Officer of Health, who was carrying out a survey on noise levels.

The Chief Public Health Inspector was informed of the decision and wrote to the planning department in July 1972, stating that he was surprised that the application had not been referred to his department for comment. In his view the close proximity of the site to the Gravelly Hill interchange made it unsuitable for housing purposes because of noise. If development did proceed, care would be needed in design, orientation and sound insulation. The developers were invited to discuss the matter with the Chief Public Health Inspector before finalising plans. The developers, on receiving the planning permission, wrote that the unopenable window was an unfair condition since, provided it was double-glazed, it was at the occupant's discretion to open or close it. The planning authority agreed that 'no action would be taken to secure compliance with the condition'. In 1973 another house became derelict and a notice was served requiring its demolition.[59]

The site of this proposed flat development is located in a very noisy environment, levels probably being in excess of 70 dB(A) on the L_{10} (eighteen-hour) scale. The conditions relating to double glazing are not particularly effective, since the air space between the glazing was not specified and normal integral units are not the most effective sound insulators. In any event, the external environment of the flats remains extremely noisome. The lack of consultation on noise matters in the early stages of dealing with this development is notable, as is the concern about living rooms and not bedrooms. It appears that this was a decision which would probably not have been made a year later, when investigations by the council into noise problems were more advanced. Now the development would either be refused or the blocks would be moved farther back. (Ideally the land might have been rezoned for commercial use, but that would have caused its own pollution damage to neighbouring areas.) There would also have been scope, had the application been submitted later, for better design against noise. No mention was made of air pollution from motor vehicles throughout, although Birmingham Public Health Department were among the first to demonstrate real interest in, and concern about, this problem.

It must be added that the planning permission had not been implemented at the time of writing (1975).

New Street station
An informal meeting was held in November 1962 between the British Railways Board (London Midland Region) and senior officers and elected representatives of Birmingham Corporation to discuss the redevelopment of New Street station, the city's main rail node. Shortly afterwards a planning application for outline permission to reconstruct the railway station, to close a road and to build shops, offices and a cinema was submitted. The applicants were not anxious to attract publicity to the application until they had gained the

approval of the Ministry of Transport. Accordingly, since a cinema proposal had to be advertised, they submitted a second application deleting this facility and merely applying for railway-related development. The city had approved this course, agreeing to consider commercial development informally.

The planning authority consulted the City Architect, the Chief Constable and the Chief Public Health Inspector. The City Engineer and Surveyor, who was responsible for planning, was anxious to avoid an extremely large, low building in the city centre, seeing the need to preserve the 'city scale'. The Chief Public Health Inspector was very concerned about flue gas discharge and noise from ventilation shafts and wished to be consulted when detailed proposals were received. He was conscious of the dust and noise produced by railway operations (partly because his department's offices overlooked the station) and suggested that decking be extended to cover the whole of the station site to control pollution.

The various comments were reported to the Public Works Committee by the City Engineer and Surveyor, who also mentioned that the developers foresaw difficulties in building a hotel or offices. As a consequence it was suggested that the House Building Committee be requested to give consideration to the erection of a residential tower block in collaboration with the developers. Planning permission for the redevelopment of the station only was given in May 1973 and approval in principle for development above the station was also given. An outline application for a full-scale commercial development was then submitted by the Railways Board and specialist developers. It was publicised and there were no objections. In June the developers decided that a hotel would be appropriate to the site, but they declared that they were opposed to point blocks of offices on the grounds of inadequate density of development.

It was suggested within the corporation that flats would be both architecturally and socially valuable on the site. It was felt there should be little problem from fumes, with the demise of steam locomotives, and that noise could be countered by double glazing. The developers continued to oppose the use of point blocks and argued against covering the whole of the tracks because of the difficulty of ventilating diesel fumes. They were also doubtful about the commercial viability of providing residential accommodation.

The corporation pressed ahead and planning approval for a

twenty-one storey block of one- and two-bedroom double-glazed flats was granted in July 1964, despite some initial doubts expressed by the architect's department. Noise was often mentioned in discussions. With a change of developers, the proposals for shops, a hotel and a ballroom were altered marginally. The corporation continued to look favourably on these proposals, despite the developers' opposition to covering the whole site. Planning permission for the redevelopment was granted in July 1964, without complete decking, but in 1968 the developers decided to construct offices rather than a hotel. The Public Works Committee agreed to grant planning permission in September 1970, after much discussion.

The Chief Public Health Inspector became involved in Building Regulations discussions and insisted that flues on the flats, the offices and the main station be extended to disperse air pollutants more effectively.[60] The finished redevelopment is known as the Birmingham Shopping Centre and consists of shops, offices, an entertainment complex and a multi-storey car park. The flats were not constructed over the railway tracks, but to one side of the site, and were easily let. Some complaints about noise have been subsequently received from residents by the Chief Public Health Inspector,[12] but these cannot be said to have been numerous. The more serious pollution problems, which have now been solved, arose, ironically, from the burning of oil in the station boiler installations.

It seems that the original advice regarding noise and fumes tendered by the Chief Public Health Inspector was retained in mind throughout the development. The Health Department were again consulted subsequently but it is debatable how they viewed the construction of dwellings, albeit for childless households, so close to a source of noise. (It should be stated that air and noise pollution from railways has decreased considerably over the years.) The flats appear to have been an aesthetic design consideration—a vertical feature in the scheme—and the pressure for redevelopment of this crucial site appears to have outweighed pollution considerations. It was felt that the design, location and method of construction would safeguard the possibility of pollution damage arising. The chairman of the Public Works Committee is known to have been favourably inclined to the principle of extensive redevelopment of this prestige site and the chief officer was similarly concerned throughout. In the last analysis it appears that both the absence of decking and the construction of flats were accepted because they were expedient at the time. The flats could certainly have been better protected from noise.

The reputation of Birmingham in both noise and air pollution control, incidentally, is excellent. The Health Department of the corporation have sponsored research and taken action on a wide range of pollution problems, and have instituted the formation of scientific advisory and industrial liaison committees on environmental pollution.[61] It is perhaps the more surprising that the Copeley Hill and New Street redevelopments were permitted in a form which allowed pollution effects to be created. As in the more serious case of Copeley Hill, it is quite possible that more concern for pollution control would have been displayed had events at New Street station taken place a few years later.

Elton

Elton is a small village just east of the Shell refinery at Stanlow, to the south of the Mersey. Apart from Shell installations there are various other companies operating within the complex. Oil refining was commenced by Shell in 1923 and their activities were much enlarged during the war. The refinery has grown considerably since. A power station was later constructed just to the north of the village at Ince, to serve an atomic fuel processing plant in the locality. A fertiliser plant was constructed to the north-east of the village in the 1960s, following an inquiry at which the protection of the Green Belt was an issue and pollution was discussed. The applicants were able to produce expert evidence to dispel fears about pollution, just as the Central Electricity Generating Board did at an inquiry into a second power station in the early 1970s. These large-scale industrial developments nevertheless do give rise to some pollution.

Cheshire County Council had anticipated that the population of the village of Elton might be expanded from about 300 to 1,750 in their 1961 West Cheshire Green Belt submission. In 1965 a development company acquired a considerable amount of land at Elton and informally submitted a master plan for a village of 5,000–6,000 people. In October 1966 it was agreed with the developers and the local authority (Chester Rural District Council) officers that the ultimate population figure should be about 2,500. Consultations were held with the Mersey and Weaver River Authority and with the Ministry of Agriculture, who both agreed to the proposals. An outline application for residential and shopping development was submitted and advertised as a departure from the approved County Development Plan. The development was within 400 yards of the refinery and the County Planning Department had reservations about residential expansion so close to the industrial complex. The District Council, however, were content to recoup expenditure from additional ratepayers on the sewerage and sewage dispersal facilities constructed in the area, and further consultations were carried out, the Minister being sent the application under the departure procedure. No objections were raised and the Minister informed Cheshire that they should themselves determine the decision. Outline planning permission was granted in July 1967, subject to detailed approval of landscape treatment and other matters.

Six months later, discussions relating to expansion of the approved population took place, and it was agreed after deliberation about sewage disposal facilities, that a population of 4,500 might be acceptable. An application was submitted, and approval granted in February 1969, relating to 1,200 dwelling units on about 100 acres of land, some rather closer to the refinery than the original site. Extensive fringe planting was to be carried out and road access altered. Detailed plans for various phases of the development have subsequently been submitted and approved, although some permissions have been refused on design grounds. House construction commenced in July 1969 and the first residents began to move in shortly afterwards. They complained about pollution, and particularly about odours, from the industrial complex.

Other landowners in the area also submitted applications for residential development. One relating to land between the main development and the trunk road to the south was submitted in October 1970, after three previous applications had been refused. The letter accompanying the application stated: 'the land around the holding is mostly developed for industrial or residential use. The holding is not large enough to be worked so as to provide a living and the factory effluence in the air does not encourage good grass to grow. In consequence, we feel that residential development is the only logical use to which this land can be put'. The water authority were consulted, and raised no objection, but the Public Health Inspector and the Alkali Inspector were not asked for their views. Cheshire County Council refused the application in December on

Green Belt grounds.

The landowner appealed and an inquiry was held. The inspector visited the site and, while mentioning the refinery in his report, was much more concerned with traffic noise from the trunk road, which he considered was not sufficiently bad to preclude development. He felt 'that housing development should be kept well away from the large industrial complex' but decided that 'the appeal site was just sufficiently far away so as not to be unduly affected by it'. He recommended that permission be granted subject to the provision of a 150 ft planted strip between the road and the houses. The Minister accepted this conclusion and gave permission in June 1972.

The original developers then applied for planning permission on land much closer to the refinery. The County Planning Department were becoming very worried about pollution, especially since numbers of complaints were increasing as more houses were occupied. A letter from Cheshire to the local authority stated that 'in view of the pollution and environmental problems existing in this district, I consider it extremely important to retain the buffer of open land between the new housing and the refinery and trunk road'. The application was rejected, however, on Green Belt grounds. Further applications relating to land in the area were made and the planning authority continued to refuse permission, the stated grounds never relating to pollution, because the authority were not confident that such a reason was valid.

The planning authority consulted Shell in September. In October Shell wrote a letter objecting to development close to the works on general planning grounds and stating that 'large areas of land to the west of the refinery have attendant noise and air-borne effluent'. They did not lay great emphasis on this point, but implied that the original planning decision had been questionable and then proceeded to buy some of the land in dispute. Discussion arose about the desirable width of marginal buffer land between the refinery and housing.

The Alkali Inspectorate had been very concerned about developments, partly as a consequence of the complaints they were receiving, and stated their opposition to housing too close to the refinery. A note expressing disapproval of the proximity of housing and the consequent possibility of further dwellings on other faces of the refinery was drafted. Shell, who had become even more aware of the problem because of growing numbers of complaints about odours, enlisted the support of the Department of Trade and Industry in endeavouring to prevent further development. The various bodies concerned have now grouped together to resist additional housing which would be affected by pollution.[62]

The Alkali Inspectorate has asked to be consulted on all developments within one kilometre of the refinery, this being a fairly standard distance for large-scale industry. It is now clear that Shell were perhaps unfortunate in not objecting to the village expansion when it was originally advertised, although the company was never approached about the application. It is also clear that the county's concern about pollution was overridden by local politics concerning sewerage and sewage disposal expenditure. Had they taken the advice of the Public Health Inspector or the Alkali Inspector in the first place, events might have turned out differently. Similarly, in view of the growing number of complaints about the refinery from people living in Elton (including some from the developer), pollution should have been an important issue at the inquiry into the village extension (especially since the applicant implied the site was not clean enough for cattle). Only when that decision had been made did the various bodies concerned become fully aware of the undesirable situation which had arisen and begin to mount serious opposition to further encroachment. (The new residents were particularly vocal because they had been seeking a house in a rural area.) This appears to be another example of a development control issue which would have been determined differently if it had arisen a few years later. Indeed, it seems very likely that pollution would now be offered as a valid planning reason for refusal of planning permission rather than Green Belt objections. A full discussion of the issues with all parties would probably then have ensued and needless pollution damage could have been avoided.

The grant of planning permission for residential development at Elton should be compared with the refusals of similar development at Carrington. It is clearly right that the use of planning powers should be employed to restrain potentially sensitive receptors from locating close to pollution sources. However, this type of action offends against the 'polluter pays' principle (Chapter 4), since owners of land are deprived of benefit by pollution originating elsewhere and receive no compensation. It is, unfortunately, difficult to see how a planning authority can correct this inequity.

There can be no doubt that pollution is considered in development control decisions taken by local planning authorities and in inquiries into these or 'called in' decisions. It is equally clear that pollution is currently a much more important factor in development than it was ten years ago, since pollution control is now both more likely to be considered and to have more weight attached to it in making a decision. Pollution grounds can now stand on their own as the reason for refusing planning permission for development if the situation is sufficiently bad.

Pollution still appears to be considered in a very generalised manner in development control, with little regard being paid to the costs of control or to detailed planning means of control. The various techniques available appear not to be widely recognised in development control practice and there are seldom operational criteria available against which to judge a pollution problem. There is certainly no evidence that the optimal level of control is taken into account in making decisions or that standards are generally striven for. The way that pollution is weighed against other planning factors in taking decisions is rarely explained clearly (even simple rankings are seldom used), and in some cases this process does not seem to be carried out, although such balancing can give rise to pollution control decisions which probably approach the optimum.

Clearly, conditions relating to pollution control are sometimes attached to planning permissions by planning authorities. Many of these may exceed the legal powers of the authorities and developers may either adhere to them or ignore them, in which case the authorities may decide not to attempt to enforce them. There appear to be a substantial number of successful bluffs, however, with developers being content to fulfil pollution control conditions which may not be legally defensible. In general, in the case of planning controls upon emissions, only noise and solid waste conditions appear to be appropriate and conditions relating to air or water pollution either impinge on other areas of responsibility or are unenforceable (as in the case of some of the conditions quoted in this chapter). After taking appropriate advice, the issue is always whether to allow the development or not. This is the local planning authority's burden and the basis of their pollution control power.

Once permission has been granted, the service of a discontinuance order to stop the polluter or the imposition of conditions (by means of a modification order) to the same end can be implemented only on payment of compensation, which is often considerable. Such measures are seldom employed, therefore. The enforcement of conditions originally attached to the permission can also be difficult, so it appears that development control decisions allowing development made at one point in time are often insensitive to unforeseen circumstances, such as changing technology or lack of compliance with planning conditions, which may cause pollution to become a more serious problem. An additional problem may arise where planning permission is granted following a public inquiry. It is not possible to include conditions which demand the fulfilment of all the various statements made on behalf of the applicant and, for a number of reasons, the level of pollution generated by the development once constructed may differ considerably from that predicted at the inquiry.

REFERENCES

1   Cheshire County Council (1974) *Planning standards: noise* CCC, Chester.
2   Committee on the Problem of Noise (Wilson Committee) (1963) *Final report* Cmnd. 2056, HMSO London.
3   Surrey County Council (1970) *London Gatwick airport: an environmental study* SCC, Kingston.
4   Manchester County Borough (1971) *Manchester airport—noise development control policy* MCB, Manchester.
5   Cheshire County Council (1972) *Interim development control policy for the area around Manchester airport* CCC, Chester.
6   Cheshire County Council (1973) *Manchester airport noise: development control policy* CCC, Chester.
7   Greater London Council (1970) *Greater London development plan inquiry Proof E12/1: transport* GLC, London.
8   Greater London Council (1966) *Traffic noise* GLC, London.
9   Telford Development Corporation (1971) *Traffic noise* Planning policy bulletin 4, TDC, Telford.
10   Manchester County Borough (1972) *Road traffic noise* MCB, Manchester.
11   Ward, E. W. (1971) Air pollution and planning *Proc. Symp. on Environmental Pollution* North West Association of Public Health Inspectors, Wigan.
12   Ward, E. W. (1971) Air pollution and town planning *Proc. Second Int. Clean Air Congress* Washington.
13   G.F.P. (1972) Pollution, people and planning *JRTPI, 58* 485.
14   McLoughlin, J. B., and Webster, J. N. (1971) *Development control in Britain* Centre for Environmental Studies, London.

15 Pollution Research Unit (1970) *Results of interviews of chief planning officers* University of Manchester, Manchester.

16 Pollution Research Unit (1971) *Results of questionnaire to river authorities in England and Wales* University of Manchester, Manchester.

17 Pollution Research Unit (1971) *Results of questionnaire to sea fisheries committees* University of Manchester, Manchester.

18 Peak Park Planning Board (1972) Personal communication.

19 Extracted from decisions by the Peak Park Planning Board and other planning authorities.

20 Ministry of Town and Country Planning (1948) *Selected planning appeals. Bulletin III* HMSO, London.

21 Ministry of Town and Country Planning (1948) *Selected planning appeals. Bulletin V* HMSO, London.

22 Ministry of Town and Country Planning (1948) *Selected planning appeals. Bulletin VI* HMSO, London.

23 Ministry of Town and Country Planning (1948) *Selected planning appeals. Bulletin IX* HMSO, London.

24 Ministry of Housing and Local Government (1957) *Selected planning appeals. Bulletin XII* HMSO, London.

25 Heap, D.(—) Selected planning appeals *Encyclopaedia of planning law and practice 3* Sweet & Maxwell, London.

26 Ministry of Housing and Local Government (1969) Use of clay pit for tipping of industrial waste *JPL (1969)* 220–31.

27 Ministry of Housing and Local Government (1970) Extension of established non-conforming industrial use *JPL (1970)* 549–50.

28 Department of the Environment (1971) Planning permission for oil refinery: regulation of noise and smells *JPL (1971)* 475–8.

29 Department of the Environment (1972) Erection of dwelling house: main sewage disposal works inadequate *JPL (1973)* 170–1.

30 Department of the Environment (1974) Residential development: evidence of effect on existing sewage works: evaluation by Department *JPL (1974)* 681–2.

31 Department of the Environment (1974) Measurement of noise and its effects *JPL (1974)* 731–2.

32 Gregory, R. (1971) *The price of amenity* Macmillan, London.

33 Bracey, H. E. (1963) *Industry and the countryside* Faber & Faber, London.

34 Ministry of Housing and Local Government (1970) *Report of inquiry into Portsmouth (River Itchen) draft water order* MHLG, London.

35 Department of the Environment (1973) *Decision letter on appeal by Plumpton Racecourse Ltd* APP/1985/A/63314, DoE, London.

36 Department of the Environment (1971) *Decision letter on appeal by Connolly Construction Co. Ltd* APP/1923/A/49986, DoE, London.

37 Department of the Environment (1971) *Report of inquiry into appeal by St Michael's Convent and W. J. Hull* APP/2303/A/53069 DoE, London.

38   Department of the Environment (1972) *Decision letter on appeal by St Michael's Convent and W. J. Hull* APP/2303/A/53069 DoE, London.

39   Department of the Environment (1971) *Report of inquiry into appeal by Tonrin Property Co. Ltd* APP/2050/A53511 DoE, London.

40   Department of the Environment (1972) *Decision letter on appeal by Tonrin Property Co. Ltd* APP/2050/A/53511 DoE, London.

41   Department of the Environment (1972) *Report of inquiry into appeal by Shirestead Ltd and Mr and Mrs R. J. Osborn* APP/1097/A/58996 DoE, London.

42   Department of the Environment (1972) *Decision letter on appeal by Shirestead Ltd* APP/1097/A/58996 DoE, London.

43   Ministry of Housing and Local Government (1970) *Report of inquiry into application to build sewage treatment works at Howdon* MHLG, London.

44   Department of the Environment (1971) *Decision letter on sewage treatment works at Howdon, Tynemouth* DoE, London.

45   Department of the Environment (1972) *Report of inquiry into appeal by Capt. J. H. Rosier and Miss H. L. N. Littlewood* APP/2044/A/59222, DoE, London.

46   Department of the Environment (1972) *Decision letter on appeal by Capt. J. H. Rosier and Miss H. L. N. Littlewood* APP/2044/A/59222, DoE, London.

47   Ministry of Housing and Local Government (1969) *Report of inquiry into appeal by Ruiprops Ltd* APP/4419/A/34570, MHLG, London.

48   Ministry of Housing and Local Government (1970) *Decision letter on appeal by Ruiprops Ltd* APP/4419/A/34570, MHLG, London.

49   Department of the Environment (1972) *Decision letter on appeal by Abbott Bros (Southall) Ltd* APP/4418/A/55594, DoE, London.

50   Ministry of Housing and Local Government (1970) *Report of inquiry into application for planning permission: Luton airport* MHLG, London.

51   Ministry of Housing and Local Government (1970) *Decision letter: application for planning permission: Luton airport* MHLG, London.

52   Department of the Environment (1972) *Report of inquiry into developments at Luton airport* DoE, London.

53   Department of the Environment (1973) *Decision letter: Luton airport—proposed development* DoE, London.

54   Department of the Environment (1971) *Report of inquiry: china clay working and waste disposal at Lee Moor* DoE, London.

55   Department of the Environment (1972) *Decision letter: china clay working and waste disposal at Lee Moor* DoE, London.

56   Cheshire County Council (—) *Carrington files* Planning Department, CCC, Wilmslow.

57   Ministry of Housing and Local Government (1968) *Report of inquiry into application by Shell Chemicals (UK) Ltd, Carrington* MHLG, London.

58 Ministry of Housing and Local Government (1968) *Decision letter: proposed chimney and associated plant at Carrington* MHLG, London.
59 Birmingham County Borough (—) *Copeley Hill files* Planning Department, BCB, Birmingham.
60 Birmingham County Borough (—) *New Street Station files* Planning Department, BCB, Birmingham.
61 Birmingham County Borough (1973) *Birmingham: the city that cares* Public Health Department, BCB, Birmingham.
62 Cheshire County Council (—) *Elton files* Planning Department, CCC, Chester.

188

Local planning authorities have not always fulfilled their pollution control role in the past. Their powers of control are now considerable, and their effectiveness in fulfilling this function generally appears to be increasing. There is, however, room for improvement.

CHAPTER 11

Conclusions and recommendations

This final chapter is concerned with drawing together the material presented earlier in order to resolve the four fundamental questions raised in Chapter 1. It will be recalled that the examination of twelve theoretical and practical issues was a prerequisite to answering the questions and these are therefore considered first. The conclusions which emerge about the nature of the planning control of pollution suggest that a number of deficiencies are currently reducing the potential contribution of planning. Several recommendations are accordingly made to assist in overcoming these and to improve the effectiveness of planning control.

CONCLUSIONS ON THE TWELVE ISSUES

1 *The potential of planning to bridge gaps in present methods of controlling pollution* was dealt with in Chapter 2 and, to some extent, in Chapter 4. The planning authority can exert control at most stages in the pollution process, but their most powerful contribution is potentially at the first, in determining the nature and location of new development and redevelopment. The local planning authority, because of their control over land use, exercise an important influence on the spatial origin of wastes and consequently upon pollution levels and their distribution. The authority are undoubtedly the pre-eminent controlling body at this stage in the pollution process, whether they recognise this position or not. Planning is also able to exercise control at later stages in the pollution process, for example by attaching conditions to planning permission. The number of areas where the powers held by planning authorities conflict with the powers of other agencies is small and disagreement is likely to arise only over the way in which planning powers are exercised, not over whether or not they are exercised. Planning, therefore, possesses a very real potential to bridge gaps in other methods of controlling pollution.

2 *The powers of town planning to control pollution* were discussed in Chapter 3. It is clear that the very considerable powers of pollution control which are vested in planning authorities are increasing both in

scope and in recognition. While the responsibilities urged upon local planning authorities are very considerable, there is room for further development. Nevertheless, if planning authorities were to discharge all the powers and responsibilities reviewed in Chapter 3, there would be little need for further instruments to strengthen the powers of planning. However, a number of recommendations arise from a consideration of the more practical issues and these are made later.

3   *The overall potential effectiveness of planning as a method of pollution control* was examined, together with other issues, in Chapter 4 and is obviously dependent on the degree to which planning powers and techniques are used to control pollution. There is no question that planning could be extremely effective, especially at the plan-making stage, where potentially polluting and sensitive land uses can be separated. At the development control stage the refusal of planning permission could prevent pollution damage by limiting development of either pollution sources or receptors. The control of pollution through the use of planning conditions has not always been effective, partly because of the problem of duplicating the powers of other pollution control authorities and partly because there have been some enforcement difficulties. Planning would, therefore, become a more effective method of control if the power to grant or refuse permission was coupled with the enforceable use of conditions relating to pollution.

4   *The selection of appropriate objectives and criteria for pollution control by land use planning* has been discussed in a number of chapters, and particularly in Chapter 4. Among other difficulties in using planning to achieve the optimum level of pollution control is the fact that planning is not a particularly sensitive method of controlling pollution. Unlike the systems of control which it complements, planning does not generally have a continuing interest in, or day-to-day control over, the pollution from a particular activity. Once the planning decision has been made, it can be altered only on payment of compensation. However, the local planning authority could ensure that standards relating to air, land, water or noise pollution were met both by design at the plan-making stage and by granting or refusing planning permission for, or imposing conditions on, new developments at the development control stage. Standards may be fixed either nationally or locally, but to be most effective pollution standards enforceable by planning measures need to be agreed locally

between the pollution control authorities and the planning authority. Whether standards are employed or not, pollution control objectives need to be phrased precisely so that the extent to which they are achieved by planning methods can be evaluated, preferably quantitatively.

5 *The reconciliation of conflicting considerations* has been raised in several of the planning practice chapters and in Chapter 4. The large number of objectives (including those directed to controlling pollution) which must be considered (either implicitly or explicitly) in the planning process implies that the reconciliation of all the various objectives will inevitably involve compromise in arriving at the final land use pattern or in deciding to grant permission for a particular development. For example, the inevitable conflict between the objectives of dispersing air pollutants and of maintaining visual amenity by limiting the height of chimneys has to be resolved. Planning objectives are generally stated in terms which do not take account of the contingent or conflicting objectives, and the weighting of pollution and other objectives (whether explicit or not) is thus an essential part of the planning process. The incorporation of pollution control into the planning process in any meaningful way, therefore, requires that pollution control objectives be defined, that they be weighted against other objectives and that planning solutions be based upon them. This again argues that it is essential for objectives to be carefully phrased to enable the process to be carried out meaningfully.

6 *The range of potential techniques for pollution control available to planners* was discussed in Chapter 5. While it could not be claimed that the review presented there was fully comprehensive, it is apparent that despite the limited treatment of pollution in planning textbooks and, with some exceptions, in planning journals a very large number of techniques do exist to control air, land, water and noise pollution. Although many of these techniques can be utilised only at the plan-making stage, others can be employed by planners responsible for development control. Some of these techniques conflict with each other, but many are quite compatible. The local planning authority are, potentially at least, very well armed in any endeavour to control pollution.*

---

*Before examining the remaining issues raised in Chapter 1 it is appropriate to mention one or two examples of pollution control in planning practice

7   It is probably fair to say that many *planning authorities* have
come to *accept that they have a distinctive role in the control of pollution* but that this acceptance is still by no means universal. Certainly
planners have taken pollution into account in making certain decisions, as the review of development control practice in Chapter 10
indicates. However, the examinations of regional, sub-regional and
new town studies in Chapters 6 and 7 lead to generally disappointing
findings because of the lack of appreciation of the distinctive role of
these plans in the control of pollution. The review of structure plans
in Chapter 8, on the other hand, suggests that recognition of this
distinctive role and of the more detailed roles of planning in the
control of pollution is growing.

Greater recognition of these roles within the planning profession as
a whole is required if changes of attitude are to be consolidated. Two
recent addresses to the Royal Town Planning Institute have set a
useful example because, in each, the control of pollution was seen as
a crucial issue. In the first (a presidential address) it was stated that
there was an urgent need to measure the extent of pollution and to
agree standards for its control, which must henceforth be regarded as

---

which could not conveniently be included in Chapters 6–10. They are all
concerned, to a greater or lesser extent, with recreational planning.

The pollution generated by visitors to an area of high amenity is a problem
to which recreational planners have had to address themselves. The noise
and, to a lesser extent, the air pollution created by motor vehicles in quiet
national parks are becoming matters for consideration,[1] whereas the problems created by litter and by sewage discharges to waterways and lakes have
been recognised for some time.[2] The creation of country parks has sometimes
encouraged water authorities to apply more stringent controls in order to
improve water quality where water sports or water features are important.
For example, a joint committee including water authority representatives has
been set up in the Lee Valley Regional Park to examine the causes of pollution and to suggest remedial action.[3] Again, the condition of a stream
polluted by animal wastes was improved by preventing discharges when a
large Midland country park containing extensive facilities for water sports
was set up. Similarly, consent conditions on effluents from a steel works and a
sewage works were tightened because the centrepiece of a Scottish country
park was to be a new lake.

The undertaking of local improvement schemes such as the landscaping of
a canal and the creation of a 'linear park' can also bring about improvement
in the control of pollution. For example, a dye works discharging highly
coloured effluent into a Manchester canal switched to the use of sewers when
proposals for the improvement of the canal came to be implemented.

a major determinant in physical planning.[4] The second (a lecture by a past president) stressed the need for planners to recast their plans to maximise renewable resources, and emphasised that 'air and water pollution will be of paramount importance'.[5]

Chapters 5 and 10 indicate that there is probably not so much need for greater recognition of the general role of the planning authority in controlling pollution by the other professions concerned, although it would appear that more knowledge of the detailed roles which planning could implement might well be valuable. Indeed, planning assistance in controlling pollution has been requested in a number of articles in the journals of the professions concerned. Some of these requests may have gone unheeded because particular planning authorities have not considered that their responsibilities encompassed the control of pollution.

8   It would appear that *local planning authorities* seldom fully *discharge their powers and responsibilities relating to the control of pollution.* There are probably three reasons for this failure. First, planners may well not be aware of the full range of powers or of all the responsibilities incumbent upon the local planning authority. Second, planners may feel that the powers at their disposal are insufficient or are unlikely to be supported at central government level. Third, planners may have only a partial knowledge of pollution problems and therefore of the need for planning action. Each of these issues is addressed in the recommendations section below.

There is, however, the question of the limit of the local planning authority's jurisdiction. It has been demonstrated that the consideration of pollution is a proper planning matter and that development may be refused purely on the grounds of the pollution it would generate or that it would be exposed to (even though there are often other factors to be considered). Consequently, the planning control of pollution can extend as far as the limits of general planning powers or practice, provided that this does not have the effect of duplicating control which can be better achieved under other legislation. Thus, on the one hand, noise conditions may be imposed because there is no other law in operation under which soundproofing can be specifically required but, on the other hand, emissions (or effluents) cannot be controlled because such control is more properly administered under other legislation. In the field of air pollution, however, the planning authority can exert control on the location of emissions within a site, on the arrangement of buildings or plant to disperse pollutants and on planting to absorb pollutants—all measures potentially equivalent in effectiveness to the imposition of planning conditions to control the level of noise emissions.

9   On the evidence of the earlier chapters it appears that *planning authorities do not control pollution in the most effective manner* at present. The reasons for this probably lie largely in the generally inadequate grasp of planning roles, techniques, powers and responsibilities. Additionally, however, the techniques employed by planners might not always be appropriate. It is possible that local planning authorities may occasionally, for example, insist that trees be planted to reduce noise where vegetation has little attenuation effect, or they may be contriving to provide a buffer strip around a particular land use when source control has advanced to the point where this is superfluous. There are clear signs from the structure plans in Chapter 8, from the implementation case study in Chapter 9 and from the recent development control decisions in Chapter 10 that some planning authorities are beginning to seek much more effective control of pollution.

10   It is not always easy to discern the *principles which guide local planning authorities in the use of pollution control techniques and powers.* It is quite clear, however, that, because of the absence of operational pollution control targets there is no conscious effort to attain the optimum levels of pollution control or to implement any particular pollution standards. Indeed, many local planning authorities do not have expressly formulated pollution control objectives, although they may consider pollution in making certain decisions (for example, in limiting development until a sewage works can treat the increased effluent to a satisfactory standard). Many planning decisions relating to pollution control (including some of the development control decisions outlined in Chapter 10 and, indeed, the inspector's recommendation in Chapter 9) are made without reference to any obvious principles other than 'planning considerations'. Those planning objectives which are utilised in the control of pollution are not always clear or defensible, and many of the authorities which have formulated objectives have, in their phrasing, weighted them towards the 'control' side of the optimum level of pollution control (for example, 'minimise pollution'), although it seems that the resulting planning solution seldom reflects this weight,

because of the need to reconcile conflicting objectives. Indeed, planning decisions sometimes appear to result in pollution levels higher than the optimum.

11 *Pollution control considerations are* very definitely *modified by the planning authority's other objectives,* as intimated above. It would be unrealistic to expect pollution control to preponderate in every decision (as it does in many of those selected in Chapter 10) but it is seldom possible to trace exactly how the process of reconciliation takes place. Nevertheless, two examples are quoted in Chapter 6, where objectives were specified and weighted, and Chapter 9 was concerned with another example where the objectives pursued were originally reasonably clear. However, the decisions in these chapters and most of the examples in Chapter 10 make it plain that pollution control objectives are generally compared in a subjective manner with other planning considerations, the weight attached to particular objectives varying in the light of local circumstances.

12 *Planners use* some of *the pollution control techniques which are available to them,* but others lie fallow. In regional, sub-regional, new town and many other planning studies the cursory attention paid to pollution and its control has, until recently, been largely confined to attempts to locate major new pollution sources such as industrial areas so that prevailing winds disperse air-borne pollutants away from residential areas (sometimes without considering whether this is the most logical course) and, similarly, to relocate 'non-conforming' industrial uses presently situated among housing. The reclamation of derelict land and the restoration of areas after mineral working has also been given some attention. The general tendency towards integration of some industries and housing areas in the interests of dispersing journey-to-work patterns is not necessarily helpful in controlling pollution.

Although the awareness of techniques in both development control and structure plans has recently begun to broaden, many techniques are still relatively unused. For example, on the basis of the reviews in Chapters 6–10 it would appear that the orientation of buildings and streets and the use of vegetation to reduce air pollutant concentrations, the use of noise barriers, the control of industrial estuarine development to reduce wastes released to saline water and the generation of industrial solid waste are probably inadequately considered. Again, the use of pollution models and standards is generally neglected. Despite the general paucity of information about pollution and its control by various planning techniques in the planning literature there have been numerous articles relating to the control of pollution by planning in the technical control literature. It is conceivable that many of these references are ignored by the pollution control authorities and are not seen by planners. It is thus possible that the information is not utilised by either, in spite of consultation between the two.

CONCLUSIONS ON THE FOUR FUNDAMENTAL QUESTIONS

1   *Land use planning does have a distinctive role in the control of pollution* in addition to, and in co-operation with, various other pollution control authorities, each with their own powers and jurisdictions. Apart from the various roles of planning in relation to the stages of the pollution process, local planning authorities also have a focal role in pollution control because of the wide range of consultations carried out in plan making (and, to a lesser extent, in development control) and their ability to co-ordinate environmental improvement on a broad scale in co-operation with other pollution control agencies. In general, planning authorities have seldom discharged these roles fully in the past.

2   *Extensive planning powers and responsibilities relating to the control of pollution exist.* While some of these powers are utilised, many responsibilities are not discharged by local planning authorities. The reasons for this state of affairs may include ignorance of the extent of powers, the perceived inadequacies of the powers, and failure to recognise circumstances in which there is a need to employ them.

3   *The discharge of these responsibilities,* where they are acknowledged, *is not governed by principles concerning the 'optimal level of pollution control'.* While the optimum may be inadvertently achieved, this is a result of compromise with other planning considerations (both related and unrelated to pollution control objectives) and not of following firm principles. It seems doubtful whether many planners are aware of the existence of an optimum level of pollution control. The need for locally determined standards for pollution levels is probably also generally unappreciated.

Town planning embodies a comprehensive range of techniques appropriate to the implemenation of its role in pollution control. Some of these techniques are regularly employed by planning authorities but many are seldom used, probably because planners are unaware of their importance or even of their existence.

DEFICIENCIES IN THE PLANNING CONTROL OF POLLUTION

A comparison of the potential roles, techniques and powers of local planning authorities with their practical application reveals that while many authorities recognise pollution as an issue in certain decisions, the full force of planning as a method of pollution control is not harnessed. Since it has been established that the planning control of pollution has a very significant contribution to make in improving the environment, the question of why this contribution is not being rendered more effectively arises.

The comparison suggests that there are a number of deficiencies which require attention before town planning can assist more effectively in the control of pollution:

Information. Planners may not be sufficiently aware of planning powers and responsibilities in controlling pollution, of techniques of pollution control or, indeed, of the pollution problem generally.

Objectives and standards. The absence of operational pollution control criteria deprives local planning authorities of a framework within which to administer their powers. Similarly, the lack of realistic planning objectives relating to pollution control (formulated with or without operational criteria) weakens the potential contribution of planning.

Powers. Certain relevant information (such as the pollution likely to arise from a particular land use), the provision of which could be a statutory requirement, is frequently not available to local planning authorities. Authorities do not always impose conditions relating to pollution control which are legally enforceable upon planning permissions.

Techniques. The appropriate means of pollution control are frequently not applied. One reason for this is probably that the numerous techniques available to the planner have never been gathered together from the wide range of publications in which they are described.

Knowledge about pollution. A pollution problem may remain un-
solved because the planner is unaware that there is a problem. He
may not know that certain types of land use can give rise to pollution, that information about local pollution problems exists or
that assistance on pollution matters may be available.

Consultations. Some avoidable pollution problems appear to arise
because of inadequate consultations between the local planning
authority and the relevant pollution control authorities or between
planning authorities.

These deficiencies, while serious, are capable of being overcome. The
recommendations which follow are designed to remove the identified
deficiencies and hence to increase the effectiveness of planning as a
method of pollution control.

RECOMMENDATIONS

1 Pollution circular

A central reason for the lack of effectiveness of local planning
authorities in controlling pollution has been the ignorance of many
planners about the problem and their ability to help solve it. The best
way to ameliorate this situation and to provide a stimulus for planning control would be the issue by the Department of the Environment of a circular devoted to pollution (or of a manual on the subject
accompanied by a circular—recommendation 5). The circular should
explain the roles of the planning authority in controlling pollution,
outline the techniques at their disposal and remind authorities of
their powers and responsibilities. This could probably be achieved by
listing or incorporating previous circulars on air, land, water and
noise pollution—the draft circular on planning and clean air
described in Chapter 3 should be included. (The development plan
manual, referred to in Chapter 8, should be revised to contain specific
advice about the inclusion of structure plan policies to control pollution.)

The circular should emphasise the need to set precise objectives
and to observe standards (recommendation 2) by co-operating with
other pollution control authorities and co-ordinating related
activities. It should advise the setting up of a central point within the
local authority to which planners and others could refer on pollution

problems (recommendation 6). It should also specify the need for extensive consultations when certain types of pollution question arise (recommendation 7). Such a circular need not await the results of further research (although it could intimate that additional information would be forthcoming) but could be published with little delay. It should help to eliminate many difficulties arising from lack of awareness about pollution and doubts about legal powers.

2   Standards and objectives

It is recommended that local planning authorities co-operate with other pollution control authorities in setting pollution control standards. It is important that attempts to impose undue uniformity through failure to take account of variations in local conditions should be avoided. For example, high chimneys may constitute intolerable visual intrusion in one situation but not in another. Again, the reservation of open areas to make a buffer may be justified where land is inexpensive but not where it is costly. Once standards have been set it is important that local planning authorities make the pollution control objectives they pursue explicit. Indeed, the same is true in the absence of standards, although objectives will necessarily be defined less clearly. These objectives should be sufficiently precise to be readily translated into operational terms and to be reconciled with other planning objectives (in goals achievement matrices, in cost benefit evaluations or in any other appropriate manner) by planning authorities. The framing and publication of such objectives would undoubtedly bring about an improvement in the contribution of planning to pollution control.

3   Planning powers

Although there are sufficient powers available to those local authorities which are seriously concerned about controlling pollution, it is suggested that the General Development Order[6] be amended to urge two further types of consultation upon all authorities. It is recommended that it should be a statutory requirement to consult the Alkali Inspectorate whenever certain types of development (to be defined by the Inspectorate) or development adjacent to them are proposed. The public health authority should be consulted whenever certain noisy types of development or development adjacent to them are proposed. These developments would be specified by the Noise

Advisory Council, but should include major roads, airports and certain mineral operations. The results of consultations would be given the same weight as those with regional water authorities and highway divisions at present,[6] and should be publicised.

In addition, it is recommended that it should be made obligatory for a developer to specify the precise nature of his proposal (perhaps by amendment of the Use Classes Order[7]) and to state the nature and extent of the air, land, water and noise pollution resulting from the development. This could be effected by amending planning application forms, no alteration to the General Development Order[6] appearing to be necessary. Where pollution problems are likely to arise, the local planning authority would require the developer to elaborate in a separate document, thus ensuring that pollution factors are considered from the outset and that the best feature of the environmental impact statement—its comprehensiveness—is incorporated simply into British planning practice. (The requirement could be extended to other impacts.) The use of planning application forms which contain a section requiring that airborne emissions from industrial establishments be described has been put forward elsewhere[8] and it is recommended that this should be extended to other uses and pollutants.

It is suggested that the possibility of amending the law relating to enforcement by increasing the penalties for non-compliance with planning conditions designed to control pollution be investigated. This recommendation forms part of a larger issue concerned with giving local planning authorities more effective powers, and more confidence, to enforce planning conditions (another aspect of which is the careful phrasing of conditions).

4   Techniques
There is a need to identify the most suitable planning techniques by which pollution control objectives might be implemented. A review of such techniques was presented in Chapter 5 but it is recommended that the widely dispersed information on the techniques and their effectiveness be collated into a set of guidelines for practising planners. For example, explanatory statements of the effects of the various abatement techniques for industrial, traffic and aircraft noise (distance, barriers, insulation, etc) are required. Again, in the case of air pollution, guidelines on the widths of buffer strips around differ-

ent types of polluting land user are needed—there being no question of a uniform strip sufficing. (Some uses, like carbon black manufacture, are such bad neighbours that they should be completely isolated.)

The precise effects of the techniques, where these have not yet been ascertained, require evaluation. A series of research projects to enumerate planning guidelines is needed, despite the fact that some work in this field is being carried out in the United States.[9] For example, research is needed to establish the reduction in air pollutant concentrations created by a planted buffer strip of a specified nature close to a specified pollution source. Similarly, the effects of city size and population density on pollution levels need evaluation,[10] as do the precise consequences of different materials, housing arrangements, building designs and locations and roadway characteristics[11] on noise and air pollution.

Research is also needed on the costs of applying the various techniques—for example, information relating to the costs and benefits of long-distance transportation of solid wastes to restore land. Similarly, the costs of implementing a zoning policy alongside a major road or around an airport should be investigated so that planners may begin to compare them with the costs of pollution damage.

It is recommended that planning authorities should participate in the construction of comprehensive waste and pollution models (designed to enable authorities to calculate the likely pollution arising from large new developments, to compare this with standards and hence to reach an informed planning decision) and in the implementation of the resulting strategies. Such models could, in the case of air pollution and noise, for example, evaluate the effects of different highway alignments, or of different industrial locations. Ancillary research on the capacity of air basins and river systems to accept wastes would be needed. Such sub-regional models would also provide the basis for setting and evaluating pollution standards prior to their implementation by zoning land uses.[10] Alternatively, different arrangements of large new increments of development (for example, regional growth proposals) could be evaluated. Much of the necessary material for such models already exists—for example, refuse disposal sub-models have been prepared for several urban areas. It is also recommended that pollution parameters be included in planning models. There is no reason why suitable variables should not be incorporated, as noise was in one of the third London airport studies.[12]

5   Information

The local planning authority have a number of information needs if pollution is to be effectively controlled. First, they need to know which pollution problems are serious and which are less important. If pollution standards are set, they need to decide priorities in meeting them. They require information about pollutants, their sources, their control and their effects (on human health, vegetation, etc) and they should have access to advice about particular pollution problems. It is recommended that a guide to the sources of data and expertise available to the planner be prepared.

Second, they need to have a clear indication of the spatial distribution of, and trends in, pollution levels on a sub-regional and more local scale. The need to forecast levels of waste generation and pollution for these areas is implicit in the use of many planning techniques, but the use of others would be feasible on the basis of information which could easily be acquired. There is considerable scope for research to prepare a 'pollution index' (a set of pollution indicators) for planning areas which could be used to indicate the local areas suffering most from pollution and so help in determining the best use of limited pollution control resources. The need to involve the public, planning officers, the pollution control authorities and pollution scientists in the compilation of this index is apparent. (Indeed, if relevant information is to be obtained, the participation of planning officers is an important precursor to much of the research suggested here.)

Third, planning authorities need data relating to the waste and pollution from various land use activities. A guide to the expected air, land, water and noise pollution potential of each land use (probably stated as a range of figures), perhaps arranged by Standard Industrial Classification, would enable the authority to identify problems likely to arise from a particular proposal at the earliest possible stage. The guide should include up-to-date information about the effectiveness of pollution control techniques exercised in carrying out the various land use activities.

It is recommended that much of this information should be stored in a pollution data bank at the central local authority focus recommended below (6). It should, of course, be retained in a readily retrievable and usable form. It is also suggested that a pollution control manual or handbook should be prepared for distribution to local planning authorities and other relevant bodies, which would draw together much of the guidance formulated as a result of these recommendations.

6 Organisation within local authorities

Since their activities will call for the consideration of numerous and varied pollution problems, both county and district planning authorities require a central local authority focus as a point of first reference on pollution issues. This focal point could be a single officer or a small unit. It might be incorporated in the planning department, in the environmental health department (in the case of districts) or elsewhere (as in the case of the Greater London Council's Scientific Unit). It is recommended that local authorities be encouraged by the Department of the Environment to provide such a focus, which should also be the point at which information about pollution was available (recommendation 5). Further advice could then be obtained from external sources such as the pollution control authorities, via the central unit, as required.

7 Consultation and co-ordination

Although many local planning authorities already consult relevant pollution control authorities, such as the Alkali Inspectorate, the regional water authority and the environmental health inspectorate, as a matter of routine when their advice would help to resolve a planning problem, it is recommended that all authorities should be encouraged to do so. This might be achieved by means of the DoE circular (recommendation 1) which could spell out the likely development control or plan preparation situations in which help should be requested. Since it will seldom be possible to formulate precise rules (such as no development within 500 m of industry X), a climate in which planners are able to ask advice freely is desirable. Eventually a body of expertise in decisions of these types could be built up and incorporated into planning methodology.

The need for consultation between planning authorities to transmit knowledge about planning experience and the circumstances in which it may be necessary to consult independent experts (pollution scientists in government laboratories, universities or specialist consulting firms) in difficult cases should also be explained.

The metropolitan and non-metropolitan counties provide a useful focus for sub-regional co-ordination of waste disposal and pollution control. It is recommended that, in collaboration with the regional economic planning councils, they should be encouraged to co-ordinate such matters as solid waste disposal, location of certain air pollution sources in relation to meteorological conditions, recycling of water and solid waste, derelict land reclamation, etc. The county planning department could provide a natural focus for sub-regional waste and re-use planning, and this is an appropriate scale for much pollution control activity of the broader, strategic type, although responsibility for particular activities (for example, the administration of solid waste disposal planning) will often reside elsewhere. It is therefore recommended that the Department of the Environment should examine the possibility of suggesting that planning authorities co-operate with other pollution control authorities with a view to co-ordinating policies in the light of anticipated future levels of waste and pollution.

8   Education
It is recommended that a series of lectures be included in planning courses to prepare the planner for the type of pollution problems likely to be met in practice. The syllabus should include a general review of the pollution problem, an indication of the pollution arising from commonly occurring land uses, a description of the various pollution control authorities and due explanation of the role of planning in pollution control, including relevant planning powers, responsibilities and techniques. Such a course would do much to eliminate the lack of knowledge now displayed by many planners about pollution and its control. It is suggested that the Royal Town Planning Institute should recommend the inclusion of such lectures in recognised syllabuses.

REFERENCES
1   Peak Park Planning Board (1972) Personal communication.
2   Nature Conservancy (1965) *Report on Broadland* NC, London.
3   Lee Valley Regional Park Authority (1969) *Lee Valley Regional Park* LVRPA, Enfield.
4   Millar, J. S. (1972) Presidential address *JRTPI, 58* 417–21.

5   Ashworth, G. (1974) Natural resources and the future shape of Britain *JRTPI, 60* 773–78.

6   *Town and Country Planning General Development Order, 1973* SI 1973, No. 3.

7   *Town and Country Planning (Use Classes) Order, 1972* SI 1972, No. 1385.

8   Department of the Environment (1973) *Information about industrial emissions to the atmosphere* HMSO, London.

9   Fensterstock, J. C., Kurtzweg, J. A., and Ozolins, G. (1970) *Reduction of air pollution potential through environmental planning* Paper 70–14, Air Pollution Control Association, Pittsburgh.

10 Burns, L. S. (1970) *Urban planning aspects of air pollution abatement* Task Force 3, Project Clean Air II, University of California, Berkeley.

11 Kurtzweg, J. A. (1973) Urban planning and air pollution control: a review of selected recent research *JAIP, 39* 82–92.

12 Cripps, E. L., and Foot, P. H. S. (1970) The urbanisation effects of a third London airport *Environment and Planning, 2* 153–92.

Gross water pollution: there is a strong correlation between the geographical incidence of high levels of air, water, land and noise pollution. Numerous sources of information and assistance on pollution are available to the planner.

Pollution for planners

This appendix forms the background for the discussion of pollution in the main body of this work and provides a guide to information about pollution likely to be of use to local planning authorities. It should be read in conjunction with Chapter 2, to which reference is made in several places. The topics outlined are sources and types of pollution, trends in pollution levels, effects of pollutants, control of pollution (including brief mention of pollution control authorities and environmental impact statements), sources of data about pollution and sources of assistance on pollution problems.

SOURCES AND TYPES

The sources and types of pollution were discussed in Chapter 2, and it is intended only to provide one or two additional references here. It is, however, necessary briefly to mention radioactivity and persistent pollutants and to describe the relationship between pollution levels and various characteristics of urban areas.

Air pollution sources and types, [1-3] land pollutants, [4-5] water pollution [6 7] and noise [8-10] are described elsewhere in considerably more detail than in Chapter 2.

Radioactivity is potentially the most dangerous form of pollution, and while there is no evidence of significant damage at present, [11] the problem may well become more acute as a greater proportion of our power is generated by nuclear stations. [12] The nuclear fuel cycle gives rise to emissions at various stages, the principal ones being routine releases from nuclear power stations and reprocessing plants, and the generation of waste materials. [13] Emissions are very carefully controlled and monitored. Waste materials may be contaminated or highly radioactive. Contaminated materials—for example, university radioactive chemicals—are often buried or dumped at sea but high level wastes have to be stored for very long periods of time (many thousands of years). Research into the glassification of these highly radioactive liquids is under way. [5]

Persistent pollutants include pesticides (e.g. organochlorides), some industrial chemicals and certain heavy metals. Their effects are complicated by biological diffusion through the food chain. Progress in reducing the use of the more persistent organochlorine insecticides [14] has been made but the use of non-agricultural toxic pesticides is increasing and is largely uncontrolled. [5]

A study of air, water, land and noise pollutants in Greater Manchester [15] revealed that high levels of one type of pollution in a particular area were often accompanied by high levels of other pollutants. There was a marked correlation between pollution levels and population density and degree of industrial activity, the highest pollutant readings being registered in old established, densely urbanised and industrialised areas. It was also found that a strong relationship existed between pollution levels and socio-economic status, the least polluted areas having the highest proportions of high-status residents.[15] Similar relationships between air pollution levels and population density and income were found in New York.[16] These relationships make it clear that the opportunities for planning intervention to reduce existing high pollution levels are concentrated in the older, central areas but that it is also important to maintain or improve the relatively unpolluted conditions in outer, newer areas which generally house the more vocal residents.

TRENDS

By no means all air pollutants are monitored but measurements of sulphur dioxide are made at a large number of sites. Readings from either lead dioxide candles[17] or the more reliable and ubiquitous volumetric equipment[18] are available for most urban areas. Region-by-region descriptions of the sulphur dioxide position in urban and rural areas are being published.[2 19 20] The downward trend in concentrations for the country as a whole, shown in Figure 3,[15 21] is reflected in most of its constituent parts (and is quite distinct from the trend in emissions or wastes) but sulphur dioxide levels in the central areas of certain cities are not responding to the implementation of the Clean Air Acts.[22 23] Isolated measurements of other pollutants such as carbon monoxide,[24] oxides of nitrogen, ozone and other constituents of photochemical smog have been made. Significant concentrations of ozone have been detected on hot days in London,[25] indicating that photochemical smog can no longer be ignored in Britain. The trend in the concentrations of these pollutants is almost certainly upwards, as they derive mainly from motor vehicles.

Smoke is widely monitored and urban concentrations are again generally available.[18] The trend in levels is more sharply downward than in the case of sulphur dioxide, and the pattern is fairly uniform throughout the country, being very much in line with emissions.[2 19 20] (See Figure 4.[15]) A measure of local dust and grit conditions is provided by deposit gauge readings.[17] The conclusion that the fall-out of deposited matter is not changing appreciably over the country as a whole[2] was not reflected in the Greater Manchester area, where dust concentrations were found to be diminishing.[15] Emissions from several industries have certainly fallen since they came under the control of the Alkali Inspectorate.[26]

Data on certain land pollutants are available. During the last decade the quantities of mineral wastes (the most important of which is mining spoil[27]) animal wastes and sewage sludges[28] have all increased. Similarly, the quantity of domestic refuse is rising and is expected to continue to grow as its nature changes from a low-volume, dense waste to a high-volume, lower-density material. The data on industrial wastes are very incomplete but it appears that quantities of these have also risen substantially and that they are more extensive than household wastes.[29] (Figures of 23 million and 18 million tonnes per annum respectively have been quoted for the UK as a whole.[5 30] Figure 5 shows the amounts of various solid wastes arising during 1973.[5 15])

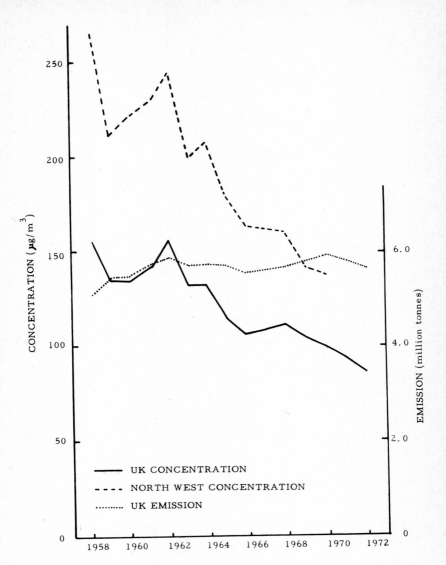

FIGURE 3 Sulphur dioxide emissions in the UK and urban concentrations in the UK and the North West, 1958–72

Despite some disposal at sea, the greater part of each type of solid waste is deposited on land. No general data exist, however, on trends in disposal

methods, and these are critical in determining whether pollution from this
source has increased proportionately. It is known that the methods of dis-

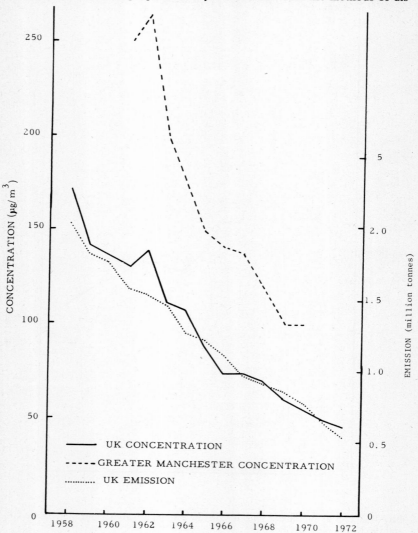

FIGURE 4   Smoke emissions and urban concentrations in the UK and concentrations
in Greater Manchester, 1958–72

posal are by no means always satisfactory in the sense of avoiding pollution of air or water or direct damage to amenity.[4] [5] [27-30] The Control of Pollution Act, 1974, should ensure that the generation and disposal of waste become better documented.

Statistics on derelict spoil heaps and tips can be obtained for each part of

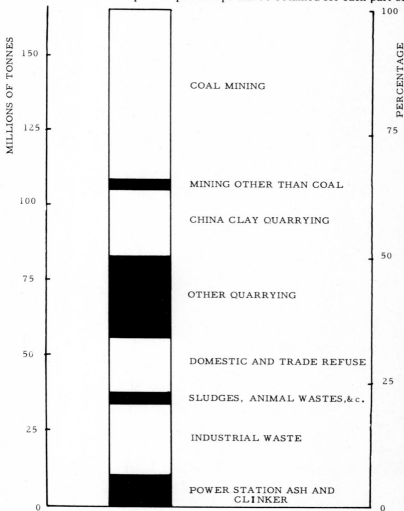

FIGURE 5   Masses of solid wastes arising in 1973

the country.[31] The previous definition of dereliction, however, precluded much polluted land from being incorporated in derelict land surveys and the official definition has now been widened.[32] Nevertheless, for the country as a whole the acreage of derelict land under the narrower definition is increasing,[31] though the rise may be partially due to changes in surveying practice. A study in Greater Manchester showed that even the figures reported under the widened definition[32] underestimated the actual situation by a factor of at least two.[15] There can be little doubt that pollution from litter of all types is increasing, and is likely to continue to grow.

River quality is described by means of such analytical measures as biochemical oxygen demand and suspended and dissolved solid content and is divided into four chemical categories. On this basis, the results obtained from surveys of rivers[33,34] show a significant improvement in their quality during the last fourteen years (Figure 6)[35] and proposed expenditure is expected to improve further the condition of rivers by 1980.[36] The state of a river in any part of the country can be determined from the survey reports.[33] Insufficient data exist to construct a trend for concentrations of such water

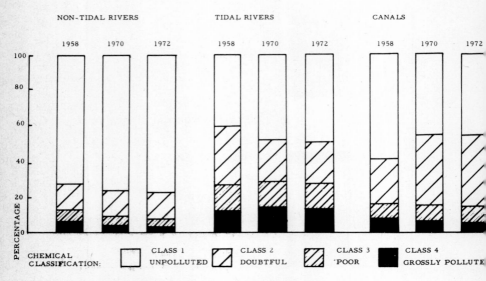

FIGURE 6   River quality in England and Wales, 1958–72

L. I. H. E.

THE MARKLAND LIBRARY

STAND PARK RD., LIVERPOOL, L16 9JD

pollutants as zinc, phenols and pesticides but the trend in certain other pollutants (for example, nitrates) is almost certainly upwards.

British estuaries are generally in a very polluted state, and the condition of the most polluted stretches appears to be worsening.[35][37] Evidence of the deterioration of the marine environment proper by pollution exists, but the pattern is by no means uniform. It is possible that coastal pollution by sewage and oil will decline as stricter control over discharges is implemented.

Noise has been defined as 'sound which is undesired by the recipient'[8] and is consequently a subjective concept—a sound which is undesirable to one person may be entirely acceptable to another. Despite this subjectivity there is fairly broad agreement on the main types of sound which cause annoyance, the most important probably being road traffic noise, aircraft noise and neighbourhood noise. Noise contours for airports based upon frequency of aircraft movements and noise (the Noise and Number Index) have been constructed.[38] Similarly, traffic noise contours along roads have been calculated, using a weighted decibel scale (db(A)) to measure noise which exceeds a certain level for 10 per cent of the time between 6 a.m. and midnight (eighteen hour L_{10}).[39]

It is not easy to calculate trends in noise from each type of source. Train noise, however, has decreased with the declining range of services and with electrification. It is unlikely that the level of either this type of noise or of domestic noise will show a sharp increase in the future. Industrial and constructional noise, on the other hand, could well show a considerable rise if the amount of power used in industry increases,[40] so that prevalent neighbourhood noise problems may well increase in severity,[41] particularly in the absence of controls on noise from public places.[42] With the rapid growth of air and road traffic, noise levels have risen markedly during the last decade and these sources are likely to generate substantially more noise in the future. Aircraft noise is more acute than traffic noise but is limited in its geographical incidence (although 'suffered' by approximately 2½ million people[41]—an underestimate), whereas that from road traffic is more prevalent but generally has lower peak levels. Figure 7 shows the proportion of the urban population likely to be exposed to certain traffic noise levels in 1980, assuming that no change in the noise characteristics of vehicles occurs.[43]

It is extremely difficult to establish trends in the concentrations of radioactive pollutants, and no general statement can be made. The levels of persistent organochlorine pesticide residues, after initially increasing, appear to have been declining during recent years. Considerable attention has recently been devoted to trace metal levels, but general trends in their concentrations cannot yet be established.[5]

EFFECTS

The effects of the various types of pollution are quite distinct, although they may all be included in the categories of damage to human health, materials, agriculture, wildlife or amenity. Individual pollutants within each medium have their own particular effects, and it is difficult to generalise about, say, water pollutants as a whole.

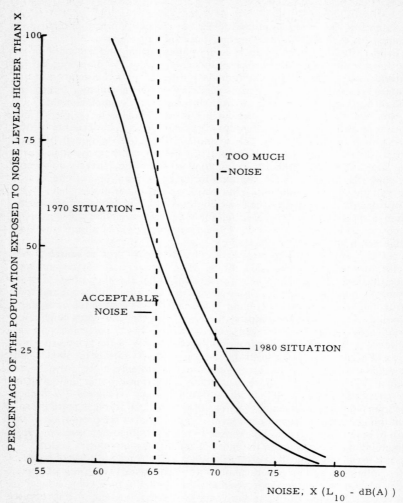

FIGURE 7 Traffic noise exposure of the urban population in 1970 and 1980

Air pollutants[1] are associated with bronchitis, emphysema and lung cancer, corrosion of metals, of stonework, of painted surfaces and of fabrics, attacks on farm animals and crops such as potato, lettuce, etc, diminution in bird species, in hours of sunshine and in visibility and general environmental degradation. Noise[8] is associated with certain mental illnesses, insomnia and general 'annoyance' as well as with impairment of hearing. The concomitant vibration can cause failure of stonework and other materials. The disturbance of amenity by noise is a common phenomenon in any industrial country. Water pollution[6] is not, nowadays, normally associated with health hazards, though it may increase corrosion of materials. The effects of pollutants on freshwater and marine shell fisheries are marked, although recreational resources probably suffer most damage. The effect on amenity of highly coloured, lifeless water containing much detritus and perhaps giving rise to obnoxious gases is apparent, particularly in urban areas. Apart from the fortunately rare tragedy, the direct impact of land pollution on human health is slight, although solid wastes often attract rodents. The obliteration of otherwise valuable land and the visual damage to amenity (spoil heaps and tips generally being very unattractive) are probably more serious than the effects of air and water pollution which often arise from solid waste disposal.

Despite the very considerable difficulties associated with the establishment of damage (dose/response) functions, approximate threshold concentrations (below which most types of damage are minimal) are beginning to be established for several pollutants, particularly air contaminants.[44] There have been a number of attempts to make an economic assessment of pollution in the United States, but few have been essayed in Britain. The one major UK exercise to date involving air pollution reached the tentative conclusion that the mean total national cost was currently in the range of £200 million to £600 million per annum, most of which was attributable to damage to health and agriculture.[45] It appears that the domestic fire, industrial and electricity generation sources and the motor vehicle (in that order) are probably the most important contributors to air pollutant damage in this country.

CONTROL
The control of pollution was briefly discussed in Chapter 2. It is appropriate, however, to provide some additional details here.[46] Common law is ineffective in containing air pollution and, although there are certain powers under the Public Health Acts, the main legislation consists of the Clear Air Acts, 1956 and 1968, and the Alkali, etc, Works Regulation Act, 1906 (and subsequent orders [47,48]), together with the Control of Pollution Act, 1974. The Clean Air Acts control the emission of dark smoke, dust and grit from chimneys as well as the height of some industrial chimneys and the designation of smoke control areas. This legislation is administered by local authorities and relies in some measure on certain standards. The Control of Pollution Act, 1974, has given local authorities the means to enforce regulations relating to the composition of motor fuel and the sulphur content of fuel oil and to obtain and publish information about emissions to the atmosphere from all non-domestic premises in their areas.

The Alkali Act, to be superseded to some extent by the Health and Safety Act, 1974, which controls the emission of noxious or offensive gases from a variety of industrial processes, involves the use of the 'best practicable means' of control, and allows scope for continual upgrading of requirements. This legislation is administered by the Alkali Inspectorate, which although

H

quite separate from the local authorities, does in practice co-operate with them. The Construction and Use Regulations, 1973, control the emission of smoke, carbon monoxide and hydrocarbons from motor vehicles to a limited extent[49] but the police appear to have done little to enforce this legislation. A voluntary scheme controlling the lead content of petrol (and hence lead emissions) is in force. The burning of solid waste is only partially controlled by legislation.

There are various technical methods of removing gases and aerosols from chimney emissions such as scrubbing with water, trapping and electrostatic precipitation.[1][21] Emissions are dispersed from high chimneys in many cases, although this method of control is being increasingly criticised.[50] Although they are not widely employed in Britain, there are many devices available for controlling automobile exhaust gases.

Legislative control over solid waste pollution was very patchy until recently. Common law has provided little control, and although the Public Health Act, 1936, the Litter Act, 1958, and the Civic Amenities Act, 1967, have given some support, the main means of controlling solid waste pollution have been found in the Town and Country Planning Acts. Now however, the Control of Pollution Act, 1974, has provided for waste disposal arrangements, the preparation of plans and the licensing of disposal sites. It makes special provision for dangerous wastes and encourages re-use.

Some use may be found for many solid wastes, if they are conveniently located, and technical treatment such as exfoliation or sintering can transform wastes into useful products. The chief methods of dealing with solid wastes, however, are to suitably locate, cover, shape and landscape them.

Common law has proved slightly more effective in controlling freshwater pollution than air pollution, but the main legislation has been found in the Rivers (Prevention of Pollution) Acts, 1951–61, which are to be virtually replaced by the Control of Pollution Act, 1974. These Acts are administered by the regional water authorities (set up under the Water Act, 1973) and they endeavour to impose standards on all discharges to rivers, estuaries and coastal waters.

Technical control centres on physical methods, such as settlement and the use of interceptors and screens, and on biological treatment (for example, activated sludge, biological filtration). These methods can effectively remove most pollutants.

The Noise Abatement Act, 1960, is to be replaced by the Control of Pollution Act, 1974, which provides local authorities with extensive powers for the control of certain kinds of noise, together with the capacity to introduce noise abatement zones. Rather limited control of aircraft noise arising from certain airports is exercised under the Air Navigation General Regulations, 1972,[51] and the law governing noise from motor vehicles is to be found in the Construction and Use Regulations, 1973.[49] Insulation of certain buildings against traffic noise is a duty under the Noise Insulation Regulations, 1973.[52] The imposition of conditions relating to noise under the Town and Country Planning Acts is also a powerful method of control.

Control over emissions of noise from industrial processes, motor vehicles and aircraft could be achieved by radical redesign, although a measure of abatement can be obtained relatively easily. The use of soundproofing methods of varying types and effectiveness around permanent sources is well established.[9] Moving sources of noise can be controlled by limiting their use, but otherwise control techniques centre on planning methods and are described in Chapter 5.

The Control of Pollution Act, 1974, while granting the power for the Secretary of State or the control authorities to set certain standards, continues the traditional 'best practicable means' approach to the abatement of certain kinds of pollution (particularly air and noise pollutants) which has served reasonably well in the past. An account of the application of the best practicable means of controlling air pollution from registered works has been published.[53]

In principle it should be less difficult to obtain estimates of expenditure on pollution control than of damage. In practice, figures are by no means readily available. In the case of air pollution, however, the total cost of control is probably not more than £60 million per annum.[21][45] Even were desulphurisation of fuels, more stringent controls on motor vehicles and the removal of lead from petrol to be implemented the additional cost would, at £100 million to £160 million, be less than that estimated to be attributable to the pollutants concerned.[45] The same situation may well apply in other media, though the level of control will obviously determine the balance between damage and control costs.

Control authorities
The various authorities empowered to control pollution were listed in Chapter 2 and, in particular, the role of the local planning authority in controlling pollution was discussed at length in that and other chapters. Other publications provide excellent reviews of the responsibilities of pollution control authorities,[5][46] and one of these presents tables listing the duties of central and local government.[5] In general, the responsibility for exercising controls on pollution rests with the local and water authorities, but powers relating to the control of emissions to air from registered works, the limited control of aircraft noise (in conjunction with local authorities owning airports), the control of pollution from radioactive materials and the control of pollution caused by agricultural chemicals, are administered by central government. Other concerns of central government include the legislative framework for controls and the provision of guidance to local and water authorities.

There are considerable variations in different parts of the country in the allocation of responsibilities between county and district local authorities. The counties are responsible for the disposal of solid and toxic wastes in England and sewage in Scotland. At district level, environmental health oficers are charged with controlling air pollution arising from non-registered works or domestic sources, and with noise nuisances. District councils are also responsible for sewers as agents for the water authorities.

The regional water authorities are responsible for the giving, and subsequent supervision, of consents to discharge pollutants to rivers, tidal stretches of rivers, estuaries and the sea. The eighty-eight disposal divisions of the water authorities administer the treatment and disposal of domestic sewage and the trade effluents discharged to sewers. Sea fisheries committees have certain powers to make and to enforce bye-laws prohibiting or regulating the deposit or discharge, within the three-mile limit of territorial waters, of any solid or liquid substance detrimental to sea fish or sea fishing.[5] These powers are soon to be lost to the regional water authorities. The British Waterways Board has some control, as owner, over discharges to canals.

Environmental impact statements

It has frequently been suggested that a way of improving the effectiveness of the planning control of pollution would be to introduce environmental impact statements to enable planning decisions to be made in the light of the full range of environmental considerations, including all types of resulting pollution. It is therefore appropriate to consider briefly the possible role of the environmental impact statement in British planning.

The US National Environmental Policy Act, 1969, established a national policy on the environment and placed new responsibilities on federal agencies to take environmental factors into account in their decision making. Every recommendation or report on legislation or on other major federal actions significantly affecting the quality of the environment must include a detailed statement concerning the environmental impact of the action, adverse impacts that cannot be avoided and alternatives to the proposed action.[54] It would be possible to institute a similar system in Britain in which all the potential pollution (and other environmental) effects were catalogued by the developer when applying for planning permission.

A body of expertise relating to environmental impact statements has been built up in the United States[55] and their usefulness in ensuring that environmental effects are considered in major developments has been improved. However, the quality of information and analysis presented in impact statements has not always been good.[56] There has frequently been inadequate discussion of the identified environmental impacts and inadequate consideration of alternatives and their environmental impacts. The quality of statements does, however, appear to be improving.[56]

Reservations have also been expressed about the use of environmental impact statements on the grounds that knowledge of effects is often inadequate, or cannot be measured quantitatively, that statements are slanted towards the proposers of the development and that their preparation and evaluation cause serious delays. (Case study investigations indicate that delays are more usually due to cumbersome and often poorly defined administrative requirements and the absence of co-ordination in decision making rather than to the actual analysis of environmental impacts.[57]) In addition, environmental impact statements have been criticised because they can give a false concreteness and justification to what is, in reality, a value judgement.[58]

Some of the best environmental impact statements are very good. A comprehensive study of the highway alternatives for the west side of Manhattan presents excellent assessments of the air pollution, noise and water pollution impacts of the various strategies,[59] drawing on thorough and exhaustive research.[60] However, many of the social and economic implications which have to be taken into account in the US were inadequately analysed and the impact statement was rejected. Some of the worst American statements are very poor. One or two impact statements have been prepared in Britain, in relation to the effects of major North Sea oil developments.[61 62]

The merits of environmental impact statements have to be compared with the planning application and inquiry system employed in Britain. There is no doubt that developments causing major pollution problems are sometimes permitted without adequate consideration of the resulting damage because planning consent is granted in the absence of objections. In other cases, exhaustive analysis of environmental problems is provided by opposing experts and advocates at public inquiries. This type of situation is almost certainly preferable to a bald statement, however good, because environmental evidence is subject to detailed refutable criticism. The role of environmental pressure groups in ensuring that full objection to possibly damaging developments is made is invaluable.

It is quite possible that environmental impact statements could be used as an adjunct to the present British procedure, rather than as a replacement. The present system is certainly very patchy and a check list of factors to be considered in every case where developments of certain types are proposed (one of the environmental impact statement procedures) would be very useful in improving the control of pollution by planning. The full paraphernalia of environmental impact statements on the American model, with the accompanying lengthy court procedures, does not, however, appear to be appropriate in a planning system where environmental concern is taken to be a central consideration.

POLLUTION DATA

A guide to the data available to local planning authorities in compiling pollution levels for their area may be found in a recent study of Greater Manchester.[15] In that exercise published sources, unpublished sources and questionnaires were employed to generate information and similar methods could obviously be used by any authority.

In the case of air pollution a general review of smoke and sulphur dioxide problems in the area will be available.[2|19|20] Readings of sulphur dioxide, smoke and grit and dust concentrations can be obtained for points within the local authority from published sources.[17|18|63|64] The number, location and types of process carried out at registered works can be obtained from the local District Alkali Inspector, as can an indication of complaints about these works and their seriousness. The district authority environmental health inspector, who should be the planner's first point of enquiry on all air pollution data questions, will be able to provide information about complaints relating to other establishments, about air pollution problems generally and perhaps about levels of road traffic pollutants. Emission figures may also be available.[15]

In the case of land pollution the local planning authority will have their own statistics on dereliction (and possibly on despoiled land) but there are also returns which are published annually.[31] The waste disposal authority will be able to provide data on solid wastes in the area, and the environmental health inspector should provide an indication of the pollution to which they give rise.

The quality of rivers in a planning authority area can be gauged from a central government survey.[33] More recent information about pollution in rivers and canals should be available from the water authorities, who can also supply detailed analyses at particular points. Details of effluents are published for large areas[36/65] and the water authorities should be able to provide more specific details. Sea fisheries committees can give an indication of marine conditions.

Few published sources relating to local noise conditions exist, but airport noise contours are available from the operating authority and noise contours can be calculated for urban roads.[15] Otherwise the environmental health inspector provides the best indication of noise problems and should be able to supply records of noise complaints. Much of this information (and details of the other pollutants already mentioned) should be found in the annual reports of the local authority's medical officer of health.

There may well be other sources of information in a particular area. For example, the management of a large industrial concern (such as a power station or refinery) probably records pollution levels in and around the site concerned. Again, the local university or polytechnic may be monitoring certain pollutants, or the director of parks may be knowledgeable about air pollution.

There is, in general, no reasonable guide to the air, land, water and noise pollution likely to arise from various land uses. In the case of air pollution and noise, however, problems can be anticipated to arise from most of the uses listed in the Use Classes Order, 1972.[66] Even changes of operation within a given use can give rise to noise or air pollution, as where an art gallery is converted to a public hall which is open late at night, or where a community centre begins to operate much longer hours of opening. The problem of noise in public places has often been ignored by planners,[42] as have the odours and effluents arising from intensive agricultural development.[5] Industries involving reclamation and those concerned with mineral working can be expected to give rise to land pollution problems and a wide variety of uses can generate water pollution, if only from surface run-off. The land uses not causing pollution of some nature are in a distinct minority, and it behoves the local planning authority to examine all applications for permission to develop carefully.

SOURCES OF ASSISTANCE

The various organisations mentioned above should be able to provide any necessary assistance. In general, the district environmental health officer should be consulted whenever an air pollution or noise pollution difficulty arises. His department may well be able to help solve the problem without further assistance, or he may recommend reference to the Alkali Inspectorate (registered works and other air pollution problems) or to some other authority. His department may also be able to assist on certain solid waste pollution problems but the waste disposal authority should, in any case, be asked their opinion. The rivers division of the water authority should be consulted on all water pollution problems. Between them the authorities will probably provide all the assistance needed in most cases.

There will be times, nevertheless, when the planning authority may need additional advice. The government departments listed elsewhere[5] should be able to help in these cases. For example, Warren Spring Laboratory can probably give an opinion about the effects of siting a new office block in a polluted area consisting mainly of smaller buildings. In a few cases, however, it will be necessary to seek independent advice about the nature of a problem or its proposed solution. University departments and private consulting firms will certainly be able to provide the necessary expertise, although it may be necessary to seek recommendations (perhaps from the environmental health department) before the appropriate expert assistance can be located.

REFERENCES

1 Stern, A. C. (ed.) (1968) *Air Pollution* (three vols) Academic Press, London.
2 Warren Spring Laboratory (1972) *National survey of air pollution 1961–71, 1* (United Kingdom, South-East, Greater London) Department of Trade and Industry, HMSO, London.
3 Smith, A. R. (1966) *Air pollution,* Monograph 22, Society of Chemical Industry, London.
4 Department of the Environment (1971) *Report of the working party on refuse disposal,* HMSO, London.
5 Royal Commission on Environmental Pollution (1974) *Fourth report* Cmnd 5780, HMSO, London.
6 Klein, L. (1967) *River pollution* (three vols) Butterworth, London.
7 Institute of Petroleum (1971) *Water pollution by oil* IP, London.
8 Committee on the Problem of Noise (Wilson Committee) (1963) *Final Report* Cmnd 2056, HMSO, London.
9 Lord, P., and Thomas, F. L. (1963) *Noise measurement and control* Heywood, London.
10 Beranek, L. L. (1960) *Noise reduction* McGraw-Hill, London.
11 Dunster, H. J. (1969) The avoidance of pollution in the disposal of radioactive waste *Atom, 162* 65–70.
12 Farmer, F. R. (1967) *Siting criteria—a new approach* SM89/34, United Kingdom Atomic Energy Authority, Health and Safety Branch, Risley.
13 Dunster, H. J., and Warner, B. F. (1970) *The disposal of noble gas fission products from the pre-processing of nuclear fuel* AHSB(RP)R101, United Kingdom Atomic Energy Authority, HMSO, London.

14   Agricultural Research Council (1970) *Third report of the research committee on toxic chemicals* HMSO, London.
15   Wood, C. M., Lee, N., Luker, J. A., and Saunders, P. J. W. (1974) *The geography of pollution: a study of Greater Manchester* Manchester University Press, Manchester.
16   Zupan J. M. (1973) *The distribution of air quality in the New York region* Resources for the Future, Johns Hopkins Press, London.
17   Warren Spring Laboratory (1960–) *The investigation of air pollution: deposit gauge and lead dioxide results* Department of Trade and Industry, Stevenage.
18   Warren Spring Laboratory (1960–) *The investigation of air pollution: national survey: smoke and sulphur dioxide* Department of Trade and Industry, Stevenage.
19   Warren Spring Laboratory (1972) *National survey of air pollution, 1961–71, 2* (South West, Wales, North West) Department of Trade and Industry, HMSO, London.
20   Warren Spring Laboratory (1973) *National survey of air pollution, 3* (East Anglia, East Midlands, West Midlands) Department of Trade and Industry, HMSO, London.
21   Department of the Environment (1973) *Towards cleaner air,* HMSO, London.
22   *Clean Air Act, 1956.*
23   *Clean Air Act, 1968.*
24   Reed, L. E., and Trott, P. E. (1971) Continuous measurement of carbon monoxide in streets, 1967–69 *Atmos. Environ.,* 5 27–39.
25   Derwent, R. G., and Stewart, H. N. M. (1973) Elevated ozone levels in the air of central London *Nature (Lond.), 241* 342–43.
26   Department of the Environment (1974) *Clean air today* HMSO, London.
27   Collins, W. G. (ed.) (1970) *Proceedings of the derelict land symposium, Leeds 1969* Iliffe Science and Technology Publications, Guildford.
28   Working Party on Sewage Disposal (1970) *Taken for granted* Ministry of Housing and Local Government, HMSO, London.
29   Technical committee on the disposal of solid toxic wastes (1971) *Report* Ministry of Housing and Local Government, HMSO, London.
30   Department of the Environment (1972) *Pollution: nuisance or nemesis?* HMSO, London.
31   Department of the Environment (1965–) *Results of derelict land surveys* DoE, London.
32   Department of the Environment (1973) *Derelict land surveys* Circular 7/73, DoE, London.
33   Department of the Environment (1971) *Report of a river pollution survey of England and Wales, 1970, 1* HMSO, London.
34   Department of the Environment (1972) *River pollution survey of England and Wales, updated 1972—river quality* HMSO, London.
35   Department of the Environment (1973) *A background to water reorganisation in England and Wales* HMSO, London.

36 Department of the Environment (1972) *Report of a river pollution survey of England and Wales, 1970, 2* HMSO, London.

37 Royal Commission on Environmental Pollution (1972) *Third report* Cmnd 5054, HMSO, London.

38 Commission on the third London airport (1970) *Papers and proceedings, 7* HMSO, London.

39 Scholes, W. E., and Sargent, J. W. (1971) Designing against noise from road traffic *Applied Acoustics, 4* 203–4.

40 H.M. Chief Inspector of Factories (1970) *Annual report, 1969* Cmnd 4461, HMSO, London.

41 Noise Advisory Council (1974) *Noise in the next ten years* HMSO, London.

42 Noise Advisory Council (1974) *Noise in public places* HMSO, London.

43 Road Research Laboratory (1970) *A review of road traffic noise* Report LR 357, Department of the Environment, Crowthorne, Berks.

44 Environmental Protection Agency (1970) *Air quality criteria for sulphur oxides* Publication AP–050, US Government Printing Office, Washington.

45 Programmes Analysis Unit (1972) *An economic and technical assessment of air pollution in the United Kingdom* Report PAU M 20, HMSO, London.

46 McLoughlin, J. (1972) *The law relating to pollution* Manchester University Press, Manchester.

47 *Alkali, etc, Works Order, 1966* SI, 1966, No. 1143.

48 *Alkali, etc, Works Order, 1971* SI, 1971, No. 960.

49 *Motor Vehicles (Construction and Use) Regulations, 1973* SI, 1973, No. 24.

50 Swedish Royal Ministry for Foreign Affairs and Swedish Royal Ministry of Agriculture (1972) *Air pollution across national boundaries* SRMFA, Stockholm.

51 *Air Navigation (General) Regulations. 1972* SI, 1972, No. 322.

52 *Noise Insulation Regulations. 1973* SI, 1973, No. 1363.

53 Department of the Environment (1974) *110th Annual report on Alkali, etc, works, 1973* HMSO, London.

54 Council on Environmental Quality (1970) *Environmental quality: first annual report* US Government Printing Office, Washington.

55 Dickert, T. G., and Domeny, K. R. (1974) *Environmental impact assessment: guidelines and commentary* University Extension, University of California, Berkeley.

56 Council of Environmental Quality (1973) *Environmental quality: fourth annual report* US Government Printing Office, Washington.

57 Goldsmith, B. J. (1974) *Delays in initiating construction of energy facilities in the United States due to environmental review procedures* Group of experts on the environmental impact of energy production and use, Organisation for Economic Co-operation and Development, Paris.

58 Greenberg, M. R., and Hordon, R. M. (1974) Environmental impact

statements: some annoying questions *JAIP, 40* 164–75.

59   United States Department of Transportation Federal Highway Administration and New York State Department of Transportation (1974) *West Side Highway Project: draft environmental impact statement* NYSDT, New York.

60   Bolt, Beranek and Newman (1974) *West Side Highway Project: technical report on noise impact* BBN, Cambridge, Mass.

61   Polytechnic of Central London (1973) *Impact: oil-related development in north-west Scotland* PCL, London.

62   Sphere Consultants (1973) *Environmental impact of alternative platform construction sites* SC, London.

63   Warren Spring Laboratory (1969) *The investigation of air pollution: directory 1: daily observations of smoke and sulphur dioxide* Department of Trade and Industry, Stevenage.

64   Warren Spring Laboratory (1970) *The investigation of air pollution: directory 2: deposit gauge and lead dioxide observations* Department of Trade and Industry, Stevenage.

65   Department of the Environment (1974) *Report of a river pollution survey of England and Wales, 1970, 3* HMSO, London.

66   *Town and Country Planning (Use Classes) Order, 1972* SI, 1972, No. 1385.

APPENDIX 2

Structure plan objectives, policies and criteria

One of the objectives of the Warley structure plan is to ensure that the detrimental environmental effects of mineral extraction are kept to a minimum.

TEESSIDE

The following amenity policies (which are direct quotations with minor editing) were designed to implement the structure plan objective 'to minimise all forms of environmental pollution and dereliction' (p. 113).

1   *Emission of atmospheric pollutants from new industrial plant will be minimised by use of the control powers vested in local authorities under the Clean Air Act, 1968.* The most obvious form of pollution on Teesside is atmospheric pollution. The concentration of heavy industry alongside the Tees produces grit and dust, sulphur dioxide, smoke and fumes. These policies are therefore designed to reduce atmospheric pollution from industrial sources. The powers available to local authorities are limited, so success in reducing pollution depends greatly upon the co-operation of industry and willingness on its part to invest funds into pollution control.

2   *Emission from existing plant will be continuously monitored and action taken to effect reductions where the provisions of the Clean Air Act, 1968, are contravened.*

3   *Negotiations will be held with firms which emit pollutants in an attempt to persuade them to 'clean up' existing plant over which there is only limited control.*

4   *Strict control will be exercised over the location of new plants or factories from which emission of atmospheric pollutants might be anticipated.* Such installations will be restricted to: [three specific locations].

5   *Land available for development or redevelopment which suffers serious atmospheric pollution will be allocated for non-residential purposes.* This policy will be applied to the following areas: [three specific locations].

6   *Housing will be cleared from areas suffering serious atmospheric pollution and generally poor environmental conditions.* It must be accepted that it is unlikely that atmospheric pollution can ever be entirely eliminated from a heavy industrial area such as Teesside. Accordingly this policy is intended to minimise the harmful impacts of atmospheric pollution upon the community.

7   *Smoke control orders (smokeless zones) will be extended to cover all housing in the county borough.* This policy, together with the clearance of unfit housing in the inner areas, where domestic smoke is most troublesome, should effectively eliminate domestic smoke.

     By mid-1974 all major areas of new housing and the majority of houses in the following areas will be smoke controlled: [six specific locations].

     The area of smoke control will be increased to cover virtually all housing within the county borough by 1980.

8   *The council will give every assistance to the Northumberland River Authority in controlling the discharge of pollutants into watercourses.* The Northumberland River Authority has power vested in it under the Rivers (Prevention of Pollution) Act, 1951–61, to control the discharge of pollutants into watercourses from new industrial plant. The council will, whenever possible, assist the river authority in improving the Tees and in attaining the ultimate objective of a river quality which will support the passage of migratory fish at all states of the tide and freshwater flow.

9   *Negotiations will continue with the firms at present discharging pollutants to tidal watercourses, where such discharges are subject to only limited legislative control, to persuade them to reduce the polluting effect of such discharges.* No statutory powers exist to control pollutant discharges into watercourses which have been in operation since before 1960. At present the only means of reducing the effect of this discharge is by negotiation with the firms concerned. A Steering Committee and an Officers' Technical Committee were established in connection with the Teesside Sewerage and Sewage Disposal scheme to tackle this problem and consist of representatives from Teesside CBC, the Northumbrian River Authority and members from the Confederation of British Industry. The council will continue to give every assistance and encouragement to the Steering Committee and the Officers' Technical Committee in the implementation of this work and in the continued negotiation with those firms at present discharging pollutants to tidal watercourses. (NB. The

Control of Pollution Act, 1974, now provides power to control all discharges to rivers and estuaries.)

10 *All domestic sewage will be suitably treated before being discharged to the river or estuary.* Apart from the recently enlarged works in an urban area, and the works which serves a rural area, there are at present no sewage works on Teesside for domestic effluent. The untreated effluent is discharged directly to the river Tees, or into the sea in the case of coastal development. To combat this problem and to assist in realising the full amenity potential of the coast and the river Tees all existing discharges of sewage will be intercepted and given appropriate treatment before being allowed to flow into the'river or sea. To this end the following action is, or will be, taken:

(i)   New sewage treatment works will be constructed at: [two specific locations].

(ii) A system of intercepting sewers is being constructed which, together with major modifications to some existing trunk sewers, will enable sewage flows to be diverted to the new treatment works. Five main intercepting sewers will be constructed at: [five specific locations].

(iii) Investigations are being carried out into the possibility of combining the existing outfalls at one location into a single new outfall which could also serve other coastal development in nearby locations.

11 *New industrial development likely to cause noise will be located away from residential and commercial areas.* Heavy industry will be restricted to: [the same three specific locations nominated under policy 4]. General industry will be accepted at: [four specific locations].

12 *Residential development will not be allowed close to likely noise sources.* Green wedges or landscaped 'buffers' will be maintained between: [three pairs of specific locations].

13 *In areas allocated for labour-intensive industry or service and storage industry, close to residential or commercial areas, strict control will be exercised over the types of industry and activities to ensure noise and vibration nuisance is not caused.* These policies are designed to minimise the effect of noise created by industrial activities.

Noise from motor vehicles should be reduced at source by changes in engine, exhaust, tyre and road surface design, which will, however, be a long-term policy. Whilst vehicle noise control is possible under the Road Traffic Acts, the projected large increase in the number of motor vehicles is likely to lead to an increase in the amount of traffic noise.

The impact of traffic noise upon the public can be reduced by reorganising the road network and introducing improved standards of highway design.

14 *New main roads will be located and designed to minimise the noise level experienced in adjacent residential properties.* This policy may be achieved by putting distance between houses and roads, by putting the road in a cutting, and by earth moulding alongside new highways. Atten-

tion to design will ensure that the new roads, in removing traffic and associated noise from existing main roads, do not transfer the noise nuisance to properties alongside their route.

Noise standards will be established based on the findings of the Urban Motorways Committee report and subsequent research and legislation, which will then be applied to all noise sources within the county borough.

15 *All derelict land within council ownership will be reclaimed.* A programme of reclamation will be pursued, dealing with about 540 acres which meet the Department of the Environment definition of dereliction and 660 acres of 'active' dereliction (eg. industrial tips).

16 *Negotiations will be carried out with owners of derelict land to persuade them to reclaim the derelict land or to sell to the council to enable reclamation proposals to go forward.* The main areas for reclamation within the Department of the Environment definition are: [five specific locations]. The main areas for reclamation which do not fall within the Department of the Environment definition are: [five specific locations].

Where landowners wish to restore derelict land themselves the necessary advice and assistance will be given on the technique of reclamation. Statutory undertakers will be encouraged to remove their disused buildings and equipment.

17 *Small areas of disused or untidy land will be made tidy, either through negotiations with owners followed by voluntary remedial work, or using powers under the Town and Country Planning Act, 1971, or the Civic Amenities Act, 1967.* Whilst policies set out in 15 and 16 for the reclamation of derelict land will do much to improve the visual environment of Teesside, the many small areas of untidiness or disuse are much more immediately unpleasant to the public, because they are found where people live, shop and take recreation. Unless these small eyesores are dealt with just as comprehensively as larger blocks of derelict land the untidy image of Teesside will persist.

WARLEY
The fifty-five objectives of the structure plan (p. 118) are grouped into three tiers representing a general level of importance. The first tier of fifteen objectives are themselves ranked into order of importance. It proved impracticable to rank the second and third tier objectives. The following objectives (quoted almost verbatim) relate to pollution and its control:

First-tier objectives
To maintain and improve, as much as possible, the quality of the environment of the Borough.

Second-tier objectives
Employment and industry. To reduce the detrimental effects of working establishments on the external environment and to ensure that new establishments do not adversely affect the environment.

Transport. To ensure that all future development and use of the transport system keeps to a minimum the adverse environmental effects on other land users.

Public utilities. To ensure that provision of services is achieved with maximum efficiency which is compatible with minimum detriment of the environment.

Environment. To reduce and prevent atmospheric pollution and pollution by noise. To ensure that no harmful pollution is carried to the land users and watercourses by domestic and industrial discharges.

Third-tier objectives

To eliminate or minimise the effect of derelict land, obsolete buildings and other physical factors which mar the visual environment.

To ensure that the detrimental environmental effects of mineral extraction are kept to a minimum.

SOUTH HAMPSHIRE

The policies below are a sample of those quoted in the written statement. The explanation of the policy is followed by examples of the criteria to be pursued in local plan preparation and development control (p. 126). They are derived from the objectives and other matters considered in the structure plan. (The quotations have been subject to minor editing to preserve continuity.)

Employment: to reserve locations for industrial and commercial uses with special siting criteria. This policy underlies such proposals as the reservation of a specific location for port-oriented activities.

For this purpose the local planning authorities will reserve land for industrial and commercial developments which require special facilities at strategic locations which should be used for the purpose on account of ability to accept industrial/commercial developments which may generate a high level of noise, fumes or other pollution.

Employment: to provide for the requirements of firms displaced by development proposals. This policy is concerned that provision should be made for the relocation of firms at present unsatisfactorily sited or which will be affected by new development or redevelopment. This policy continues the existing policies of all three local planning authorities.

For this purpose the local planning authorities will, in the preparation of local plans, seek to relocate non-conforming uses which create nuisance.

Countryside: to permit only development appropriate to the countryside. Appropriate development will normally include development essential to the proper functioning of the primary rural activities in the countryside and other uses, such as recreation, as may be proposed in the structure plan and as set out in the references to countryside areas or (from time to time) in local plans or which can be shown to have an *overriding* need for a countryside location.

In their consideration of proposals in the countryside the local planning authorities will have particular regard to the generation of noise, fumes and other forms of nuisance or pollution which would detract from the enjoyment of the countryside.

Countryside: to take positive action to maintain and improve the landscape resources of the countryside and coast. This general policy underlines the determination of the local planning authorities to ensure that the character and quality of the landscape of South Hampshire is not harmfully changed. Action will, of course, be determined by the circumstances prevailing, if or when specific problems are identified during continuing studies as part of the process of continuous monitoring of the plan. The principal powers available will be those of the Countryside Act.

Where existing uses materially detract from the landscape resources of the countryside and coast the local planning authority will, where practicable and finance is available, take active steps to abate or extinguish the detracting use. Such uses are defined as those which generate a high level of noise, smoke, fumes or other pollutants.

Built environment: to maintain and improve the existing built environment in South Hampshire. This policy is to maintain and improve the quality of the environment in the existing built-up areas, and will form the basis for further positive action through local improvement schemes (often associated with housing improvement) and the definition of General Improvement Areas. It also includes the development and improvement of open space systems and landscaping, the adoption of amenity environmental areas in the preparation of local plans so as to exclude through traffic, the pedestrianisation of shopping and other centres, the relocation of non-conforming industrial and commercial uses harmful to the local environment, and the temporary use of land and buildings which would otherwise remain vacant and deteriorate in appearance.

1   In preparing local plans or design briefs or in considering other proposals for change in the existing built environment: the local planning authorities will:

   (a)   Seek to remove or discourage through or extraneous traffic from residential areas where the local planning authorities consider that congestion is too great, the environment is being degraded by noise, vibration or other intrusion, or where personal safety is at risk.

   (b)   Introduce traffic management and other measures so as to reduce existing congestion and parking problems where the local planning authority consider that these are at levels such as to be detrimental to the environment and/or dangerous to residents.

   (c)   Secure the relocation or removal of uses which are noisy, noxious or otherwise objectionable, particularly in residential areas.

2   New development or expansion of existing uses will not normally be permitted where it is likely to affect the existing or new built environ-

ment, in terms of the generation of an inappropriate level of noise, fumes or other nuisance.

Built environment: to require a good standard of layout and environmental design in proposals for development or redevelopment. In preparing local plans or design briefs for areas of new development, the local planning authorities will ensure that the areas are planned to minimise nuisance from noise and unsightly and unpleasant uses.

Minerals: all mineral working schemes will be expected to provide for planned working and reinstatement in preparation for a specified after use in conformity with the general policies for the area concerned. This policy makes provision for beneficial after use of mineral workings and is to ensure that the traffic and environmental effects of mineral extraction are kept within acceptable levels. It should be read in conjunction with appropriate Countryside and Built environment policies and criteria.

In considering proposals for the extraction of minerals the local planning authorities will take account of the provision for:

(a) Avoiding nuisance to adjoining uses by virtue of noise, dirt, dust or other pollution.

(b) The siting and type of plant, spoil heaps.

Foul and surface water drainage: development requiring foul or surface water drainage facilities will only be permitted where such facilities can be made available. This policy is to ensure that development takes place only where adequate provision for foul and surface water drainage can be made available at reasonable cost, and that neither harmful pollution nor technical or administrative difficulties in the provision and maintenance of main drainage systems are created by piecemeal development and the use of local disposal systems, cesspits and septic tanks. The local planning authorities will ensure that no development takes place:

(a) Which cannot be served by foul and surface water main drainage at reasonable cost.

(b) Which will create other problems in terms of maintenance of the disposal or surface water system, or proliferation in the use of local disposal systems, cesspits and septic tanks.

(c) Until adequate drainage facilities, capable of catering for likely future demand, can be made available. See also Built environment policies above.

Foul and surface water drainage: no development will be permitted which would hinder the efforts of the drainage authorities to avoid harmful pollution of the rivers, watercourses, estuaries, harbours and sea of the plan area. This policy is to ensure that no harmful pollution is caused to the rivers, watercourses, estuaries, harbours or sea by domestic, industrial or agricultural discharges.

1   No development will be permitted which would overload existing or proposed facilities such as to cause harmful pollution.
2   No industrial or other uses will be permitted which would discharge harmful wastes or effluents.

Foul and surface water drainage: planning powers will be used to assist the drainage authorities in exercising their functions including, where necessary, the provision of water pollution control works on suitable sites, the safeguarding of foul and surface water drainage sewers and channels and other appropriate matters.

1   In considering sites for water pollution control works the local planning authorities will have particular regard to:
     (*a*)   The supporting criteria of the relevant Built environment and Countryside policies.
     (*b*)   The ability of the proposed works to cater for future expansion of growth if necessary.
     (*c*)   Minimising the visual effects of such works by requiring that all engineering works are incorporated into a landscape scheme of high standard.
     (*d*)   Minimising the adverse effects of smell or other nuisance.
     (*e*)   Minimising the costs of development, commensurate with environmental considerations.
2   No development will be permitted which would:
     (*a*)   Conflict with potential water pollution control works sites.
     (*b*)   Interfere with major foul and surface water drainage sewers.

Refuse disposal: to reserve suitable sites in local plans and schemes for refuse disposal. Their detailed location will be ascertained by reference to the appropriate criteria in local studies (these criteria will include such matters as access, appearance, effect on adjacent uses, alternative land use possibilities, smell and noise, with the addition of any other factors of local significance). Sites will only be reserved at the request of a refuse disposal authority or organisation.

Refuse disposal: to permit refuse disposal only at sites meeting the above criteria, where the local planning authorities are satisfied that no harmful pollution of land, air or water is likely to occur, having regard to the type of refuse to be disposed. This policy will ensure that the methods of refuse disposal adopted do not harm the important natural resources of the area and cause the least possible disturbance to the existing rural and urban areas.

Airports: to avoid harmful effects on the environment. This policy is to ensure that airport use and development does not cause harmful disturbance by noise and that the safety and safeguarding requirements of airports do not have harmful effects on land use.

1   No new residential development will normally be permitted where it would be subjected to an unacceptable (excessive) level of noise or other pollution from existing, or proposed, airport facilities.

2   No expansion or extension of existing airport facilities will normally be permitted which would subject existing or proposed residential areas to excessive (unacceptable levels of) noise or other pollution.

Transport: to avoid harmful effects on the environment. This policy forms an essential element in the development of a satisfactory transport system, in order that the adverse effects of traffic are minimised. These adverse effects include accidents, pedestrian/vehicle conflict, noise, fumes, visual intrusion and intimidation.

1   The local authorities intend to take measures to restrict extraneous traffic from using local streets in residential areas, shopping and commercial centres, and other environmental areas:
   (*a*) By defining the network of primary and secondary routes in either the structure plan and/or supporting local plans, and hence identifying potential environmental areas.
   (*b*) By the use of traffic management and other measures which will ensure as far as practicable that such extraneous traffic is restricted to the defined primary and secondary highway network.
2   The local authorities intend to safeguard or improve environmental conditions in urban or rural areas adjoining traffic routes and other major transport facilities by:
   (*a*) The provision of noise barriers, embankments or screens.
   (*b*) The establishment of suitable landscape features.
   (*c*) Careful consideration of the alignment and profile of new routes.
   (*d*) Careful consideration of the location and form of new development in relation to such routes.

Index

252166